Altruism and Economy

A STUDY IN NON-SELFISH ECONOMICS

Altruism and Economy

A STUDY IN NON-SELFISH
ECONOMICS

David Collard

Oxford University Press
New York

First published in 1978 by Martin Robertson & Company Ltd. 108 Cowley Road, Oxford OX4 1dF

Published in the U.S.A. by Oxford University Press, New York.

Library of Congress Cataloging in Publication Data

Collard, David A
  Economics and altruism.

  Bibliography: p.
  Includes index.
  1. Economics—Moral and religious aspects.
2. Altruism. I. Title.
HB72.C56   330.1   78-7496
ISBN 0-19-520066-7

Typeset by Santype Ltd., Salisbury
Printed and bound by Richard Clay Ltd.,
at The Chaucer Press, Bungay, Suffolk.

Contents

To perform an act of benevolence towards one's neighbour is called, in Hebrew, *to do justice*; in Greek *to take compassion* or *pity*; in Latin *to perform an act of love or charity*; in French *to give alms*. We can trace the degradation of this principle through these various expressions: the first signifies duty; the second only sympathy; the third, affection, a matter of choice, not an obligation; the fourth caprice.

P. J. PROUDHON, *What is Property?*

Sympathy – the one poor word which includes all our best insight and our best love.

GEORGE ELIOT, *Adam Bede*

Preface

For two hundred years economists, unlike other social scientists, have assumed a self-interested economic man. This small book seeks partially to redress the balance and to some extent fulfils a commitment made several years ago in my Fabian Tract, *The New Right: A Critique* (1968). I there wrote:

> I have given an unusually prominent place to the economics of altruism and have argued on normal liberal and individualist, but not necessarily selfish, grounds that private markets are unable to deal adequately with situations where altruism is important. [p. 19].

That an interest in non-selfish economics is now in the air may be seen from the appearance of Boulding's *The Economy of Love and Fear* (1973) and Phelps's *Altruism, Morality and Economic Theory* (1975).

I attempt to deal as simply as possible with the implications of non-selfishness for economics. It will be obvious to the reader that I owe a great intellectual debt to Edgeworth, who attempted, as I explain in Chapter 6, 'to incorporate the more general case into the theory of exchange, at its very moment of inception'. Again, in Chapter 2, the analysis is Edgeworthian and closely follows my *Economic Journal* article of June 1975.

The book is divided into two parts. I have called the first part 'Theory' and the most important chapters in this part are Chapters 2 and 4. I have called the second part 'Illustrations' rather than 'Applications' because a really tight coherent theory of altruism remains to be worked out so that its empirical predictions may be properly tested. There are still many grey areas where a sophisticated self-interest competes with altruism as an explanatory hypothesis and where it is very difficult to devise 'tests'. To that extent this book presents fragments of a research programme still incomplete. My excuses for presenting them now are (i) that I sense a general interest in the subject matter and (ii) that it is sometimes necessary to unburden oneself of one's mental scribble.

The reader will see from the contents list that I have not provided a concluding chapter. Each chapter (except the last) does, however, carry a summary, and for the reader who wants a quick impression of the book I suggest a reading of Chapters 1 and 7 together with a look at the chapter summaries.

I have tried out various chapters of the book, in draft form, on seminars at Birkbeck College and at the Universities of Bath, Birmingham, Cardiff, Keele, Kent, Manchester and Reading and on the 1975 History of Economics Conference at Piraeus. I wish to thank my colleagues at Bristol for their encouragement and for allowing me a study term in 1976. I am also grateful to Amartya Sen for very helpful comments on an earlier draft. Responsibility for those errors that persist remains, of course, with me.

David Collard
University of Bristol
September 1977

Part I
THEORY

1 Altruism and Economics

My thesis in this book is that human beings are not entirely selfish, even in their economic dealings. It may seem strange to a layman, or even to his fellow social scientists, that the economist should consider such an assumption to be in any way remarkable or controversial. Yet it is the case that self-interested 'economic man' dominates the textbooks. Indeed rationality and self-interest are often taken as one and the same thing. This book, on the contrary, deals with rational altruistic man.

Though non-selfishness is not the standard mainstream assumption in economic theory it has been a significant minor theme for at least 250 years. Neither has it been restricted to minor writers: Hume, Smith, Edgeworth and Marshall all treated it seriously. In the more modern literature it has formed a relatively neglected part of the theory of externalities. It has even received a mention in a prominent introductory textbook (Samuelson 1973 p. 505). It raises not only interesting technical difficulties but also fundamental questions of the nature of man in society and the possibility of socialism and economic justice.

Examples of apparently non-selfish behaviour are not at all difficult to find, particularly where kin relationships are close. Some biologists have argued (see Chapter 5) that all such behaviour may be explained on the hypothesis of the 'selfish gene'. But in human society non-selfishness is not confined to genetically close individuals. Numerous instances may be given: individual contributions to charity, voluntary work for non-profit-making organisations like youth clubs and hospitals, voting in favour of welfare payments to the poor, the donation of blood, saving for future generations, etc. The reader will be able to think of many more.

3

RIVAL EXPLANATIONS

It may be objected that some altruistic acts are only apparently so; that an explanation in terms of self-interest can very often be provided. This is undoubtedly true. There are two kinds of counter-argument. One is to assert that there nevertheless remains a residue of truly altruistic behaviour when all else has been separated out. The other argument is less satisfactory but has to be used; i.e., that the alternative explanation cannot easily be handled by the economist and therefore has to be brought under the same umbrella as altruism. Some of these alternative explanations are now briefly considered.

One set of explanations runs in terms of *enlightened self-interest*. My apparently altruistic behaviour will rebound to my advantage indirectly or in the future. A crude example is the ingratiating employee who holds a door open for his superior. The reader is doubtless able to think of numerous other illustrations. This sort of case is absolutely straightforward on the definition already adopted provided we define my present goods and expected future goods as accruing to the same person. But see Nagel (1970). My actions are then explained in terms of my own bundle of goods. No novelty is involved in this; it is a standard part of the economist's analysis of inter-temporal choice. As for indirect but current benefits, these are simply a question of not drawing the boundaries too narrowly. With perfect information there is no difference between self-interest and enlightened self-interest.

Then there are explanations based on *reputation*. Like the eighteenth-century writer Mandeville, many people would have this bear pretty well the whole explanation. I give to a beggar so that he and others will think well of me. I endow university chairs so that future generations will respect my memory. A real difficulty is presented by this sort of case. Reputation and respect imply psychic returns but they generally do not (though they may) lead to an identifiable return flow of bundles of goods.

Some gifts are based on *reciprocity* or *implicit exchange*. Presents, invitations to dinner and baby-sitting are sometimes of this kind. An economist would see these as simple barter transactions which can easily be handled within the framework of self-interest. Even so, it would very often be necessary to introduce more subtle factors relating to uncertainty. Gifts may be made to another so as to build up his *goodwill* towards oneself. The gift may then be reciprocated if ever one should fall upon hard times. Normally we would not wish to label these actions 'altruistic'.

Acts of giving may be associated with the reinforcement or confirmation of *status*. A parent's gift to his child may be of this kind (Schwartz, 1967). In accepting the gift the recipient confirms his status *vis à vis* the donor. Such motives cannot be distinguished, in our analysis, from truly altruistic motives.

Lastly, acts of giving or self-abnegation may be due not to love or benevolence but to their opposite, *fear*. A blackmailer may threaten unpleasant action unless he is paid off. An employer may threaten a lock-out unless wage cuts are taken. Fortunately this does not present a definitional problem. The consequences make themselves felt through the individual's bundle of goods and services and no altruistic motive need be assumed. But it may sometimes present a problem in prediction: for the same act of behaviour could be explained either in terms of altruism or fear. One must tread carefully.

Once these various sorts of motivation have been allowed for, does there remain a truly altruistic residual? It is a tenet of this book that there does. The most convincingly argued example is blood donation, but this can be taken as the leading species of a large genus. If the altruistic residual were trivial much of the analysis presented would nevertheless be useful in handling some of the actions described in the paragraphs above. But this book itself would then be trivial and its conclusions unimportant.

A DEFENCE OF SELF-LOVE

Self-interest is an extraordinarily powerful assumption. The reasons for its dominance have been partly normative and partly positive. One of its great but paradoxical strengths is that it can be worked into a social harmony doctrine. Each, in pursuing his own narrow selfish interest, unconsciously promotes the common good. In its more sophisticated form this doctrine appears as one of the so-called 'basic theorems' of modern welfare economics: that every competitive equilibrium is a Pareto optimum. Essentially this part of the theorem is an elegant restatement of Smith's original proposition described in Chapter 6. Modern welfare economics has shaken, though not destroyed, this doctrine by laying stress on the various sorts of 'market failure' that occur in real economies: for example, monopoly, increasing returns, externalities, distributional injustice and so on. Criticisms based on market failure may be countered to some degree by an adequate analysis of property rights, but it would be fair to detect a widespread disbelief in the social harmony, or 'invisible hand' doctrine. That doctrine now provides only a poor defence for self-love. It is weakened still further by the failure of self-interest to lead to desirable outcomes in games of a socially co-operative nature. In these sorts of games, self-interested players may easily find themselves trapped in non-co-operative equilibrium. (see Chapter 4).

The self-interest assumption derives its support, however, only partly from its normative aspects. It is, in addition to these, a rich and plausible assumption yielding falsifiable predictions about human affairs. Consider some hum-drum matters of economic policy. Regional incentives are offered to firms on the assumption that they are profit-seeking institutions. Banks seeking greater deposits offer higher interest rates than their competitors. On the whole the work-a-day assumption of self-interested behaviour turns out to be quite a useful one. Practically the whole of (neoclassical) economic theory is built upon self-interested individuals maximising utility and firms maximising profit or minimising cost. It is an assumption not lightly to be abandoned or even modified.

One further defence of the self-interest assumption needs to be made: that it is by no means extreme. Economic man is often thought, particularly by non-economists, to be a particularly unpleasant and reprehensible abstraction. He is brutish, unsympathetic and probably misanthropic. This ıs a mistaken view. To be sure, economic man is incapable of sympathy, benevolence or love. But he is also incapable of envy, malevolence or hatred. In short, he is splendidly neutral to others. He is concerned *only* with the bundle of goods and services he is to receive. Self-interest, it may therefore be argued, is a neutral or middle assumption and certainly morally more attractive than envy, malice or hatred.

Taking these three types of argument together, self-interest may be defended on: (a) grounds of normative or welfare economics – that self-interest leads to socially good outcomes, (b) grounds of positive economics – that it leads to good empirical predictions, (c) moral grounds – that its motives are not ignoble.

ATTRIBUTION

A puzzle about definitions must now be faced. The assumption of self-interest is sometimes defended in a way that renders it tautologous. The man who drowns in rescuing a child or the martyr at the stake are said to be serving their own interests just as a man eating cream cakes or seeking promotion is serving his. Every rational individual reveals his preferences in his behaviour. The fallacy in the argument is that self-interest has been assumed, not proved. But it does bring out a real problem: how are we to know when preferences (or behaviour) are altruistic and when they are not? Unless one cuts through this tangle there is little more to be done.

Fortunately, the economist has a simple way out of the difficulty. The escape is something of a fudge and merely moves the definitional problem one stage backwards. But it is an acceptable fudge and it enables one to proceed. It is customary in economics to take it as axiomatic that the bundle of goods and services going to any one individual can be defined objectively. An individual gets so many jars of jam, so much health care and so on; similarly with other individuals. If his preferences are associated only with his own bundle he is said to be selfish. If they are positively associated with other people's bundles he is said to be in some degree altruistic. Thus as long as the prior question of definition of bundles has been settled, the rest is straightforward.

In the immediately following discussion the non-specialist reader may safely skip the algebraic notation. I wish to distinguish two sorts of case, one where interdependence is *commodity-related* and one where it is *utility-related*.

Let x_i and x_j be the bundles of goods going to individuals i and j, u_i and u_j their utilities and U_i and U_j their utility-related welfares. Thus, in the two columns:

	Commodity related	*Utility related*
	$u_i(x_i, x_j),$	$U_i[u_i(x_i), u_j(x_j)]$
where		
	$\dfrac{\partial u_i}{\partial x_j} > 0$	$\dfrac{\partial U_i}{\partial u_j} > 0$

These are potentially two very different ways of presenting the thing, for it may be that in the commodity-related case my perception of how you value (or should value) your goods does not at all accord with your perception. In a sense to be used later it is useful to say that my tastes may (but not necessarily will) be 'meddlesome'. With the utility-related approach, which is obviously in some degree more genuinely concerned with the *alter*, a delicate chain of sympathy seems to be required on my part unless others wear utility-meters, as it were, on their faces.

For the present it will do for my purposes to say that people are altruistic when one or other of the above conditions holds. I must stress that the key assumption here, which I shall call the assumption of *attribution*, is precisely the assumption that economists always make, though consider too trivial to mention. It becomes crucial in the present context.

It is well-known that the assumption of attribution holds for private goods but not normally for *public goods*. The so-called pure public good is, if provided for anybody, available to everybody. This makes things rather tricky, for there is no obvious way of distinguishing between the resulting bundles of its services going to particular individuals. Let there be a public good, z, and assume that individuals are selfish with respect to their own attributable bundles, x. Then $u_i(x_i, z)$ and $u_j(x_j, z)$ and there is no way of defining their interest in z as selfish or unselfish. But often it will be possible to make such distinctions. For example, the provision of a recreational lake in one area will provide bundles of services to a fairly well-defined group of people. Some analysis along these lines is provided in Chapter 3. Whenever such attribution is impossible the distinction between the individuals' feelings about other particular individuals and collective entities like 'society' become blurred.

The assumption of attribution draws boundaries around individuals and permits a non-tautologous distinction between altruism and self-interest. It also confirms that altruism is concerned with tastes or preferences and not yet with action. Altruistic motivation is therefore to be distinguished from positive acts such as giving. Altruistic feelings may exist but be too weak to lead to action. As is pointed out in Chapter 10, altruism is neither a necessary nor a sufficient condition for giving, for weak altruism may be Pareto-irrelevant and giving may be inspired by fear as much as love.

THE AFTER-YOU PROBLEM

That 'excessive' altruism can lead to absurd results has long been recognised; see, for example, the quotations from Hutcheson and Dante in Chapter 6. At a trivial level take the case of two excessively polite individuals each of whom insists that the other pass through a doorway first: both wish to pass through but neither is able to do so. I refer to this as the 'after-you' problem. Characteristically after-you problems rarely stay unresolved for long.

> [Shubin:] 'I want love for myself: I want to be number one'.
> 'Number one', Bersyenev reported. 'Whereas I feel that the whole of one's destiny in life should be to make oneself number two.'
> 'If everyone behaved as you recommend,' Shubin said, pulling a face in protest, 'there'd be no-one at all to eat the pineapples – everyone would leave them for someone else.'
> 'That merely means pineapples are not necessities; however you needn't worry – there will always be people glad to take even the bread out of other people's mouths.'
> [Turgenev, *On the Eve*]

Bersyenev's pessimistic solution is, of course, not the only one. The parties might accept a 'fair' arbitration device (like tossing a coin or taking turns). In the rather limited sense of the after-you problem the economic problem itself 'vanishes' when altruists' concern is excessive (see the quotation from Hume in Chapter 6 and Collard, 1975).

Obviously not everyone can be entirely altruistic as there would then be nothing positive to bite upon. Thus Rawls:

> A perfect altruist can fulfill his desire only if someone else has independent, or first order, desires. To illustrate this fact, suppose that in deciding what to do all vote to do what everyone else wants to do. Obviously nothing gets settled; in fact there is nothing to decide. For a problem of justice to arise at least two persons must want to do something other than what everyone else wants to do. It is impossible, then, to assume that the parties are simply perfect altruists. [1972, p. 189]

In view of these and other difficulties I shall normally be assuming that the marginal weight I attach to the welfare of others is less than that I attach to myself, or that $\partial u_i/\partial u_j < 1$. This permits a modest degree of altruism but not enough to lead to the after-you problem.

CONSENSUS

Many, among whom are some 'utopian socialists', believe that altruism (while not leading to the after-you problem) would end economic rivalry. As will be shown in Chapter 11, extremely unequal distributions of income may be rejected by everyone even in only a moderately altruistic community. By the same logic, if everyone's social consciousness could be raised sufficiently there would be unanimous agreement about the optimal distribution of goods and services. But such a complete consensus would imply that everyone's social preferences were essentially identical. Not only is this uninteresting for the analysis of social choice: it may even be unjust or unfair. Suppose, for example, that A is very altruistic indeed but B is selfish. There would be perfect consensus in favour of allocating almost all output to B and very little to A. But this would hardly be 'fair'. As Pattanaik has argued, in the spirit of the quotation from Proudhon p. vii,

> it seems more reasonable to base social preferences on a higher order individual evaluation – ethical preferences – rather than on a lower order valuation – subjective preferences. Unless some such procedure is adopted, the individual interests of the egotistic individuals will have too great a weight in the cardinal social welfare function, and the more altruistic individuals are likely to be penalised precisely because of their altruism. [Pattanaik, 1968]

This remark is firmly in the tradition of Smith's 'impartial spectator' or Hume's 'calm moment' – that ethical judgements should be detached from hasty day-to-day action.

Short of a consensus (which may or may not be judged 'fair'), Arrow's famous problem of social choice remains, even though individuals preferences are non-selfish. The problem (Arrow, 1951) is the impossibility of deriving a social ordering from a set of individual orderings without violating one or more 'reasonable' axioms. It is often wrongly believed that nonselfishness provides a solution for Arrow's problem: but it only does so in the trivial case where altruism is such as to generate perfect consensus. In the general case, however, Arrow's formulation relies in no way upon individual self-interest. All that is required is that each individual orders social states – which may include only his own attributable bundles of goods and services but may equally well include those of others.

THE CONTAGION THESIS

It may very well be that non-selfishness has some of the qualities of an epidemic. Each individual, when considering a benevolent action, will have it in mind that others are more or less benevolent. The amount of altruism an individual displays will itself depend on his *expectations* of how others will behave. Hume (see Chapter 6) and Titmuss (see Chapter 13) could certainly be interpreted as having taken this view. For convenience I shall refer to this as the Hume–Titmuss *contagion thesis*.

The process of social dynamics implied by these writers is a complex one that cannot easily be handled by the economist (or for that matter by anyone else). A modest start may be made in terms of the theory of games (see Chapter 4). This line of investigation has some features in common with that part of genetic theory concerning itself with the proportion of 'altruist' genes in a population (see Chapter 5).

SOCIAL DISTANCE

Historically almost all writers on this theme have argued that although perhaps one ought to treat everyone the same, one in fact gives a much greater weight to some people than to others. Almost always, a greater weight is given to kin than to others. On the 'selfish gene' type of assumption the weight is precisely determined by the closeness of the genetic relationship. The relatedness between two brothers is one-half, as is the relatedness between parent and child. For first cousins, relatedness is one-eighth. 'A third cousin is not far removed from being equivalent to any old Tom, Dick or Harry as far as an altruistic gene is concerned' (Dawkins, 1976). An altruistic gene for saving the lives of more than two siblings would tend to become more numerous in the population.

The economist has normally worked with a sharply discontinuous version of this. Members of the family behave *as though* perfectly altruistic towards one another but completely selfishly towards outsiders. Becker (1974, 1976) has provided some justification for the first half of this version: if one makes some fairly stringent assumptions about the role and preferences of the head of the household it may be shown that even a 'rotten kid' will behave as though non-selfish towards other members of the family. More generally, one would want to break down this discontinuity. Human beings make complex social relationships with workmates, colleagues, neighbours, fellow club members and so on, and tend to make some allowance for how their own behaviour will affect these others. Generalised altruism towards the human race is rare and, indeed, suspect.

The meagre data on giving (see Chapter 10), relating as it does to expenditure, vastly understates its prevalence as it omits intra-family giving. To this extent the crude genetic effects and their ramifications dominate human 'gifts' just as they do those of other species. But there is also a generalised concern, not towards man-kind as an abstraction, but towards particular types of need by socially distant and unknown other individuals. The prime factor here is sympathetic identification. Few imaginations are so limited as to be able to 'sympathise' only with near relations. Thus social distance remains as one, but only one, determinant of the 'weight' attached to others.

Co-operation

The solution of the perfectly competitive game requires no formal alliances or collective acts – apart from the infrastructure of the game itself. The very existence of markets, however, presupposes under-lying trust, codes of conduct or civil force. I argue in Chapter 4 that this important aspect of economic evolution may be modelled as an *assurance game*. This is a type of game in which I will behave co-operatively if I believe others will do the same. But if I believe that they will lie, cheat and kill I will do likewise. If the game really is of this type, trust rather than altruism (or love) is sufficient for a solution. If it is nearly an assurance game but not quite, altruistic behaviour, or at any rate behaviour that appears to be altruistic, may serve to tip the balance.

Apart from these infrastructural considerations, competitive equilibrium requires no collective action. Is this conclusion upset once altruism is introduced? For an important class of cases, perhaps surprisingly, it is not at all upset. These are the cases covered by what I call the *non-twisting theorem*. The theorem states that if each individual, i, is concerned about the welfare (or utility) of other persons, j, but not about their specific choices of goods and services, then the conditions for efficient exchange are precisely those in the selfish case. External concern or altruism is simply not Pareto-relevant. The same condition may also be described in terms of i having *non-meddlesome* preferences. The outcome is an immensely attractive one, for at one blow it:

(i) preserves competitive markets as an efficient allocative mechanism *even when* consumption externalities are present,

(ii) confirms the ethically appealing nature of non-meddlesome or non-paternalistic preferences.

Comforting as it is, the non-twisting theorem is only of limited applicability. Even with non-meddlesome preferences, the altruist will sometimes wish to redistribute income from rich to poor. Admittedly this may be done on an individual basis. However, in a large community one has to take account of the *free-rider* problem; for, paradoxically, the individual altruist who wishes to give to the poor would be perfectly happy for other altruists to give instead, as long as he values his own welfare more highly than he values theirs. To avoid this free-rider problem some form of collective action seems to be required (see Chapter 3).

Redistribution apart, one must allow that people's preferences are, in general, 'meddlesome'. They are more concerned that their fellow citizens should be reasonably well fed, housed, educated and cared for in ill health than they are in their overall economic welfare. If this is so, and the empirical support for it is strong, the conditions for efficient exchange will be much more complex than in the egotistical case. The supporting price system would then require different prices for different individuals together with a policing system (like means tests) or direct provision by the state. Competitive markets would no longer lead to efficient allocation and some collective method of resource allocation would clearly be required. This is rather a pity, for the subsidy/means test system leads to great inefficiency and muddle, as is shown in Chapter 12.

Altruism, then, seems to imply a much greater scope for co-operative or collective economic behaviour both with regard to income redistribution and resource allocation. Turning the question on its head, might it not also be the case that altruism actually facilitates socially co-operative acts, even that it leads to spontaneous, voluntary, co-operation? Indeed it does, and the way in which it does so is described in Chapter 4. Essentially, what happens is that games of the rather hopeless prisoner's dilemma type are converted into assurance games if players are sufficiently altruistic. But there are important limitations on the extent to which this is possible. Spontaneous co-operation turns out to be more likely:

(i)   the more altruistic the players,
(ii) the smaller the number of players,
(iii) the greater the advantage of co-operation,
(iv) the greater the marginal impact of the individual.

(ii) and (iv) are, in fact, interdependent and are related to the question of increasing returns.

To some limited degree this lends support to Schumacher's thesis that 'small is beautiful'. Even if people are only moderately un-selfish, there is a far greater chance of voluntary social co-operation in a small than in a large community. And a great many of the important groups in our society are quite small, indeed of a "village" type. Our affections and loyalties are not to society in the large but to particular groups or clubs – to colleagues at work, to family, to local schools or play groups, to friends, to fellow political activists, to neighbours. All of these run more effectively with loyalty and affection than without. But even these groups cannot operate properly unless fickle affection is somehow hardened into duty. On the whole these smaller groups (the whole gamut from churches to gambling schools) are neglected in this book. This is a serious omission, for society is mainly a knitting together of such groups.

Difficulties arise when the number of players is large. Normally in such cases a very high degree of altruism would be required for spontaneous voluntary co-operation. Then one must introduce a quite different principle, the Kantian principle, based not upon love but upon 'reason':

> If the interest of the action can without self-contradiction be universalised it is morally possible. [Kant, 1930, p. 44]

Using the terminology of Chapter 4, such a principle would lead all participants to choose alpha (co-operative) rather than beta (non-co-operative) strategies. Each player perceives that the true choice is between fully co-operative and fully non-co-operative outcomes: that any attempt to gain at the expense of the other could not be universalised and is therefore morally impermissible.

Now it is always possible to convert the Kantian condition into an equivalent altruistic condition. That is to say, the Kantian co-operator may be said to behave *as though* he attached at least a certain altruistic weight to the pay-offs as his fellow players. Nevertheless, the principle is based on reason, not love, and may be acted upon by players who feel no love or altruism whatever towards the others:

> There is nothing in the world so sacred as the rights of the others. Generosity is a superfluity. A man who is never generous but never trespasses on the rights of his fellows is still an honest man, and if everyone were like him there would be no poor in the world. [Kant, 1930, p. 211]

It seems to me that a useful way of putting the distinction between the Kantian and altruistic principles is as follows. Suppose that A's are richer than B's and feel sufficiently altruistic towards them to wish to transfer income to them. For unspecified reasons this is best done collectively. The non-Kantian altruist considers only his own (negligible) contribution to the redistributive fund in deciding whether or not to attempt a free ride. The Kantian altruist, on the other hand, asks what would happen if other A's behaved similarly: were they to do so the B's would get nothing. The non-Kantian altruist fails to co-operate: the Kantian altruist co-operates spontaneously.

DEMOCRACY

Though I do not wish to underestimate the Kantian principle and shall make use of it in the course of this book, it *does* require people to act *as though* highly altruistic. It may very well be that in a 'calm moment' one recognises that one *ought* to behave Kantianly, but does not in practice do so. If so, the principle is of little immediate interest to positive economics.

One is then driven to a 'social contract' type of arrangement, whereby each votes in favour of a scheme *compelling* him to adopt alpha (co-operative) strategies, in the knowledge that others will be compelled to do likewise. In the simplest models such an arrangement would receive unanimous support. But more generally I shall be assuming that when social co-operation would be advantageous, the possibility and degree of co-operation will be decided by some form of *majority voting* in a democracy. (The exceptions to this are spontaneous co-operation on the basis of the Kantian or altruistic principles.) Altruism is not, of course, banished by this device, for each individual will be free to vote according to his preferences, whether selfish or non-selfish.

An advantage of this method is that it enables one to make use of well-known theorems in voting theory, principally about the relationship between simple majority rule and the role of the voter with median preferences. Admittedly the simplest results here are based on 'unrealistic' assumptions (single-issue voting, odd numbers, single-peaked preferences) but they permit useful discussion of matters such as tax rates and are not at all difficult to generalise to rather more complex majorities.

A principal issue in the modern welfare state is how much in the way of welfare services and income redistribution the 'median voter' is prepared to allow or support. For in the end a society of egotists would not be prepared to support an 'altruistic' social policy. To claim otherwise would be an odd position to take. It would imply that a group of benevolently inclined policy-makers were able to hood-wink a community of egotistical voters into accepting altruistic social policies. It has the further implication, of comfort to the élite perhaps, that the voters are generally selfish but stupid while their rulers are altruistic and wise. I find this implausible. If a society is truly selfish it can surely be manipulated into adopting non-selfish policies only for short periods: after that it will throw out those rulers who have hoodwinked it.

SUMMARY

The standard assumption of self-interest is simply a special case, though a highly important special case. It ignores those non-selfish elements in his behaviour of which man has always been conscious and has to be stretched to the very limit to accommodate everyday instances of altruistic conduct. Certainly the self-interest assumption may be defended in the most unlikely circumstances, but the modifications needed proliferate in an *ad hoc* fashion. Once this happens to a theory it is perhaps time to look elsewhere. I have suggested that an 'attribution' assumption be made in order to rescue the theory from tautology; that, in general, altruism will not be strong enough to give rise either to the after-you problem or to complete consensus; that non-selfishness may grow or decline, in a dynamic fashion and that no crude explanation of altruistic 'weights' will serve. Looking ahead a little, I claim that (except in the special 'non-twisting' case) altruism will:

(i) create a need for socially co-operative action, but

(ii) itself facilitate voluntary social co-operation.

I also claim that, particularly in a large community, altruism will have to be buttressed by duty if it is to be effective. It is interesting in this connection that the dictionary definition of altruism combines taste and duty: 'regard for others as *a principle of action*' (*Concise Oxford Dictionary*). Where neither love nor duty is sufficient to generate spontaneous co-operation, altruistic preferences may express themselves through the ballot box.

2 Exchange

In this chapter I examine the pure theory of exchange when utilities are interdependent. The case relevant to altruism is where consumption externalities (the effect of *his* consumption on *my* welfare) are positive. I do not claim that the presence of such externalities is either a necessary or a sufficient condition for altruism: it is not *necessary* because the altruist may be moved by general considerations of humanity rather than feelings towards specific others, and it is not *sufficient* because interdependence may have nothing to do with altruism (for example, my pleasure from drinking with you rather than alone). Nevertheless there is much common ground here and an analysis of utility interdependence can hardly fail to illuminate the issues.

The chapter falls into three short sections. A simple mathematical treatment is provided in an extended chapter note.[1]

THE EDGEWORTH BOX

Following Edgeworth (1881), Boulding (1962) and others[2] it is convenient to set up the problem using a suitably modified Edgeworth Box diagram. On the traditional egotistical assumption each individual's utility function is defined only over 'his' consumption. In order to map out his preferences one only needs to know the goods in his consumption set. Once the self-interest assumption is dropped, however, one's utility depends on the whole consumption set. It is useful to refer to these preferences as one's *social preferences* (defined over the whole consumption set) as opposed to one's *private preferences* (defined on one's own consumption set).

The most striking point to be made is that the individual's

18

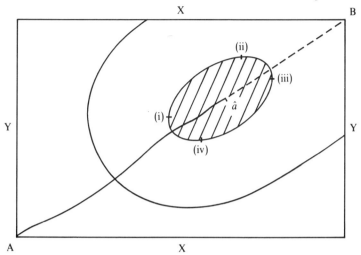

FIGURE 2.1 *The modified Edgeworth Box*

preferred set (shown as the shaded area in Figure 2.1) may become closed: that is to say, he reaches an interior 'bliss-point'. Individual A's bliss-point is at *â*. He would definitely prefer *â* to the apparently more favourable allocations to the north-east. On this account Edgeworth divided the contract curve into two parts, the pure and impure parts, and, similarly, Frisch (1971) distinguishes between the *Kooperationskurve* and *Konflictkurve*. Allocations to the north-east of *â* may be improved upon by moving to *â*, yielding the unfamiliar result that movements *along* the contract curve may be Pareto improvements! This cannot happen along the pure stretches of the curve, however.

A short conducted tour around the modified indifference curve may be helpful. The four points marked indicate the western, northern, eastern and southern extremities of the curve.

(i) – (ii)   A is allocated more of both commodities but feels no better off. His marginal rate of substitution between commodities X and Y is positive and as he is offered more Y he requires progressively more X in compensation.

(ii) – (iii)   A is allocated less Y but more X. His marginal rate of substitution is now negative, as is normal, but its curvature is perverse. As he is allocated more X he requires progressively less Y in compensation.

(iii) – (iv) A is allocated less of both commodities but feels no worse off. His marginal rate of substitution is positive but as he is allocated less X he is prepared only to take progressively smaller reductions in Y.

(iv) – (i) Over this range A's preferences are 'normal' though the curvature is greater than that of a private indifference curve passing through the same point. His marginal rate of substitution is negative and he requires progressively more Y to compensate him for reductions in X.

Boulding made interesting use of this approach to demarcate sectors of the Edgeworth Box (see Figure 2.2). For simplicity I have drawn a contract curve running to the corners of the box. Frisch discusses the path of the curve on various specific assumptions about the algebraic form of the closed curves. The easiest case to take is sector (5), in which the pure contract curve lies and where

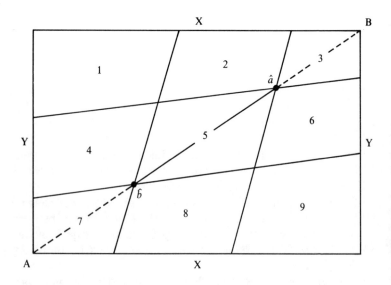

FIGURE 2.2 *Boulding's segmentation of the modified Edgeworth Box*

both parties are selfish with respect to both goods. Similarly, both parties are altruistic or charitable in respect of both goods in sectors (3) and (7). In sectors (1) and (9) both parties are altruistic in the same good and selfish in the other. In sectors (2), (4), (6) and (8) both parties are altruistic in respect of one good and selfish in the other. For example, in sector (2) individual A is altruistic in respect of Y but selfish in respect of X and individual B vice-versa. The approach is versatile in that it can take quite different preference patterns into account. For example, if A is very interested in B's consumption of X his indifference curves will be more or less U-shaped; if in B's consumption of Y they will be more or less C-shaped. One has, therefore, in the Edgeworth Box a useful exploratory tool for analysing utility interdependence. At the risk of some (slight) confusion I shall refer to the modified contract curve as the *social* contract curve, to be contrasted with the usual *private* contract curve. It has already been noticed that, when preferred sets are closed and there is an interior bliss-point, the social contract curve will be a shrunken version of the private curve. This '*shrinking theorem*' is intuitively acceptable on the assumption of diminishing marginal utility of income. At allocations near the extreme north-east corner of the box B's marginal utility must be very high and even very mild altruism on A's part would be sufficient to keep $\hat{a}$ within the box. Should altruism be extremely weak, the modified indifference curves will have greater curvature than ordinary curves but there will be no interior bliss-point. Altruism would then be completely Pareto-irrelevant: there would be no *shrinking*, neither would there be any *twisting* (see below).

Edgeworth showed (Collard, 1975) that if each individual takes only the *utility* of the other into account, the social contract curve will merely be a shrunken but not a 'twisted' version of the private curve. This very important proposition, which is not at all difficult to prove has recently resurfaced in the literature[3] and may be christened the *non-twisting* theorem. It implies that when I consider another's welfare I accept *his* marginal rates of substitution between goods, my attitude being variously described as non-paternalistic, non-specific or non-meddlesome. These attitudes almost always carry moral approval in the literature and it is difficult to find neutral but acceptable terminology. Perhaps 'non-specific' is the least prejudicial of them, though I shall frequently use 'non-meddlesome'.

EXISTENCE

Before moving on to discuss welfare propositions, one should be reasonably confident that an equilibrium exists under utility inter-dependence. Fortunately, this is not the place for a rigorous proof. It is intuitively clear that convexity must be a crucial assumption in any such proof. Provided that preferred sets *are* convex, there will be a separating hyperplane between them.

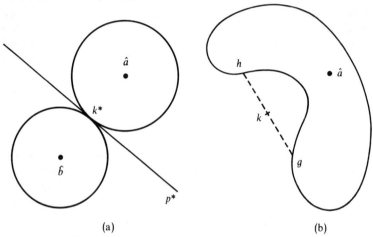

(a)   (b)

FIGURE 2.3   *Convex and non-convex preferred sets*

Thus the price line p^* supports an equilibrium at k^* in Figure 2.3(a). Is convexity of an individual's social preferences a reasonable assumption? Given that private preferred sets are convex, it surely *is* a reasonable assumption. If A is socially indifferent between h and g it would be rather perverse of him to prefer them to some linear combination k when both individuals would privately have preferred k. Socially preferred sets like the kidney-shaped set in Figure 2.3(b) seem unlikely.

Several writers, beginning with McKenzie (1955), have demon-strated the existence of competitive equilibrium with consumption externalities. The brief discussion that follows here is based on Arrow and Hahn (1971).[4] The authors make the same distinction as is made in the chapter notes between preferences *given* the allocations to others and preferences over the entire set of allocations; but they concentrate on the former as more relevant to their existence problem. Apart from a modification of their assumption of continuity to take externality into account, Arrow and Hahn essentially allow all the normal assumptions to hold, viz., transitivity, connexity, continuity, semi-strict convexity and non-satiation. The difference is that private preferences, $U_h(X_h)$, are everywhere replaced by social preferences, $U_h(X_h, w^*)$ where w^* is a consumption allocation across the whole economy. Essentially the only extra condition is that every household is 'indirectly resource-related', which seems in general to be a reasonable condition and holds trivially in a pure exchange economy.

Laffont and Laroque (1972) go considerably further by allowing for production-to-consumption and consumption-to-production externalities. On this also see Osana (1973). Additionally, as well as treating the usual formulation of utility interdependence they remark, in an annex, that:

> la notion de minimum vital social est mal représentée par la relation introduite jusqu'ici entre les preferences d'un consom-mateur et les choix des autres. Une liason avec la borne inférieure de l'ensemble de consommation parait plus adéquate. [Laffont and Laroque, 1972, p. 47]

I have not followed this suggestion here, but it is relevant to the discussion of needs and redistribution in kind in Chapter 12.

WELFARE

One is now in a position to consider what happens to the basic propositions of welfare economics when consumption externalities are introduced. These theorems are:
  (i) every competitive equilibrium is a Pareto optimum;
  (ii) every Pareto optimum may be supported by a competitive equilibrium and involuntary transfers.

Envisage them in the context of the normal Edgeworth Box analysis. The first theorem says that the process of competition will lead to a unique efficient point on the contract locus. The second theorem says that any point on the contract curve may be sustained by a combination of competition and lump-sum transfers. This second proposition is often considered to be of wider interest as

Pareto-optimal points could equally well be sustained by centrally calculated prices under market socialism.

Do these theorems still hold when externalities are allowed? A key point is that competitive equilibrium is essentially a non-collusive equilibrium reached as a consequence of individual actions. In the spirit of the introductory chapter, one has to ask whether the presence of non-selfishness makes explicit co-operation necessary for efficient exchange to be achieved. *A priori*, externalities will in general indicate an equilibrium different from competitive equilibrium: hence it will have to be achieved by another, probably co-operative, mechanism.

The first point to notice is that a competitive equilibrium might result in a point on the impure contract curve (the dotted portion in Figure 2.3(a)). A price line p' supports an equilibrium at which both marginal rates of substitution equal the price ratio. But it is obvious that k' cannot be a full equilibrium as $\hat{a}$ is preferred to k' by both parties. I imagine that this possibility was what Arrow and Hahn had in mind when they wrote:

> In the presence of externalities, the competitive equilibrium is conditionally Pareto-efficient, that is, Pareto efficient according to the utility functions and production possibility sets corresponding to the equilibrium allocation. Of course, the equilibrium is not Pareto-efficient in any broader sense; other allocations may indeed improve the utility of all, when the utility considered is a function of the entire allocation. [Arrow and Hahn, 1971, p. 132–6]

Presumably Borglin (1973) also had such points in mind when referring to examples of instability at apparently Pareto-optimal positions.

But this possibility requires only a minor modification of the basic theorems. Starting from some allocation k (Figure 2.4(b)), let there be a voluntary redistribution t (measured in terms of x) from individual A to individual B. This would put both agents on the price line $\hat{p}$ supporting $\hat{a}$. Now define $\hat{a}$ as a *net* competitive equilibrium, i.e. competitive equilibrium after *voluntary* transfers. The first theorem may then be restated:

(i) Every net competitive equilibrium is a Pareto optimum.

As for the second theorem, consider Figure 2.4(b) once more. While the redistribution t is voluntary, any further redistribution away from A, to support any point to the south-west of $\hat{a}$ on the

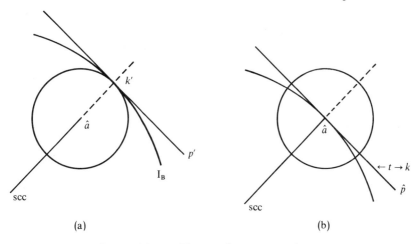

(a)   (b)

FIGURE 2.4   *Equilibrium and Pareto-optimality*

social contract curve, would be resisted. Hence theorem (ii) becomes:

(ii) every Pareto optimum may be supported by a competitive
     equilibrium and some mix of voluntary and involuntary
     transfers.

It will be convenient for the purpose of later discussion to refer
to the voluntary element in this as 'Pareto-optimal' redistribution.
Of course, the voluntary transfer element may be zero in particular
cases.

With these minor changes, then, the basic theorems seem to hold
well enough, provided, of course, that the *non-twisting* assumption
is made, i.e. that the old private contract curve coincides with the
social contract curve in its pure section. Given this, the welfare
implications are comforting. One is able, for example, to make
Wicksteed's assumption (see Chapter 6) of non-tuistic behaviour:
that is to say, not that people are selfish, but that their unselfishness
is not relevant to the process of exchange. This is an enormous
social contract curve in its pure section. Given this, the welfare
implications are comforting. One is able, for example, to make
Wicksteed's assumption (see Chapter 6) of non-tuistic behaviour:
that is to say, not that people are selfish, but that their unselfishness
is not relevant to the process of exchange. This is an enormous
gain from the informational standpoint and certainly saves one from
continual anxiety about the indirect effects of one's daily market

behaviour. As Archibald and Donaldson (1976) put it, 'optimality is attainable in the everyday world in which we do not even know the names of all our fellow-citizens, much less their preferences'.

At this stage of the discussion I must raise the spectre of Kantian versus non-Kantian behaviour. If individual agents behave non-Kantianly difficulties are created even for the apparently simple *non-twisting* case. Though he did not use this terminology, Winter (1969) essentially argued that the first theorem would fail to hold whenever optimality required voluntary transfers. Assume that a Pareto optimum relative to social preferences has to be a position where no one is in poverty.

> There may easily be competitive equilibria which, in the absence of gifts, would leave some individuals in poverty [the last figure will serve for this purpose]. Does the possibility of gifts make a difference? Only if some individual can, by redistributing *his own income*, lift everyone out of poverty (without going into poverty himself). Other-wise no single individual can improve his situation in any degree by giving any part of his income away.

The implication of this line of argument is that some form of social co-operation would be necessary if a Pareto optimum were to be achieved. Winter is much less pessimistic about the second optimality theorem, which holds even when externalities are intro-duced. However, he carefully restricts his comments to the case which one now knows to be relatively straightforward, where each individual's Bergsonian welfare function, $w^i[u^1(x_1)...u^m(x_m)]$, depends on the own-preferences of others. In his own words, 'the amended theorem points up the fact that there is more scope for reliance on the price mechanism in a community of men of goodwill than in a community of ill-will – *provided that the goodwill is accompanied by respect for each other's tastes*' (my italics). The italicised clause is simply a statement of the non-twisting condition.

Such pessimism about the first theorem, even under apparently favourable assumptions, has its roots in the co-operative nature of efficient redistribution. For this part of the discussion I shall assume that voluntary co-operation is Kantian rather than empathetic. Both A and B perceive the macroscopic effects of their actions as simply the two-person case writ large. Each asks himself, in a Kantian fashion, what the effects of his action would be if each A or each B behaved as he did. The two-person case (see extended n. 1 to chapter) is misleadingly simple in that the effects of one individual's conduct on the other's allocation is obvious and direct (if A has one unit less B has one unit more). Now let there be n_a and n_b individuals of type A and B and let individual A believe that, when he consumes one unit less, a proportion r of A's will do likewise. Then as n becomes large (or indeed if $n_a = n_b$), A's expectation of the macroscopic effects of his action comes to depend entirely on r. If each A expects r to be unity or feels he ought to behave *as though* it were unity then the effect is still -1. But suppose, on the contrary, that each A expects no one else to reduce consumption at the same time. Then the expected effect will approximate to 0 and each individual's social marginal rate of substitution will be exactly the same as his private rate. Figure 2.5 illustrates the easy case of nonmeddlesome preferences where k is a point on the private-social contract locus and the indifference curves passing through k nest within one another as r rises.

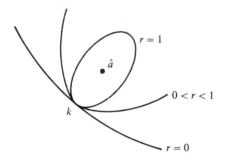

FIGURE 2.5 *Modified indifference curves through k with alternative assumptions about r*

Thus the Kantian altruist's preferred set will correspond to his true social preferences whereas the non-Kantian's will approximate to the egotist's. The non-Kantian may feel altruistic towards the poor, but, he will argue, his individual contribution is of no importance: the Kantian will voluntarily take part in appropriate collective action on the dictates of his categorical imperative. But the non-Kantians would nevertheless find it worthwhile to accept a *social contract* whereby they could collectively redistribute to the poor.

These remarks about collective action apply *a fortiori* when *twisting* takes place (or preferences are 'meddlesome'). It may be shown (see Chapter 12) that meddlesome concern implies different prices for the same commodity between persons, depending on the degree of social sympathy they excite. The same difficulty arises as with Winter's discussion of transfers: even though I feel altruistic towards the poor, I will not, being non-Kantian, trade necessities with them on favourable terms unless I can be confident that other A's will behave similarly.

Where altruists are non-Kantian, doubtless the general case, the outlook for the first optimality theorem is rather bleak. It

> requires strong conditions excluding almost completely the external effects of preference relations, . . . externalities in preference relations are great obstacles for a competitive process to achieve an optimal resource allocation. [Osana, 1972]

The prospects for the second optimality theorem are nothing like as bleak so long as preferences are non-meddlesome.[5] It will then be possible for a central authority to choose prices that support a socially optimal allocation. Individual agents will then take these prices as given and reach socially preferred positions subject to them. But if the non-twisting condition fails, or if preferences are meddlesome, not even a market socialist solution will do, as trade will be subject to discriminating prices.

MALEVOLENCE

Benevolence is a fundamental theme of this book. Yet it has been correctly argued by de Graaff (1957), Scott (1972) and Brennan (1973) that voluntary redistribution could come about through the opposite motive, malevolence. In the extreme case, if all members of a community were jealous of one another, it might be possible to increase welfare by reducing everyone's goods. Indeed, some of the earlier discussions of consumption externalities seemed particularly fascinated by this pathological case (see for example, Mishan, 1960, p. 253).

Brennan puts up a particularly strong case for assuming malice and envy. Thus:

> individuals motivated by malice and envy may also be prepared to contribute to redistributive programmes, not because they value increased consumption by the poor, but because they value reduced consumption by the rich, . . . it does appear as if malice

and envy may not be wholly unmitigated evils – which is perhaps reassuring, since they do seem to exist in some abundance. [Brennan, 1973, p. 183]

Brennan's analysis is similar to de V. Graaff's, though more explicit. Consider three individuals A, B and C, the former two being rich and C being poor. In de Graaff's analysis A and B envy one another but not C; thus it is possible for both to become better off by redistributing to C. In Brennan's analysis envy is more generalised and A and B could be made better off by the destruction of one another's income,[6] and indeed all three become better off because C, too, is envious. But if we now assume that A and B are indifferent between destruction of their goods and redistribution to C, and if C has a vote, then giving to C will be Pareto-optimal. Scott is concerned with the two-person case and with a diagrammatic generalisation of altruism and envy taken together.

This line of approach is quite a useful one, though not the subject matter of this book. However, I cannot agree with Brennan's remark that malice and envy are 'more in keeping with the spirit of this dismal science, and with the nature of *homo oeconomicus* as traditionally conceived'. The great beauty of the self-interest assumption (see Chapter 1) was its neutrality towards others.

Summary

Interdependent preferences may usefully be examined in the Edgeworth Box tradition: they generate a 'social' contract curve that will not in general coincide with the old 'private' contract curve. It is convenient to think of it as a shrunken and twisted version of that curve. However, the *non-twisting* theorem states that, whenever external concern is non-specific, non-paternalistic or non-meddlesome, the contract locus does not twist, and no interference, except in the matter of transfers, is required.

Various writers have demonstrated the existence of competitive equilibrium with consumption externalities and there is no great difficulty about this provided that preferred sets remain convex. However the 'basic theorems' of welfare economics require considerable modification except where individual agents behave as Kantian altruists. Short of this, Pareto optimality may require collective action.

3 The Free-Rider

It was hinted, at the end of the last chapter, that the free-rider problem is fatal to voluntary social co-operation. This chapter constitutes a brief note on its nature and possible ways of circumventing it.

Most readers will be familiar with the problem. Consider some socially co-operative act (like the maintenance of law and order) which everyone (or nearly everyone) favours. It will be in the narrow interest of each to evade his share of the cost while continuing to enjoy the benefits. Left to their own devices people will attempt a free ride, but these attempts will be frustrated in the aggregate. This line of argument provides a rationale for collective provision since it will not be possible to rely on spontaneous voluntary co-operation. In the language of the next chapter, it would be in the interest of everyone to pursue alpha, or co-operative, strategies whereas each separately will adopt beta, or non-co-operative strategies. No such co-operation is required in a competitive market.

At first sight altruism might be expected to unite the selfish with the collective interest, thus overcoming the free-rider's temptation. An economy of altruists would then be characterised by private exchange in ordinary commodities and voluntary co-operation in public goods within a very minimal collective framework. But it is easy to see that this would require rather an implausible degree of altruism in that each (in the pure cost-sharing case) would need to give the same weight to each other person as to himself. The most common forms of altruism consist in attaching some positive weight to one's family and friends, neighbours and even strangers, but certainly they do not extend to an equal degree to everyone. Were this so, it would be like having everyone adopt a purely utilitarian point of view or having him follow the Kantian precept of asking himself what would happen if everyone behaved as he did.

Socially conscious behaviour of an apparently extreme sort is part of the subject matter of this book so I certainly do not wish to rule it out. Indeed, participants may be led to socially desirable or alpha strategies by behaving *as though* altruistic, or by doing their 'duty' or by an almost unconscious awareness of the superiority of co-operation. This type of behaviour is essential to the understanding of some aspects of our society. But I shall try not to rely upon it where there are plausible alternatives. There is, then, a substantial 'free-rider' problem in spontaneous voluntary co-operation, especially when the action called for is not militaristic or heroic but of a mundane economic nature.[1]

The standard allocative rule for pure public goods – lighthouses, public clocks and parks, law and order – is that:

the *sum* of the marginal rates of substitution between Z (a public good) and X (a private good) over all individuals should equal the marginal rate of transformation between them in production.

How is this Samuelsonian rule to be interpreted when individuals are altruistic? As hinted earlier, there is a conceptual difficulty here in that the benefits of a pure public good (as distinct from their valuation) are collective in nature so cannot be split among individuals. It is therefore not meaningful to make a distinction between altruistic and non-altruistic preferences for public goods.

This seems rather a severe limitation. One useful way round it is to consider the whole class of quasi-public goods which seem to generate quite different bundles of services to different individuals. One is then able to make a legitimate distinction between the public good itself, which is jointly supplied to *everyone*, and the flow of services generated by that good. A useful example is a public park, which is jointly supplied to everyone but yields differential services to, say, nearby residents, young children, old men and dog-owners. Another example would be an urban motorway, which is, again, jointly available to all but yields different services to the inner urban poor and the dormitory town commuters. The altruist will presumably take some of these services into account when valuing alternative levels of quasi-public good provision.

It turns out that an analogue to the *non-twisting* proposition holds when the altruist takes into account only the *utilities* that others derive from a quasi-public good (i.e. when he allows other people's preferences to count) without adopting a paternalistic or 'meddlesome' view. This important point deserves some elaboration. If the rich feel that public parks are good for the poor, there will tend to be a greater provision of parks (*ceteris paribus*) than otherwise. But if the rich are interested in the utilities of the poor directly, the Samuelsonian rule[2] is unchanged. All that is required is some redistribution of income from the rich to the poor – an important matter certainly, but not one that requires a new rule for public good provision.

A *Lindahl* equilibrium for the public good Z is located where the sum of individual 'marginal valuations' of the good equals the marginal cost of provision.[3] Where this is so (Z^*) provision is said to be optimal with respect to the initial allocation of income. In the general case Z^* will not be the same under selfish and non-selfish assumptions. However in the non-twisting case the two Z^*'s will differ from one another only to the extent that, under altruism, some redistribution is required before the Lindahl process for Z begins to operate.

In either event, whether Z^* has shifted or not, the attainment of a Lindahl equilibrium – where competitive markets are in equilibrium and the quantity of public goods is unanimously agreed to, each individual paying a tax price equal to his marginal valuation – gives rise to a free-rider problem closely similar to that already encountered in the pure cost-sharing case. This time it will be in each person's apparent interest to understate the marginal benefit he derives from Z so as to pay a lower tax price. But if everyone does this there will be underprovision of Z and 'everyone' could be made better off by moving to Z^* and having this collective optimum enforced through a tax system.

Pressing this point, Olson (1965) attempted to explain collective behaviour, for example pressure groups of various sorts, in terms of individual rather than collective interests. Even if individuals were to some degree unselfish, each would recognise that the incremental effect of his behaviour on group achievement would nearly always be small in relation to individual costs. When applied to groups like trades unions this conclusion would appear to be somewhat embarrassing: they do, after all, manage to exist. Olson explains apparent solidarity in terms of gains to individuals, for example sickness and legal aid benefits to rank-and-file members or the sweet fruits of office to the activist. Olson's analysis is essentially a swingeing attack on notions of duty, brotherhood or altruism as explanations of group behaviour and carries some conviction when the community concerned is large and the role of the individual small. A similar point was made by Downs (1956) in the context of voting behaviour. Voting involves positive costs in time and trouble and sometimes in money, yet people must know, particularly in non-marginal constituencies, that their individual vote can make precious little difference to the result. So one predicts that *either* (a) hardly anyone will vote *or* (b) people who do vote are 'irrational'. But the fact that people *do* join trades unions and *do* vote should make us pause before swallowing the Olson–Downs argument whole.

It is perfectly possible, of course, that some individuals may be prepared to provide some public goods. For example, individual 1 in Figure 3.1 would be prepared to pay for Z_1, enjoyment of it by 2 and 3 being purely incidental. Olson's rule is:

The optimal amount of a collective good for an individual to

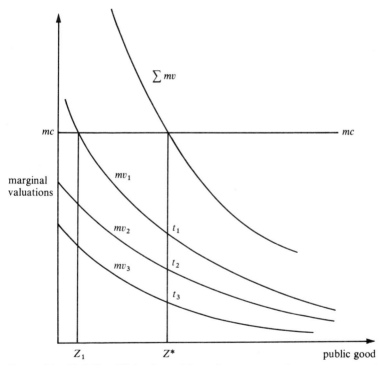

FIGURE 3.1   *Lindahl equilibrium for a public good: mc = marginal cost; mv = marginal valuation; t_1, t_2, t_3 = individual 'tax prices'*

obtain, if he should obtain any, is found when the rate of gain to the group, multiplied by the gain the individual gets, equals the rate of increase of the total cost of the collective good.

Only if the individual gives the same weight to others as to himself will private provision equal optimal collective provision.[4] As Olson remarks, the chances of individual provision are greatest in a small community with unequal incomes.

Free-riders would present no difficulty if people could somehow be prevailed upon to reveal their true preferences. A full Lindahl equilibrium could then be reached. Some recent work has suggested that the chances of this are not quite as thin as had previously been imagined (Groves and Ledyard, 1977). It may be shown that if the 'government' asks individuals to report their whole marginal valuation schedules, and if the government makes its decisions about Z on the basis of reported valuations, then individuals will be led to reveal their 'true' preferences. This happens because at each stage the individual reviews the amount of Z proposed and *finds it in his own interest* to revise his reported valuation in the direction of his true one.[5] It is too early yet to say whether this kind of work will lead to weaker conditions for true reporting of preferences. For the present it would be safer to assume that the free-rider problem will continue to be a major difficulty in public goods analysis.

Finally, the problem would vanish in a community where telling the truth was a dominant ethic (though not in the purely cost-sharing case). Each would feel it a duty to report his true marginal valuation. Hirsch (1975) has interestingly suggested, in a banking context, that 'telling the truth and keeping one's word' may be treated as collective intermediate goods, the creation of which is positively hindered by normal competitive processes. But he adds that a truth-telling ethic may be most effectively induced in small, closely knit groups. Once again, therefore, the small group seems to be more promising than the large group for voluntary co-operation.

Outside the small group situation the only way for altruistic individual preferences to find expression in collective action is through the ballot box. The outcome then depends on two sets of factors, first the prevalence of altruism in the community and second the decision-making process linking individual preferences and social choice. Simple majority voting is the easiest rule to deal with, for then (under perfect conditions) the median outcome is uniquely selected. This outcome will *not* correspond to a Lindahl equilibrium unless side-payments are allowed. With more complex majorities the property of uniqueness disappears but the outcome is still determinate.[6]

Meade's solution is wholly in the spirit of preserving non-tuistic market behaviour tempered by socially conscious voting:

> In my view the ideal society would be one in which each citizen developed a real split personality, acting selfishly in the market place and altruistically at the ballot box.... it is, for example, only by such 'altruistic' political action that there can be any alleviation of 'poverty' in a society in which the poor are in a minority. [Meade, 1973, p. 52]

SUMMARY

The 'free-rider' problem highlights the improbability of voluntary co-operation. Altruism does not in itself eliminate the problem except in the case of the perfect utilitarian. However, the attempt to explain *all* co-operative behaviour in terms of self-interest seems to put a heavy strain on that assumption. The size of the co-operating group is obviously an important factor and is a major concern of the chapters that follow. Only Kantian behaviour based on a sense of duty is strong enough to overcome the free-rider problem. Altruism, unless extensive, is not.

In large societies individual altruism has to take effect through the mechanism of political choice.

4 Non-Selfish Games

I now wish to look at non-selfish games, starting with the famous *prisoner's dilemma.*[1] The point of this class of game is that the co-operative outcome is better for all concerned than the non-co-operative outcomes. The terminology of the game is not entirely unfortunate, for it emphasises that the goodness of the outcome relates to the players taking part (be they prisoners, members of a cartel or whatever), not to society as a whole. What I propose to show in this chapter is that, for a limited class of cases, non-selfishness increases the chances of a co-operative outcome.

Some simple terminology is needed. In general, let the co-operative strategies be indicated by α and the non-co-operative strategies by β. Taking the game as symmetrical, write the pay-offs in Table 4.1. For example, Player 2 receives a pay-off $\alpha\beta$ if he plays

TABLE 4.1 *Pay-off matrix*

		Player 2	
	Strategy	α	β
Player 1	α	$\alpha\alpha, \alpha\alpha$	$\alpha\beta, \beta\alpha$
	β	$\beta\alpha, \alpha\beta$	$\beta\beta, \beta\beta$

α when Player 1 plays β. The structure of the game is determined by the relative sizes of the pay-offs. Their ranking for Player 1 is:

temptation or free-rider's pay-off ($\beta\alpha$)	>	fully co-operative pay-off ($\alpha\alpha$)	>	wholly non-co-operative pay-off ($\beta\beta$)	>	sucker's pay-off ($\alpha\beta$)

To show that $\beta\beta$ will result under selfish behaviour we may assume either that each player follows a maxi-min policy or that he pursues the temptation pay-off. In the first case he chooses β because $\beta\beta$ is better than $\alpha\beta$. In the second case he chooses β hoping for $\beta\alpha$.

36

If each is similarly motivated each chooses β and they are locked into $\beta\beta$. This is rather a shame because $\alpha\alpha$ is definitely better than $\beta\beta$ for both parties – it is, in fact, Pareto-better.

Notice that this would still be true even if Player 1 received a convincing *assurance* that 2 would play α. He could take advantage of 2's co-operative behaviour and run away with the temptation pay-off. For co-operation it would be necessary that

$$\alpha\alpha > \beta\alpha$$

i.e., that the co-operative pay-off be greater than the temptation pay-off. One would then have an *assurance game*.[2] Unfortunately, assurance games are nothing like as common in the economic context as prisoners' dilemmas. Take the simple example of keeping the neighbourhood tidy – am I more or less likely to tidy up if I believe everyone else will do so?

CONVERSION INTO ASSURANCE GAMES

Experimenters have discovered, however, that players do not in fact get locked into $\beta\beta$-type strategies as one might have expected. I turn to the question of why this is so after introducing a simple way of converting prisoners' dilemmas into assurance games.

Table 4.2 gives a numerical example. Clearly we have a prisoner's

TABLE 4.2   *An illustrative prisoner's dilemma*

	Strategy	Player 2 α	β
Player 1	α	1, 1	$-2, 2$
	β	2, -2	0, 0

dilemma, for $2 > 1 > 0 > -2$. The players will tend to choose β and become locked into $\beta\beta$ with zero pay-offs. They could both do better by moving to $\alpha\alpha$. Let us call these numbers the *primary* pay-offs. Now let each player attach a weight, v, to the other's pay-off and $(1 - v)$ to his own pay-off. So far v has been 0 and there has been no need to bother about it. How big must v be to convert this prisoner's dilemma into an assurance game? The

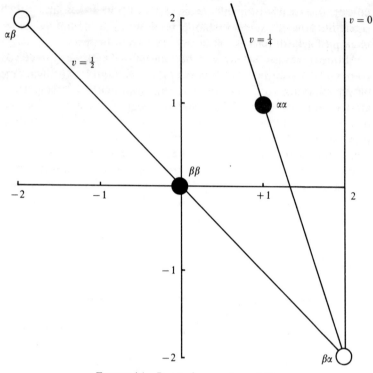

FIGURE 4.1   *Required conversion weights*

weight v^* at which the conversion takes place is $\frac{1}{4}$ in this case.[3]

If each expects the other to co-operate and attaches a weight of more than $\frac{1}{4}$ to the other's pay-off, he will himself co-operate. Both trust and 'love' are needed, love being, as it were, a catalyst of mutual gain. It is useful to have a graphical representation of the result just obtained. In Figure 4.1 the outcomes $\alpha\beta$ and $\beta\alpha$ are lightly marked as they are to some degree illusory. With zero weighting one has only to read from right to left to order the outcomes for Player 1. Similarly, one reads from top to bottom to order Player 2's outcomes. It can be seen that as 1's weight *exceeds* $\frac{1}{4}$, $\alpha\alpha$ will be chosen rather than $\beta\alpha$.

One more piece of terminology must be introduced. If there is assurance $v > \frac{1}{4}$ is required. If there is no assurance $v > \frac{1}{2}$ is required. I refer to this as an *assurance positive* game. The more assurance there is, the less unselfishness is required to yield co-operation. Intuitively one would expect this to be the case rather often. Surprisingly often, however, economic games turn out to be *assurance neutral* (or even *assurance negative*).

Another way of saying that I am (convincingly) assured of co-operation is to say that I attach a probability of 1 to the other player adopting α and of 0 to his playing β. But my belief in his co-operation will depend upon various factors including whether or not he has given an assurance, my trust in human nature, his previous record of co-operation, our subscription to a common ethic and so on. It would therefore not be at all unreasonable to use a subjective *probability* of co-operation, π. A slight generalisation of the numerical example is then possible. The co-operative strategy will be played by either player if,[4]

$$v > \tfrac{1}{2}(1 - \pi/2).$$

Any combination of v and π lying in the shaded region of Figure 4.2 will cause a player to choose α rather than β. For

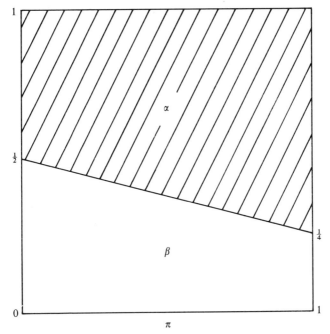

FIGURE 4.2 *An assurance-positive game*

example, if I think there is a $\frac{3}{4}$ chance of co-operation on your part and I attach a weight of $\frac{1}{3}$ to your pay-off I shall be willing to play α.

Sen's (1973b) illustration of the prisoner's dilemma during a discussion of the inappropriateness of the revealed preference axiom may be recast as in Table 4.3. With assurance, the required

TABLE 4.3   *A Prisoner's Dilemma*

	Not confess	Confess
Not confess	−2, −2	−20, 0
Confess	0, 20	−10, −10
Differences	−2, +18	−10, +10

weight for co-operation is $v = \frac{1}{10}$; with mistrust it is $v = 1$. Hence there is a strong *positive assurance tilt* to this particular game.

Sen, though not performing this exercise, remarks:

> The prisoners' non-confession will be quite easy to put within the framework of revealed preference if it were the case that they had so much concern for the sufferings of each other that they would choose non-confession on grounds of joint welfare of the two.

Maximisation of joint welfare would require a weight of unity, but, as has just been demonstrated, as long as there is assurance, non-confession is likely even at weights of very much less than 1.

In the chapters that follow I wish to retain the very simple structure of this model and to apply it to particular problems. For that reason we require a generalisation to a many-player game where α and β are still the strategies available but where the pay-offs are the pay-offs to *me* and to *each other* player. The generalisation is almost entirely notational so is confined to a footnote.[5]

EXPERIMENTAL GAMES

It is terribly easy to fall into the trap of reading more into these simple games than they can really bear, 'to develop a pantheon of player types in the study of matrix games: heroes, martyrs, cooperators, teachers and learners, selfish and selfless players' and to supply 'fanciful scenarios' (Shubik, 1975). Nevertheless, game theorists have hoped to learn a certain amount about human behaviour by observing how people act in artificial[6] gaming situations.

One such study is due to Rapoport and Chammah (1965). Although they themselves did not use the terminology, a useful distinction may be made between a *supergame* and a *dynamic game*. A supergame is just the same game played lots of times over. In a dynamic game the outcome of any one game is affected by what happened in previous games. In theory the players of a prisoner's dilemma supergame will play the non-co-operative β every time. I would certainly choose β in the very last (say 100th) game; the 99th game then becomes the last so I choose β for that, and so on. The fact that players do not seem to choose β all the time is attributed to an 'intellectual shortcoming'. Rapoport and Chammah conclude that 'the most typical feature of the time course of a prisoner's dilemma protocol is the initial decline in co-operation, followed eventually by a recovery'. They find, among other things, more variation between pairs of players than within pairs and increasing co-operation when information is readily displayed and when the sexes are mixed. The static supergame effectively becomes a dynamic game in which each player builds up expectations about how the other will behave. Among the sorts of response possible are the passive playing of a single strategy (which tends to invite exploitation), tit-for-tat responses, random responses, and threatening to drop out of the game altogether.

More recently Eiser (1975) has reviewed co-operative and competitive games and has expressed strong doubts about whether they can really be understood in terms of 'pay-offs'. He criticises gamers for concentrating solely on such pay-offs and ignoring psychological factors. His are important reservations, as the standard type of experiment consists in investigating the response of players to variations in pay-offs. Indeed, he goes beyond psychological factors to consider notions of justice and fairness. People are quite happy to behave in a self-interested way except when they see others acting in a co-operative or restrained fashion or where others make direct appeals to them. Like Rapoport and Chammah, Eiser comments that communication has a favourable effect on co-operation.

Even this very brief look at the literature is enough to suggest
that the relationships concerned are very subtle and complex. One
cannot hope to capture them successfully in any simple model.
Figure 4.3 illustrates just one simple dynamic path consistent with
the basic model I have suggested. I am concerned only with the
first player (me). Two important assumptions are made:

(i) My concern for the other player and consequently the weight
     I attach to his pay-off increases gradually to some maximum
     as the series of games progresses. The opposite assumption
     could equally well have been made. The gaming literature
     seems to suggest that close contact between the players is
     likely to produce a relatively high weight.

(ii) I initially assume that the other player will behave co-
     operatively. Perhaps we have made some sort of prior (but
     unenforceable) agreement about this, or perhaps I am merely
     naive. But I gradually learn that he is co-operating for about
     half of the time regardless of my own behaviour.

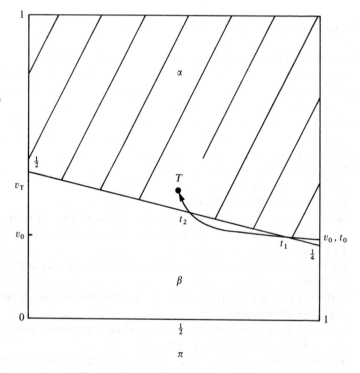

FIGURE 4.3   *An illustrative time-path*

It must be admitted that these assumed interrelationships are excessively simple. Indeed, the time path followed is typical of games in the aggregate rather than of particular pairs (Rapoport, 1974). But while it would certainly be possible to simulate much more complicated relationships, we do not yet have a sound behavioural basis for them. As long as this is so a simple illustration is probably no less helpful than a complicated simulation. Under our assumptions the line in Figure 4.3 shows the time path of v and π and therefore whether I play α or β. Initially I play α. After t_1 I change over to β, and remain at β for a while until t_2. After this I switch again to α. v_0 is the weight attached to the other player's pay-offs at the beginning and v_T the weight at the termination of the game. Between t_0 and t_1 I select α, between t_1 and t_2, β, but after t_2 I settle down to α.

ETHICAL BASES FOR CO-OPERATION

Runciman and Sen have already remarked (1965) that the prisoner's dilemma rather nicely illustrates Rousseau's distinction between the 'general will' and the 'will of all'. The general will is, of course, for $\alpha\alpha$ but each pursues his own separate will and chooses β. Each then seeks an agreement, a social contract, whereby $\alpha\alpha$ is chosen.

This seems a good moment to note a surprising confluence of ethical systems in that all roads lead, as it were, to $\alpha\alpha$. All of the following lead to co-operative behaviour:

(i)   pursuit of the general will,
(ii)   the utilitarian outcome,
(iii) 'Kantian' behaviour ('if the intent of the action can without self-contradiction be universalised it is morally possible'),
(iv) the assurance game and trust,
(v)   a prisoner's dilemma converted into an assurance game by non-selfishness,
(vi) the Christian ethic of turning the other cheek,
(vii) the Pareto principle,
(viii) the 'Rawlsian' principle that one should maximise the pay-off of the least well-off player.

These considerations reinforce Eiser's point that to concentrate simply on the pay-offs is to miss the point. People are able to make the imaginative leap to co-operative behaviour if they are aware of the social advantages of co-operation and if their self-interest is modified by an α-biased ethic. They are able to perceive that the temptation and sucker pay-offs are illusory and that the game really boils down to co-operation or non-co-operation. But if this is so, is it a matter of indifference to us whether co-operation is described in terms of (modified) pay-offs or ethics? The great and essential difference is that, by retaining a pay-off structure in which the pay-offs are self-interested, as the basis, one is able to show how powerful the ethic has to be in order to secure co-operation. The economist, in his hum-drum fashion, then feels able to predict for specific socioeconomic situations whether or not spontaneous co-operation is likely.

SUMMARY

In a prisoner's dilemma game players will find themselves locked into an inferior non-co-operative set of outcomes even though each is attempting to follow his self-interest. Under some circumstances the dilemma may be unlocked in so far as non-selfish motivation turns the game into an assurance game which is altogether more tractable. All that is then required is that each *trusts* the other to behave co-operatively. This trust is handled analytically in terms of a subjective probability of co-operation, and a simple dynamic path is briefly considered.

Finally, it is noted that almost all ethical and moral systems would point to $\alpha\alpha$ rather than $\beta\beta$ strategies: only myopic economic man is led to $\beta\beta$.

5 Egotism and Evolution

The Social Darwinist view was that altruism enhanced man's evolutionary prospects only to a minor degree: the obvious contrast is with Kropotkin, who argued that sympathy was the basis of human society. However, Herbert Spencer, the leading Social Darwinist, took nothing like as hostile an attitude towards altruism as an evolutionary force as has commonly been supposed. Indeed, I suspect that his view would have been highly acceptable to Adam Smith. Family and parental altruism should, he believed, extend to the whole of society sufficiently to permit social intercourse. His examples are low-key – honesty in dealings, an interest in public affairs, belief in justice; all the virtues of the upright Victorian male. Some examples are quaint. He complains of 'the acted falsehood of railway passengers who, by dispersed coats, make him believe that all the seats in a compartment are taken when they are not' (Spencer, 1904, ch. 12). But inadequate egoism is just as bad as inadequate altruism; viz. the poor clerk who overworks until he develops 'scrivener's palsy' and has to retire in shabby poverty for himself and family. Likewise, extreme forms of altruism (Benthamism, Christianity and the Kantian universality principle) lead to absurdities.

Along with Hume and Titmuss, Spencer believes in the contagion principle but also that the *need* for altruism decreases with the advance of society.[1] He is firmly against beneficence outside the family to good-for-nothings and even to the sick, strongly against the poor law and organised charity, and finally adopts his famous view of 'survival of the fittest' in society. In light of more modern discussions, his view of altruism among insects is especially interesting (Spencer, 1904, esp. Ch. 1 p. 14).

Kropotkin, taking an opposite view, noticed that the Darwinian struggle for suvival is not marked among animals of the same species and concluded that *co-operation*, as well as competition, was a factor in evolution. But he does not base his analysis on love or personal sympathy so much as on 'a more vague feeling or instinct of human solidarity' or man's 'perception of his oneness with each human being' (Kropotkin, 1904/1972, p. 251). He argues that mutual aid is a powerful factor among small groups, families, village communities and the poor, whereas the centralised power of the State encourages narrow individualism. Political economists are strongly condemned:

> The theory that men can, and must, seek their own happiness in a disregard of other people's wants is now triumphant all round . . .; political economists, in their naive ignorance, trace all progress of modern industry and machinery to the 'wonderful' effects of the same principle. [Kropotkin, 1904, p. 197 of 1972 edn]

The underlying question seems to be not whether altruism is desirable in itself but whether it exists and is efficient from an evolutionary standpoint. Joan Robinson (1962) nicely captures the traditional, common-sense view, i.e. that only mother love is strong and that society has to strike some balance between too much altruism and too little.

> Altruistic emotion is strong enough to evoke self-sacrifice from a mother defending her young; it is very unreliable in any other context. . . . a society of unmitigated egoists would knock itself to pieces; a perfectly altruistic individual would soon starve.

Briffault, in his classic study, *The Mothers*[2], argues that *only* mother love is altruistic, that it is the biological basis and beginning of all other bonds and sympathies. Altruism is firmly linked to the family; as a general principle Briffault condemns it as a 'discursive philosophical abstraction'.

Altruism as an efficient device in evolution has been thoroughly discussed by Trivers (1971), to whom these paragraphs owe a great deal. His discussion fits very easily into the prisoner's dilemma model already adopted in Chapter 4. The first question to be asked is whether alpha strategies are better for the species (or sub-species) than beta strategies. Trivers uses, as did Spencer, the analogy of saving a drowning man. It will be socially efficient for rescues to be attempted if the chances of success (without losing the rescuer) are high. If rescue is indeed socially efficient and if drowning is a potentially common hazard, a society of altruists will stand a better chance of survival, under those conditions, than a society of egotists. However, one still has to face the free-rider problem. The easiest case to take is that of implied exchange where similar altruistic acts are expected in return. Trivers shows that primates are good candidates for reciprocity of this kind as they are long-lived and have low dispersal rates. He then considers some simple dynamics of the prisoner's dilemma.

The pay-offs to two individuals under altruistic (A) and competitive (C) conduct are as in the matrix of Table 5.1: R = reward, T = temptation pay-off, S = sucker's pay-off and P = punishment where $S < P < R < T$. Trivers shows that, where the players are exposed to $2n$ reciprocal situations, there is a barrier to the spread of altruism unless n becomes large.

TABLE 5.1 *Altruistic and Competitive Pay-offs*

	A_2	C_2
A_1	R, R	S, T
C_1	T, S	P, P

The time lag is the crucial factor, for it means that only under highly specialised circumstances can the altruist be reasonably guaranteed that the causal chain he initiates with his altruistic act will eventually return to him and confer, directly or indirectly, its benefit. Only under these conditions will the cheater be selected against and this type of altruistic behaviour evolve. [Trivers, 1971, p. 39]

Notice that n here refers to the number of trials in a dynamic game, not to the number of players. Our earlier analysis of games suggested that the likelihood of altruistic behaviour would decrease as the number of participants rose. Putting this together with Trivers' analysis, altruism is most likely to occur when (a) it is efficient, (b) the community is 'small' and (c) all parties expect similar situations to recur over long periods.

Trivers gives three examples of altruistic behaviour. The first concerns cleaning symbioses in fish. As he remarks, there has apparently been strong selection 'to avoid eating one's cleaner' as the fish obtains substantial benefits from being able to return to the same cleaner. His second example is mating calls in birds. Such calls warn other birds but may result in the caller's death. His third example is from human behaviour – helping in times of danger, sharing food, helping the sick, the old and the injured and sharing implements and knowledge. As in so many other cases, it is difficult to distinguish at all sharply between cases of self-interest, of kinship and of wider altruism.

As Trivers points out, whether or not altruism is efficient has to be determined with respect to genes not individuals. Indeed Maddox *et al.* (1976) remarked that 'a bee is simply a device invented by a gene for making more genes'. It certainly does seem that apparently altruistic behaviour turns out to be of the kinship variety. Thus, in the social hymenoptera (bees, wasps, ants), their peculiar reproductive pattern means that sisters are extremely closely related genetically; moreover, the advantages of altruism are great. Something similar happens in the case of dogs and lions: 'it is striking that, whenever a group of animals do manage to evolve cooperative hunting, they turn out to be closely related' (Maddox *et al.*, 1976).

The discussion just referred to was based to some extent on Wilson's important book *Sociobiology* (1975). In that book Wilson reviews previous work on altruism and evolution. A role for altruistic genes is to be found in two crucial stages in the development of a society – first, the pioneering stage, where tough risk-taking behaviour will bring most community benefit, and second when the community has become so large as to be in danger of destroying its habitat. At this second stage quite a different sort of altruism is required – that of restraint and discipline. Failure can occur at either the pioneer or maturation stage. Is it possible that altruism may act as an offset to decline, even in large communities? Wilson concludes that the evolution of altruistic genes in large populations owing to differential population extinction is improbable and turns instead to *kinship* selection, i.e. selection on a much smaller scale involving families or extended families of perhaps ten to one hundred individuals. Here, using the *selfish gene* notion, he argues that the individual will consider not merely his own 'fitness' but the 'fitness' of his relations depending upon his shared heredity or proportion of genes held by common descent. If, by some degree of self-sacrifice, the individual can create more shared genes in the following generation, he will do so. Dawkins, as already noted in chapter 1, has pushed this view rather more strongly in his recent book *The Selfish Gene* (1976).

Boorman and Levitt (1973) have produced an intriguing paper

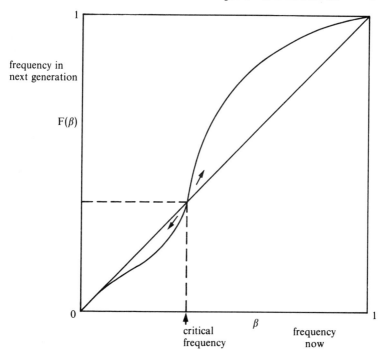

frequency in
next generation

$F(\beta)$

0

1

critical
frequency

β

frequency
now

1

FIGURE 5.1   *Critical frequencies*

on critical levels of a so-called altruism gene in the evolution of
hunting carnivores. Their thesis is that altruism is evolutionarily
efficient, in the sense already described, in a bonded pair: that
co-operation 'pays', and that above a critical frequency the altruism
gene will spread explosively. Figure 5.1 maps the frequency of the
altruism gene in the next generation against its frequency in the
present generation, using rather a special set of assumptions. The
authors argue that growth above the critical level will be exponential
but that decay below it will finally be very slow as the lower part
of the curve lies almost along the 45° line.

One is, of course, acutely aware of the dangers of drawing simple
analogies between genetic theory and social behaviour, but this
notion of critical frequencies is certainly a suggestive[3] one and bears
on the question raised in Chapters 1 and 16 of whether or not
altruism is 'contagious'. Pessimists believe that one is stuck at a low
level of altruism at around the mutational level; that altruism is

scarce and must be economised upon. Optimists believe that the frequency is not too far below the critical and that, with time, leadership, education and so on, it could rise above it, thus enabling altruism to spread to the whole population.

The crucial question posed for us by these discussions is whether altruism is, as it were, merely egotism at one remove and whether the separate analysis of altruism suggested in this book should therefore be abandoned. I do not believe these conclusions can be drawn. Admittedly, a society that displays too much or too little altruism will eventually encounter difficulties in genetic survival. But this will be of little interest to the ordinary individual in his economic behaviour. Many sorts of economic behaviour will be quite neutral as far as genetic survival is concerned, so the 'selfish gene' assumption will be of no help in judging between alternative courses of action. Over and above basic instinctive behaviour economic and social transactions are of an immense richness – why should I feel altruistic towards my genes rather than to the family next door? Indeed, Dawkins himself takes refuge in the analogous concept of the 'meme' in his brief discussion of human society.

SUMMARY

(i)   There will be some circumstances (when altruism is efficient) under which altruism will favour the establishment, stability or growth of a species.

(ii) The work of geneticists supports the often-expressed view (of Sidgwick and Edgeworth, for example) that blood ties play a large part in determining 'coefficients of sympathy'.

(iii) Altruism is more likely among small kinship groups than in larger populations.

(iv) Genetic theory offers some useful rules of change in the frequency of altruistic genes and, by analogy, offers some weak support to the contagion hypothesis.

(v)   Even though individual non-selfishness is consistent with genetic selfishness, it does not seem reasonable (for the purposes of this book) to shift the unit of analysis from the individual to the gene.

6   Antecedents

Since Kuhn (1972) historians of economics have become self-conscious about their motives in seeking historical antecedents for the positions they wish to adopt. The present writer is no exception. The analysis of non-selfishness has been a recurring minor theme in economics: more than this, it was a major theme for Smith in the years before the *Wealth of Nations,* and for the great theorist F. Y. Edgeworth. As the main object of this book is to bring these issues to the centre of the stage I attempt to show, in this chapter, the extent of earlier interest in them.

THE EIGHTEENTH CENTURY

My theme in this first section is British political economy in the period leading up to Smith's *Wealth of Nations.* The key is Smith's theory of the 'invisible hand', which made it possible to construct a political economy without resorting to notions of sympathy or benevolence except in so far as these were a precondition for the institutional framework. What was new about Smith's theory was not his doctrine of social harmony but his efficiency theorem. Thus:

> It is not from the benevolence of the butcher, the brewer or the baker that we expect our dinner, but from their regard to their own interest. We address ourselves not to their humanity but to their self-love, and never talk to them of our own necessities but of their advantages. [Smith, 1776]

But the social outcome of these individually selfish actions is desirable:

> He [the individual] . . . neither intends to promote the public interest, nor knows how much he is promoting it . . . , he intends only his own gain, and he is in this, as in many other cases, led by an invisible hand to promote an end which was no part of his intention. [Smith, 1776]

51

Not content with this rather sensational proposition, Smith further asserted that the outcome would be better than if people had behaved non-selfishly:

> By pursuing his own interest he frequently promotes that of the society *more effectually than when he really intends to promote it.* [Smith, 1776, Bk. IV. Ch. 11 – my italics]

These statements are very clear and very firm: benevolence, it seems, has no place in the *Wealth of Nations*. Smith goes some way towards proving his efficiency theorem even though his argument is far less rigorous than a modern theorist would demand. His 'proof' rests on the efficient allocation of factors of production (especially labour) in response to relative price changes.

Thus far, there is no puzzle. The first and greatest work of scientific economics put self-interest firmly at the centre and there it has remained ever since. But it is worth recalling the apparently rather different line that Smith had taken seventeen years earlier in *Moral Sentiments* (1759). Smith opened his *Moral Sentiments* thus:

> How selfish soever man may be supposed, there are evidently some principles in his nature, which interest him in the fortune of others, and render their happiness necessary to him . . . though he derives nothing from it except the pleasure of feeling it. Of this kind is pity or compassion . . . . [Smith, 1759]

But he cautioned that:

> the care of the universal happiness of all rational and sensible beings, is the business of God and not of man. To man is allocated a much humbler department . . . the care of his own happiness, that of his family, his friends, his country [Smith, 1759, Pt IV]

Smith's 'impartial spectator' judges his own actions as though viewed by impartial others. A great literature,[1] to which I hesitate to add, has grown up around the apparent irreconcilability of these two positions. Unfortunately they cannot be understood without reference to earlier eighteenth-century discussions. What we might call the Optimistic Tradition is well illustrated by the third Earl of Shaftesbury (1669). Summarised rather crudely, his view was that only by being unselfish could one be truly happy: that to concentrate too much on self-affection may make us miserable and damage the 'natural affections' which tend to the public good. To act for the common good is natural:

'Tis not more natural for the stomach to digest, the lungs to breathe, the Glands to separate Juices, or other Intrails to perform their several offices [Shaftesbury, 1669 p. 25]

The general view he takes in his *Inquiry* is that motives must be judged utilitarianly, but he also mixes up two other themes – first that non-selfishness is actually good for one's moral hygiene[2] and second that creatures sometimes seem to act for the good of the species.

Mandeville (1714), in his allegory *Fable of the Bees*, showed that the hive prospered under egotism but flagged under moral restraint. I am concerned here with Mandeville not as a precursor of defective demand but as a critic of benevolence. As he provides a surfeit of marvellous quotations, I limit myself to these:

Pride and Vanity have built more hospitals than all the Virtues put together.

neither the Friendly Qualities and Kind Affections . . . nor the real Virtues . . . but that which we call *evil* in this would . . . is the Grand Principle that makes Sociable Creatures. [Mandeville, 1714, pp. 269, 370]

Frances Hutcheson, well known as a teacher of Adam Smith, reacted to what he regarded as an excessive emphasis on self-interest in Hobbes and Mandeville by attempting to establish the central role in human behaviour of benevolence and sympathy. He believed benevolence to be based not at all on self-interest. The two were quite different forces but were jointly at work. However, the moral rightness of benevolent actions had to be judged by their consequences: thus an action motivated by benevolence, but with an unfortunate outcome, is not praiseworthy. Indeed, a fully universal benevolence could imply collapse.

There are some nearer and stronger Degrees of Benevolence, when the Objects stand in some nearer relation to ourselves. [Hutcheson, 1725, para. 145]

This universal Benevolence toward all men, we may compare to that Principle of Gravitation, which perhaps extends to all Bodys in the Universe: but, like the Love of Benevolence, increases as the Distance is diminished and is strongest when Bodys come to touch each other.

Now this increase of attraction on nearer Approach, is as necessary to the Frame of the Universe, as that there should be any at all. For a general Attraction, equal to all Distances, would by the contrariety of such multitudes of equal Forces, put an end to all Regularity of Motion, and perhaps stop it altogether. [para. 147]

No doubt Hutcheson was here influenced by Dante's passage, based on Empedocles,[3] which runs:

The universe trembled in the throes of love, whereby as some believe, the world's been brought oft-times to chaos.

Taking, as he did, a utilitarian view of these things, Hutcheson must have believed that benevolence would facilitate some co-operative acts that would benefit everyone. Hutcheson also considers that benevolence could generate what he called 'imperfect rights'.

Instances of imperfect Rights are those which the Poor have to the Charity of the Wealthy. [Hutcheson, 1725, para. 147]

He would probably have accepted two of the main themes of this book: the social 'usefulness' of altruism in the right context and its role as a sufficient condition for redistribution. For all this he concedes that, in matters of labour and industry,

Self-love is really as necessary to the Good of the Whole as Benevolence. [para. 180].

Hutcheson thus begs the central question for political economy. Is altruism at all necessary to the efficient working of an economic system?

Bishop Butler's *Sermons* (1729), written a few years after Hutcheson's *Inquiry*, are not at all helpful on this central question, looking as he does to the hereafter:

'Duty and interest are perfectly coincident; for the most part in this world, but entirely and in every instance, if we take in the future and the whole' [Butler, 1729, p. 83]

But he is more helpful on the related questions (to which I return frequently) of 'tastes versus duty'. Consider, alongside the quotation from Proudhon at the front of this book and Kant's view, Butler's second sermon, which considers conscience as a principle *superior in kind* to appetites and desires.

The last of the pre-Smithian writers whom I wish to consider is Hume. He is worth quoting at some length as his observations are remarkably full of insight.

First, he rebuts the universal assumption of self-interest:

> the descriptions which certain philosophers [e.g. Mandeville] delight so much to form of mankind in this particular, are as wide of nature as any accounts of monsters, which we meet with in fables and romances. So far from thinking that men have no affection for anything beyond themselves, I am of opinion, that though it be rare to meet with one, who loves any single person better than himself; yet 'tis rare to meet with one in whom all the kind affections taken together, do not overbalance all the selfishness. [Hume, 1736, p. 487]

Second, sympathy is not a sufficient condition for generosity:

> My sympathy with another may give me the sentiment of pain and disapprobation, when any object is presented, that has a tendency to give him uneasiness; tho' I may not be willing to sacrifice anything of my own interest, nor cross any of my passions, for his satisfaction. [p. 586]

Or, as we would now say, our concern for others need not be Pareto-relevant. Third, non-selfish 'tastes' will extend to only a limited number of individuals:

> In general . . . there is no such passion in human minds, as the love of mankind, merely as such, independent of personal qualities, of services or of relation to oneself. [p. 586]

But fourth, one should try to put these differences on one side when making moral judgements:

> tho' sympathy be much fainter than concern for ourselves, and a sympathy with persons remote from us much fainter than that with persons near and continguous: yet we neglect all these differences in our calm judgements concerning the nature of man. [p. 603].

Compare this with Butler's 'conscience', Smith's 'impartial spectator' and Edgeworth's 'calm moments'. This must mean giving different weights to others depending on taste or preference in everyday behaviour, but equal weights in moments of reflection.

Fifth, Hume is with the Optimists in so far as he believed in the contagion thesis:

> The passions are so contagious, that they pass with the greatest facility from one person to another, and produce correspondent movements in all human breasts. [p. 605]

Lastly, Hume very clearly recognised, in a brilliant passage, that the economic problem would vanish *either* if there was very great material prosperity and satiation of demand *or* if people were strongly altruistic (the 'after-you' problem). In either case everyone would reach a 'bliss-point' within the attainable set. Hume put it rather better:

> [the poets] easily perceived, if every man had a tender regard for another, or if nature supplied abundantly all our needs and desires, that the jealousy of interest, which justice supposes could no longer have place . . . encrease to a sufficient degree the benevolence of men, or the bounty of nature, and you render justice useless. [pp. 494–5]

Here we have Hume, as in his essays on economic questions, making a 'model' of great simplicity and elegance and conveyed in marvellous language.

Smith must be seen as standing squarely in the tradition of Hutcheson and Hume on the nature of sympathy. Now the dynamics of sympathy and the scientific analysis of conscience formation is no doubt a fascinating question, but it is rather outside the scope of this book. The question here is whether or not non-selfishness has to be kicked upstairs to the morality department. If so it will be of only limited interest for positive economic analysis.

The terminology of Chapter 4 will be helpful here. As in that chapter, let there be a socially co-operative strategy, alpha and a non-co-operative strategy, beta. It is shown there that, provided the context is right, non-selfishness, especially if reinforced by duty, can help in reaching a co-operative solution. Now consider an even less co-operative strategy of theft, warfare and deceit and call this a gamma strategy. If everyone plays gamma society finds itself in the Hobbesian Jungle.[4] I suggest that one may regard the transition from gamma to beta strategies as contingent upon sufficient 'sympathy' and 'trust' as to permit simple exchange to develop, markets to evolve and elementary political processes to operate. Smith, on this interpretation, believed that sufficient sympathy existed to provide the pre-conditions for an economic framework of this kind. But what of alpha strategies? We know that Smith recognised the need for 'public goods' (see Smith, 1776, Bk V) but he clearly relied in no way upon voluntary co-operation for these which would have to be provided by the state and financed by taxation and other charges.

We also know, from the quotations at the beginning of this chapter, that (apart from public goods) there was no disadvantage in pursuing beta strategies rather than alpha: this is the whole point of the 'invisible hand' passage.

The mystery surrounding Smith's apparent inconsistency in his treatment of self-love seems to be solved. Sympathy was kicked downstairs to the infra-structure and upstairs to morality. The decks were then cleared for a political economy uncluttered by consideration of altruism. It will however be argued in Chapter 16 that, once one turns to the analysis of social co-operation, Smith's notion of sympathy must be reintroduced.

BENTHAM AND MILL

Bentham included in his list of pleasures, amity, goodname, piety, benevolence and malevolence.

> The pleasures of benevolence are the *pleasures resulting from the view of any pleasures supposed to be possessed by the beings who may be the objects of benevolence*; to wit, the sensitive beings we are acquainted with; under which are commonly included, 1. The Supreme Being, 2. Human Beings, 3. Other animals. These may also be called the pleasures of good will, the pleasures of sympathy, or the pleasures of the benevolent or social affections. [Bentham, 1789, Ch. V; my italics]

It cannot be claimed that this notion in any way entered into the analysis of classical political economy. But J. S. Mill seemed to believe not only that it was one's *duty* to behave utilitarianly, but that as society progressed people would actually come to behave so. As usual Mill is many-sided. His comments on Comte are particularly revealing. Comte had written in his *Cours de Phisosophie Positive*.

> each man's happiness [is] dependent on the extension of benevolent acts and sympathetic emotions to our species as a whole, and even, by a necessary gradation, to all those sentient beings that are our subordinates, proportionally to their animal dignity and their social utility. [Comte, 1830–42, Ch. XI]

Mill's response to this was rather Smithian in his analysis of the here-and-now:

There is a standard of altruism to which all should be required to come up, and a degree beyond it which is not obligatory but meritorious. [Mill, 1865 p. 143]

Any further altruism would be of doubtful value:

May it not be the fact that mankind, who after all are made up of single human beings, obtain a greater sum of happiness when each pursues his own, under the rules and conditions required for the good of the rest, than when each makes the good of the rest his only object?' [Mill, 1865, p. 143]

In a similar vein he writes in his essay on *Utilitarianism*:

it is a misconception of the Utilitarian mould of thought, to conceive it as implying that people should fix their minds upon so wide a generality as the world, or society at large. The great majority of good actions are intended not for the benefit of the world, but for that of individuals, of which the good of the world is made up. [Mill, 1863]

Nevertheless the utilitarian should judge an action in terms of its effect on the *total* of happiness. His statements on this are sharp and unequivocal:

As between his own happiness and that of others, utilitarianism requires [one] to be as strictly impartial as a disinterested and benevolent spectator.

To do as you would be done by, and to love your neighbour as yourself, constitute the ideal perfection of utilitarian morality. [Mill, 1863, Ch. 2]

Mill seemed to believe, in a vague way, that although at the present time 'This feeling in most individuals is much inferior in strength to their selfish feelings, and is often wanting altogether,' a process of education and learning would ensure that 'The good of others becomes . . . a thing naturally and necessarily to be attended to' (Mill, 1863, Ch. 2).

Then there is the famous passage in his *Political Economy*:

Mankind are capable of a far greater amount of public spirit than the present age is accustomed to suppose possible. [Mill, 1848]

But, unlike Rousseau,[5] he made no attempt to set out an educational programme for weaning individuals from self-regard. Neither did he attempt to explain in the context of the invisible hand doctrine precisely how this secular increase in altruism would be helpful.

MARX'S VIEW

The place of non-selfishness in the socialist tradition is considered in Chapter 9 on communes. Now it can be argued that socialists and liberals share an optimistic view of human nature but with this important difference: the liberal requires time, education, leadership and example, while the socialist requires a dramatic change in environment. The change could be provided by dreaming up a *Utopia* or by establishing independent communities within a capitalist system; an implication of this line of thought is that man has a great capacity for good, provided that the environment is right. Or it could be provided by revolution.

It cannot be claimed that the analysis of altruism played a major part in Marx's analysis. Some writers[6] have argued for the essential similarity of the liberal and Marxian views of man. This must rest mainly on the following often-quoted passage from Marx's *Gotha Programme*:

> in the first phase of communist society as it is when it has just emerged after prolonged birth pangs from capitalist society [there must be inequalities]. Right can never be higher than the economic structure of society and the cultural development conditioned by it.

> In a higher phase of communist society, after the enslaving subordination of the individual to the division of labour, and therewith also the antithesis between mental and physical labour has vanished; after labour has become not only a means of life but life's prime want; after the productive forces have also increased with the all-round development of the individual, and all the springs of cooperative wealth flow more abundantly – only then can the narrow horizon of bourgeois right be crossed in its entirety and society inscribe upon its banners: 'From each according to his ability, to each according to his needs!' [Marx, 1875, p. 119]

For social consciousness to be released Marx requires more than the gradual improvement sought by the liberal. In fact, he denies the validity of the liberal programme in that social consciousness can never be released under capitalism. The striking thing is how *much* Marx requires before true social man can emerge. Not only has there to be a revolution followed by a dictatorship of the proletariat; there has also to be abundance. In this Marx comes dangerously near the utopian socialist's trick of assuming the economic problem away at both ends.

The distinction between egotism and altruism is not in any case a very useful one in interpreting Marx's analysis, for Marx saw man as a *species* or *social* being. He was hindered from fulfilling his true nature by alienation.

> [Communism] is the complete restoration of man to himself as a *social*, i.e. human being, a restoration which has become conscious . . . , it is the *genuine* resolution of the conflict between man and nature and between man and man . . . , it is the solution of the riddle of history and knows itself to be the solution. [Marx, 1844, p. 348 of 1975 edn]

SIDGWICK AND EDGEWORTH

I have put these two writers together, though Edgeworth made by far the more major contribution. Sidgwick is included because he is highly representative of late nineteenth-century utilitarianism and because of his great influence on Edgeworth's thinking. The two following quotations are sufficient to establish Sidgwick's view that one *ought* to behave purely utilitarianly but will fall short of this in practice, attaching different weights to different individuals:

> [Utilitarianism prescribes that] we *should* aim at Happiness generally as our ultimate end, and so consider the happiness of any one individual as equally important with the general happiness of any others, as an element of this total; and *should* distribute our kindness so as to make this total as great as possible.

> We should all agree that each of us is bound to show kindness to his parents, and spouse and children, and to other kinsmen in a less degree: and to those who have rendered service to him, and any others whom he may have admitted to his intimacy and called friends: and to neighbours and to countrymen more than others: and perhaps we may say to those of our own race more than to black or yellow men, and generally to human beings in proportion to their affinity to ourselves. [Sidgwick, 1874, Ch. 4; my italics]

A third quotation, though not relevant to Edgeworth, anticipates the treatment of the need for collective redistributive action in Chapter 11:

> it is doubtful whether 'distributive justice' – so far as this diverges

from the result brought about by open competition – can be effectively promoted by the voluntary action of private persons. [Sidgwick, 1903, p. 540]

I now come to Edgeworth (1881), who made by far the most important contribution to the analysis of non-selfish economics of any economist, notwithstanding that he wrote nearly a hundred years ago. I quote his first-rate analytical achievement at length.

between the two extremes of Pure Egoistic and Pure Universalistic there may be an indefinite number of impure methods; wherein the happiness of others as compared by the agent (in a calm moment) with his own, neither counts for nothing, nor yet 'counts for one', but *counts for a fraction.* [Edgeworth, 1881, p. 16]

between the frozen pole of egoism and the tropical expanse of ulitarianism [there is] . . . the position of one for whom in a calm moment his neighbour's happiness compared with his own neither counts for nothing, nor yet 'counts for one', but counts for a fraction. We must modify the utilitarian integral by multiplying each pleasure, except the pleasure of the agent himself, by a fraction – a factor doubtless diminishing with what may be called the social distance between the individual agent and those of whose pleasures he takes account. [pp. 102–3]

we might suppose that the object which X (whose own utility is P), tends – in a calm, effective moment – to maximise, is not P, but $P + \lambda\pi$; where λ is a *coefficient of effective sympathy.* And similarly Y – not of course while rushing to self-gratification, but in those regnant moments which characterise an ethical 'method' – may propose to himself as end $\pi + \mu P$. What then will be the contract curve of these modified contractors? *The old contract curve between narrower limits* – as these coefficients of sympathy increase, utilitarianism becomes more *pure*, the contract curve narrows down to the utilitarian point. [p. 53 n.1]

it appears that the pure and impure parts of the contract curve are demarcated by the points where $DP/D\pi$ changes sign, that is (in general) where either $DP/d\sigma$ or $D\pi/d\sigma$ ($d\sigma$ being an increment of the length of the contract curve) either vanishes or becomes infinite. Accordingly the maxima and minima of P and π present demarcating points. [p. 25–6]

I have found it convenient to refer to these as the shrinking and non-twisting theorems[7]. The reader is invited to consider the extent of Edgeworth's achievement here. Not only did he see egotism as just a limiting case, but he showed us how to incorporate the more general case into the theory of exchange, at its very moment of inception. This contrasts very strongly with the *obiter dicta* of almost every other economist who had considered the question. Furthermore, on the assumptions he was making here, his conclusions were perfectly correct. The shrinking of the contract curve indicated that what we would now call Pareto-optimal redistribution was needed. Its non-twisting indicates that, given redistribution, market processes would lead to efficient exchange. His case corresponds to what I have called the 'non-meddlesome' case.

THOSE WHO ALSO RAN

Carver (1915) is worthy of brief mention for declaring, in the spirit of Edgeworth, that:

> Both benevolence and selfishness, as actual facts in the world, must be found somewhere between the two extremes, one of which allows no preference whatever for self as compared with any other being, and the other of which allows no interest whatever in any other being. [Carver, 1915, p. 61]

He also drew an interesting parallel between social distance and time:

> The present self estimates or appreciates the interests of the future self according to a law quite analogous to . . . that according to which it appreciates the interests of others. [p. 71]

However, apart from drawing partial equilibrium marginal diagrams he did not pursue the analysis.

Whitaker has shown that 'economic chivalry' was a recurring minor theme in Marshall's writings; indeed, he even flirted with the view of some 'German writers' that collective aims were tenable. Marshall seemed to believe there was quite a lot of unselfishness and sense of duty about:

> There is much more economic chivalry in the world than appears at first sight. [Whitaker, 1975, p. 14]

In particular, Marshall suggested the notion of compromise benefit [Whitaker, 1975, note 12] such that a monopolist might wish to maximise a weighted sum of profit and consumer's surplus. Notice that with *equal* weights he would be led to the competitive solution! Whitaker notices that Marshall came to rely more upon public approbation than on benevolence and remarks, caustically, that:

[Marshall] was placed in the comfortable position of being able to argue that socialism would not work without economic chivalry and would not be necessary with it. [Whitaker, 1975, p. 15]

The recently published *Early Writings* of Alfred Marshall (Whitaker, 1975) show that he had given some thought to the symmetrical treatment of time and social distance:

If we take account of the fact that the total happiness will be best promoted generally by each man taking special account of the happiness of those around him, and not dissipating his attentions over space, we may introduce another factor $e^{-\lambda r}$, where r is the distance – measured perhaps partly in terms of geography and partly in terms of kindred – of a man from the several units. Thus we should get the aim for any man, (maximise),

$$\iiint e^{-(kt+\lambda r)} \cdot dp \cdot dt \cdot dn.$$

[Whitaker, 1975, p. 318]

Marshall also discussed the possibility of using awards and decorations as incentives to work for the common good. Devices such as knighthoods, the Queen's Award to Industry, etc., may be quite effective for eliciting certain types of non-selfish behaviour. He remarked, in the spirit of Mill:

No doubt men are capable of much more unselfish service than they generally render; and the *supreme aim* of the economist is to discover how this latent social asset can be developed more quickly and turned to account more wisely. [Marshall, 1890, p. 9; my italics]

In spite of this quotation, it cannot be fairly said that Marshall devoted any substantial part of his analytical attention to this 'supreme aim'.

These bits and pieces of analysis indicate that Marshall had considered non-selfishness and was certainly capable of providing a serious analysis of it.

Wicksteed's *Commonsense of Political Economy* must be mentioned, if only for his introduction of the term 'non-tuism', which is used several times in this book. He believed that market transactions constituted a game which one played according to the rules.

Selfishness or non-selfishness did not come into it:

> The proposal to exclude 'benevolent' or 'altruistic' motives from consideration in the study of Economics is therefore wholly irrelevant and beside the mark. [Wicksteed, 1910, p. 179]

Trustees, to take his example, may be altruistic, but they strike hard bargains. When A and B conclude a bargain A is not thinking of B nor vice-versa but each may be thinking of others. Economic relations are, he argues, characterised not by 'egoism' but by 'non-tuism'. A similar point has been made by Nagel in relation to competitive fighting according to the rules.

Pigou has a rather lame discussion of non-selfishness in *Economics of Welfare* (1920), where he quotes Marshall with approval and makes the point about the inadequacy of voluntary transfers, quoted in Chapter 11. He is clearly aware of the work of Carver, to whom he refers. He also has an interesting footnote[8] on inter-generational transfers, in which he manages, in one short paragraph, to include altruism, discounting and generational overlap.

SUMMARY

Great attention was devoted to 'sympathy' in eighteenth-century discussions, but Smith showed that, while sympathy was necessary to move society out of the Hobbesian jungle into an institutional framework for exchange, it was not necessary or desirable in exchange itself. After Smith, discussions of sympathy or benevolence tended to be confined either to ethics or to discussions of the ideal society. Edgeworth was the first economist to attempt an integration of 'love' into economic theory, and various other writers pursued it as a minor theme. Apart from Smith and Edgeworth, no major economist has paid it the compliment of sustained economic analysis.

INTERLUDE

7 Recapitulation

Two routes to the analysis of non-selfishness have been followed in earlier chapters: first, the theory of exchange and second, the theory of games.

When modified to allow for selfishness, the theory of exchange indicates that some redistribution may be voluntary or 'Pareto-optimal'. I referred to this as the *shrinking theorem*, and it is an important basis for Chapters 10 ('Giving and Income'), 11 ('Taxation'), and 14 ('Disasters'). It is not argued that altruism is either a necessary or a sufficient condition for redistribution, but it obviously plays a major part in any total explanation.

It was also shown that, in a larger community, the individual will behave *as though* in the two-person context, only if he is a *Kantian altruist*. That is to say, he asks himself what the consequences of his own action would be if generalised and makes this a basis in principle for his actions. The same problem arises here as in the case of public goods, where each is tempted to be a free-rider with the consequence that socially inferior decisions are made.

But redistribution is not the only consequence of non-selfish preferences. At least as important is the question of what happens to exchange itself. Surely the prices and market configurations reached under selfish competition can no longer be relevant? Even to attain efficient exchange a set of taxes and subsidies or some equivalent device seems to be called for. Perhaps surprisingly this is not true if each individual's preferences are separable in the goods and services going to others; that is, he allows their preference to 'count' when he takes account of their welfare. This proposition I have called the *non-twisting theorem*. It requires that altruistic individuals are 'non-meddlesome' or 'non-paternalistic'. Whenever this condition does not hold, departures from market price will indeed be required and implications of enforcing these departures are discussed in Chapter 12. Because of the non-twisting theorem, the most general result to come out of the discussion of exchange is the optimality of some collective acts of redistribution.

The second approach is via a simple development of the famous prisoner's dilemma game. The writer is not a game theorist and the analysis is at rather a low level. Nevertheless, the conditions for a prisoner's dilemma to turn itself into an *assurance game* are explored. These are potentially important conditions (involving 'trust' as well as 'love') because trials suggest that people get locked into socially inferior situations less often than one might have imagined. Altruism seems to be important here in two quite different ways which may be usefully examined in terms of *contractors* and *third parties*. First, think of a two-person game where maximin policies would lead to Pareto-inferior outcomes. If there is an assurance game, the contractors will co-operate so as to achieve a superior outcome provided that they trust one another. Each contractor will have done better for himself by being non-selfish (or at any rate behaving *as though* non-selfish).

Now imagine, instead, a three-person game, in which effective social decisions are made by two people (the contractors) who have an altruistic concern for the third person, the third party. But altruism towards the third party may not be sufficient to induce altruistic behaviour on the part of contractors unless they behave like Kantian altruists. Clearly, if the contractors felt selfishly towards the third party, Kantian principle, or duty, would dictate no redistribution. Kantanism and altruism *can* lead to the same result, but it is perfectly possible to have one without the other.

Third parties are introduced in the first illustration of Part II (on wage restraint) and are relevant to the chapters on giving, taxation and redistribution. But they do not appear in Chapter 9 (on communes), where all the parties are contractors. Post-disaster co-operation within a community will be among contractors in the stricken area but outsiders considering transfers will see them as third parties. As for inter-generational choice, the third party might be some distant target generation while intervening generations will be fellow-contractors. Obviously then, trust among contractors is important and altruism oils, as it were, the wheels of social co-operation. Without altruism, however, no action will be adopted favourable to third parties.

Some attempt is made throughout the discussion (but see particularly Chapters 4, 13 and 16) to emphasise the dynamic relationship between altruism, trust and duty. A thorough and satisfactory treatment of this central issue is outside the writer's present competence and poses a major research challenge for the social sciences.

I have put considerable stress, particularly in Chapter 6, on the continuity of the theme of non-selfishness in the history of economics, though it has usually been a somewhat minor theme. The *illustrations* of Part II all deal with acts that *could*, with ingenuity, be explained in terms of self-interest. But the more these acts multiply, and the more intricate the explanations, the greater is the temptation to make a clean sweep and abandon self-interest as a universal assumption. Indeed, there is much to be said for making non-selfishness the general case – especially as there will be many circumstances where the individual contractor finds it best to behave *as though* completely selfish. Similarly, there will be circumstances where non-selfish behaviour would be predicted; for example, in small groups, in voting behaviour and in matters such as life-support, where empathy is strong. In other words it may now be appropriate to turn the usual argument on its head: it is not that selfish men sometimes appear to behave unselfishly, but that unselfish men sometimes appear to behave selfishly.

Part II
ILLUSTRATIONS

8 Voluntary Wage Restraint[1]

This chapter was stimulated by the UK experiment known as the 'social contract' and set out (albeit imprecisely) in the Labour Party Manifesto of October 1974. Broadly, it was an agreement between the trades unions and the Labour Government whereby the unions would exercise wage restraint in order to reduce the rate of inflation and the government would help the less well-off.

> Naturally the trade unions see their clearest loyalty to their own members. But the social contract is their free acknowledgement that they have other loyalties – to the members of other unions too, to pensioners, to the lower-paid, to invalids, to the community as a whole.

To quote from Harold Wilson's forward to the document,

> It is not simply, or narrowly, an understanding about wages. It is about justice, equality, about concern for and protection of the lower paid, the needy, the pensioner and the handicapped in our society. It is about fairness between one man and another, and between men and women. It is about economic justice between individuals and between regions. It is about cooperation and conciliation, not conflict and confrontation.

These are lofty sentiments. I am concerned here with the rather more restricted question of how unselfish the unions are being asked to be under such an arrangement. I make use of the assurance game analysis, already outlined, and a number of heroic assumptions. A particularly heroic assumption is that the level of unemployment is not determined *primarily* by the rate of wage inflation and may therefore be left out of account.

Collective Restraint

The unions may follow one of two strategies, exercise restraint (α) or pursue free collective bargaining (β), the latter being a non-co-operative strategy. In what sense might it be better for *all the unions taken together* to pursue α rather than β? It is not at all clear that it would be in their self-interest to do so. Prices are not likely to rise (at least in the short term) to the full extent of money wage increases. Thus, while any money wage increase will be eroded to some extent by price increases, it will not be eroded altogether. Self-interested unions could not reasonably be expected, under these circumstances, to forgo free collective bargaining. But it would not at all be in the spirit of the social contract to ignore the interest of other members of the community.

If increased money wages push up the rate of inflation, then other groups with weak bargaining power will suffer losses in real terms. Let us imagine that there is one such weak group, called 'pensioners', and that the unions attach some weight to their welfare. To cut a long story short, it may be shown[2] that the unions will collectively choose to exercise restraint, or adopt an α strategy, so long as each trades unionist gives a weight to each pensioner of at least

$$\frac{1 - r}{1 - r(1 - n_3)}, \tag{8.1}$$

where r is the responsiveness of the rate of price inflation to the rate of increase of money wages, and n_3 is the ratio of 'pensioners' to trades unionists.

A numerical illustration may help to make this a little more concrete. Let $r = 0.8$ and $n_3 = 0.5$. The required weight is then 0.33. A great deal clearly depends on what the unions believe about r: whether, for example, they believe inflation may be due to factors other than money wage increases. The size of n_3 depends on the size of the group towards which the trades unions feel altruistic. The illustrative value is very roughly the ratio of pensioners to all trades unionists. Provided that the correct figures do not generate an unreasonably high value for (8.1), it is not at all unreasonable to look to unselfishness behaviour on the part of the unions taken as a whole.

RESTRAINT BY INDIVIDUAL UNIONS

But this is not at all the same thing as restraint by individual unions. All we have said so far is that, *if* there is sufficient altruism about, $\alpha\alpha$ will seem more attractive to the union than $\beta\beta$. Unfortunately, this only gets us to first base. One has to go much further than this to show that the individual union will adopt α. In the language of Chapter 4 I have shown that we could, with sufficient altruism, have a prisoner's dilemma rather than a wholly non-co-operative game. What I have yet to show is that it could be converted into an assurance game.

Common sense suggests that a higher weight (more unselfishness) would be required because the individual union, given the behaviour of the rest, will have a small effect on the rate of wage inflation. The larger the union the larger the effect, but in any case we know that the largest union (TGWU) does not have much more than one-tenth of total union membership. The general rule is fairly straightforward,[2] and I have selected two extreme cases for presentation here.

(1) *Zero weight to other unions.* The individual union is concerned with the real incomes of its own members and of pensioners. It will exercise restraint provided that the weight which each unionist attaches to each pensioner is greater than

$$\frac{1 - rl}{1 - rl(1 - n_3')} \tag{8.2a}$$

where l is the ratio of the union's membership to total union membership and n_3' is the ratio of pensioners to that union's membership. For example, putting $l = 0.1$ and $n_3' = 5$ gives a required weight of 0.7, leaving only $(1 - 0.7)$ or 0.3 for themselves! Thus to ask for restraint on the part of individual unions is asking rather a lot.

Notice that in the special case where $l = 1$ (and therefore $n_3 = n_3'$) the expression (8.2a) reduces to (8.1).

The more nearly an individual union swallows up the rest, the less likely it is to renege on what the unions have collectively decided.

(2) *Equal weight to other unionists and to pensioners.* The union is now concerned not merely with pensioners but with the effects of its restraint on the real incomes of other trade unionists. The required weight will now be

$$\frac{1 - rl}{1 - rl(1 - n_2' - n_3')}. \tag{8.2b}$$

The same illustrative weights may be used as before. It is not necessary to assume a value for n_2' as it is already determined by the assumption of 0.1 for l. It has to be 9, therefore. Expression (8.2b) then becomes 0.45. Notice that although the weight required for pensioners is less in (8.2b) than in (8.2a), the *same* weight is being attached to other unionists as to pensioners. Therefore each unionist gives a total weight of 0.8 to others, leaving only 0.2 for himself. Again, a high order of altruism is required. (8.2b) also reduces to (8.1) when $l = 1$.

Expressions (8.1), (8.2a) and (8.2b) taken together confirm the common sense view as to when to expect co-operation.

CONTINGENT GRANTS

A curious feature of the discussion so far is (to use the language of Chapter 4) the absence of an *assurance tilt* to the game. It doesn't seem to matter to the individual union whether the other unions are behaving co-operatively or not: the difference to its own position, and that of the other two classes, generated by its co-operation is precisely the same whichever strategy the other unions are following. Though this appears odd the reason for it is obvious. Price changes are assumed to be linearly related to increases in money wages – the coefficient r is assumed not to rise when money wages rise. If it rose a union would do more damage by failing to co-operate when others were also co-operating than when they were not. This would be a little awkward to take into account as it stands, and I am not sure there would be any empirical basis for it. However, a similar assumption is now considered.

Let the government announce a 'contingent grant' to be awarded to pensioners *if and only if* all unions co-operate in the wage restraint policy. The weaker assumption, that the grant would be paid *in any case*, would not serve. All it would do would confirm and strengthen the attractions of $\alpha\alpha$ over $\beta\beta$ to the unions as a whole. It would do nothing to strengthen the appeal of co-operation to individual unions as the grant would be paid whether they co-operated or not. It would fail to give the game a positive assurance tilt. Hence the brutal assumption that g is truly contingent on co-operation. Under this assumption it is absolutely clear to the individual union that if it adopts β the pensioners will forgo their grant.[3]

Let the government announce, then, that pensioners will receive a percentage increase in their grant equal to g if the unions adopt $\alpha\alpha$. The earlier condition (8.1) for unions to co-operate collectively has to be modified to

$$\frac{1-r}{1-r+n_3(g/m+r)} \tag{8.3}$$

where g/m is the ratio of the contingent grant increase to the money wage increase that could be achieved under collective bargaining. The reader can easily see that this reduces to (8.1) when $g = 0$. The chances of collective restraint must be greatly enhanced by the contingent grant. Using the same illustrative figures as before but assuming $g/m = 0.5$, it is now necessary for the unions to give the pensioners a weight of approximately 0.23 rather than 0.33.

The grant has a much more dramatic effect at individual union level. The easiest comparison is with (8.2a), which assumed a zero concern for other unions but a positive concern for pensioners. This yields a required weight of

$$\frac{1-rl}{1-rl+n_3'(\pi \cdot (g/m) + rl)} \tag{8.4}$$

which reduces to (8.2a) when $g = 0$. Using the same illustrative figures as before ($r = 0.8$, $l = 0.1$, $g/m = 0.5$ and $n_3' = 5.0$) and letting $\pi = 1$ the required weight is now only approximately 0.24 rather than 0.70 as in expression (8.2a).

Introducing the contingent grant has given a strong positive tilt to the assurance game. The bigger is π, the less the degree of altruism required. A union is then definitely more likely to co-operate if it believes that others will do so. Though the contingent grant introduced here must be viewed only as a proxy for more sophisticated arrangements, something like it is required if reliance on the selflessness of unions is to be a major plank of anti-inflationary policy.

One returns, as in the previous chapter, to the theme that deeper, ethical considerations are at work than those captured in the pay-offs. Once the unions have agreed collectively to restraint, an aura of moral rightness grows up around α behaviour. A 'norm' is established. Loyalty to the government is demanded. For all this richness I maintain that the prisoner's dilemma and assurance game framework gives a good indication of when a voluntary policy is likely to be feasible and when it is not.

SOME LESSONS OF 1974–7

The 'social contract' experiment eventually collapsed for various reasons.

(i)   Unions began to doubt whether $\alpha\alpha$ really was better than $\beta\beta$ as it became clear that cost-push wage inflation was simply one ingredient in the inflationary process. Such doubts were reinforced by the revival of 'monetarist' doctrines during this period. Thus, support for the policy began to crumble even at the highest levels of union leadership. For indeed, even if unionists (collectively) felt altruistic towards pensioners or some other 'third party' group, they were also aware of the relatively minor effect of their wage claims on the whole inflationary process and subsequently upon third party real incomes.

(ii) The policy of a 'package' such that tax cuts were partly conditional upon acceptance of voluntary pay limits worked in 1976 but had worn rather thin by 1977. Unions suspected that a mere token acceptance of the policy would be sufficient to elicit concessions.

(iii) As indicated by the analysis of this chapter, the terms of the 'conditional grant' were much less rigorous than would have been required to put a brake upon wage claims made by individual unions. A really effective conditional grant would have to have been contingent on the *behaviour* of individual unions rather than on *undertakings* given by the trade union movement as a whole.

(iv) The lump sum element in pay policy had the effect of eroding differentials. After a time this could be expected to lead to a lower average altruistic weighting of the pay-offs to other unionists by those unions whose favourable relative position was being eroded.

(v)   Even apart from the conditional grant issue, it is always the case that co-operation by the trades union movement as a whole is easier to elicit than co-operation by individual trades unions. Once the trades union leaders and the politicians realise this, less importance comes to be attached to mere 'paper' agreements at top level and more importance to the realities of grass-roots acceptance.

9   Communes

A casual survey of the literature on communal living suggests altruism as a major but not a sole ingredient. On the whole I think it is right to say that it plays a greater part in the *blueprint* literature than in accounts of actual communistic experiments. My intention in this chapter is to sort out the main strands of economic argument and then to provide a simple economic analysis of the altruistic element.

UTOPIAS AND COMMUNES

Even in Utopia the economic problem has somehow to be solved. Thomas More, in his *Utopia*, essentially solves his problem by relaxing the assumption of non-satiation. If Utopians work for six hours a day there will be more than enough for everyone's simple requirements. Wants are modest, buildings and clothes relatively durable. Rivalry is assumed away:

> no living creature is naturally greedy, except from fear of want – or, in the case of human beings, from vanity, the notion that you're better than people if you can display more superfluous property than they can. But there's no scope for that sort of thing in Utopia. [More, 1965 edn, p. 80]

This is a very easy way of solving the economic problem: satiation is reached *inside* the resources constraint. More's distinction here between real and artificial wants is persuasive and has had a long and vigorous life. Keynes made a similar distinction between absolute wants (satiable) and relative wants (insatiable) in his essay on 'Economic Possibilities for our Grandchildren' (1930). He looked forward to when 'we shall honour those who can teach us how to pluck the hour and the day virtuously and well, the delightful people . . . .'.[1] But in the meantime it was our duty to carry on being economically purposive if only for others. Ramsey, in his famous analysis of saving (1928), assumed quite a modest level of income for 'bliss'. The trouble is that in the real world outside of the blueprints, that hour is not yet. It is always in the future. People tend to feel that *if only* they had a little more they could be really happy. For the satiation escape route to be at all convincing it needs to assume, if not altruism, at least the absence of envy.

The satiation escape route is sometimes combined with an assumption of physical plenty. Perhaps this is overdoing things rather, but it certainly takes care of the economic problem. Owen (1836) had a tendency to tackle the problem from both ends at once, as it were. He is worth quoting at length because of the dominant roles of plenty and of non-selfishness.

> Scientific arrangements will be formed to make wealth, everywhere, and at all times, superabound beyond the wants and wishes of the human race. [p. xxi]

> As wealth of all kinds will be so delightfully created in greater abundance than will ever be required, *no money price will be known.* [p. xxiii; my italics]

> In this new world, the sympathies of human nature will be rightly directed from infancy, and will engender a spirit of benevolence, confidence and affection which will pervade mankind [p. xxv]

Schumpeter (1943) has remarked that even Owen's Utopia required a *deus ex machina* (Owen himself!) to bring it about. This suggests one further important ingredient, charismatic leadership to provide a driving force.

Perhaps the most striking difference between Utopian blueprints and practical experiments is the role of leadership in the latter. Religious fervour sometimes provides the key. Armytage divides English Utopian experiments into several phases, the first having a strong millenian flavour.[2] Communality of interest was reinforced by religious persecution from without. The same reliance on religion and leadership may be found in the writings of General Booth (1890).

Religion also played a major part on the three utopian sects examined by Whitworth (1975). The Shakers were founded on the charisma of Ann Lee and an abhorence of sexuality. Indeed, their celibacy made it necessary to evangelise and it was on the rock of recruitment that they eventually foundered. The Oneida Community was established by Noyes after disappointment with his literary evangelism and collapsed after he grew too old to provide the requisite leadership. Noyes was less straightlaced than Ann Lee in notions of sexuality, and an air of scandal surrounded his doings. The young men brought up in the communities found the doctrine of the 'ascending fellowship', whereby the old men (like Noyes) slept with the young women, particularly irksome. Eberhard Arnold's *Bruderhof* was modelled on early Christianity and the ideal of total selflessness and co-operation: 'All mankind would eventually be bound together in egoless harmony, united by Agape, the love stemming from the spirit of God' (Whitworth, 1975, p. 176). Each group, says Whitworth, modelled itself on the primitive church, and each assumed that economic communism was implicit in true Christianity.

The Bruderhof was an economic success because, although its communities had their roots in agriculture, they developed an adequate industrial base. A great many experimental communities are agricultural and are battling with marginal or sub-marginal land. To some degree this is deliberate and inevitable, for the motivation to form a commune is often a revulsion from the sordidness of cities and large-scale industry. Armytage labels this view the Rustic Vision and dates it from Ruskin.[3] But others, especially Owen and St Simon, embraced industrialisation and based their systems on its economies of scale. As we shall see, whether a commune has an industrial or an agricultural base is crucial to how large it can be.

Regardless of their technology, however, all communes require partial abnegation of the self, whether this be achieved by religion, ideology or love. Members of the commune must somehow be led to pursue the interest of the community as a whole. We have already noticed that the powerful mechanisms of the *invisible hand* are able, in principle, to achieve this for a private enterprise economy. In a sharing economy some other mechanism is needed.

Some of the agricultural Chinese communes illustrate the tensions between community and self as well as pointing to possible solutions. The 1959–62 changes led to much greater emphasis on relating individuals' rewards to the output of their production team. Birrell (1969)[4] puts the consequent incentive problem rather well.

The CCP is aware, of course, that the smaller the size of the production unit, the closer will be the connection the member perceives between his income and the profit of his team . . . a member knows that any reduction in the team's production that results from his work or negligence will have to be shared by all the other members of the team . . .[Motivation] depends on a number of factors, including how successfully the regime has inculcated a sense of commitment to the collective. [Birrell, 1969, pp. 410–11]

Because of this there was some tendency after the Great Leap Forward to contract output to quite small groups, even to individual households. Other things being equal, the larger the group, the stronger must be the cementing ideology.

NEEDS AND ABILITY

It might be very well imagined that the less selfish the members of the commune, the greater the proportion of total output that might be allocated on the basis of *need* rather than *ability*. Sen (1966) has shown this not to be true. It turns out that in the special case where 'social consciousness' is unity (i.e. each family attaches the same weight to the happiness of the other families as to his own), either basis of allocation is as good as the other. In all other cases the appropriate rule is very closely related to the competitive one.[5] As Sen puts it:

barring the special case, the optimum proportion to be distributed according to needs or according to work, is completely independent of the amount of sympathy that the members of the co-operative have for each other. [Sen, 1966]

This very interesting result is a special case of the result we obtained in Chapter 2, about the non-twisting of the contract curve. The optimum proportion is not unfamiliar as is seen in Figure 9.1. Individuals are identical. Each has a production function g and maximises U, a microcosm of the social welfare function. The optimum division between the two payments is as shown. By rotating wage lines through k the reader can easily see that, if payment is entirely by need, work will be under-allocated and, if by effort alone, it will be over-allocated. I have departed slightly

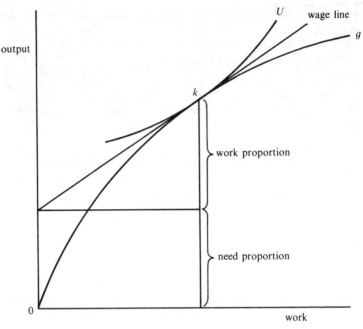

FIGURE 9.1   *Payment according to ability and need*

from Sen by depicting the case where the commune uses labour only, hiring no factors from the outside. The proportion of income to be distributed according to work should then equal the elasticity of output with respect to labour. (It can easily be shown that the ratio of work to non-work in the figure is simply a convenient geometrical method of displaying that elasticity.) The result would have to be modified if people attached weights specifically to the goods or leisure of others rather than to their utilities.

ASSURANCE

I wish for the rest of this chapter to make the extreme assumption that we are dealing with a commune in which *all* income is distributed on an equal-shares basis. The question to be posed is whether or not such a commune may be said to be feasible. On the basis of the discussion so far several features have to be modelled.

(i) The economic problem has not been magicked away by assuming satiation or plenty.

(ii) There is a technology relating the output of the whole commune to the work effort of its members.

(iii) Alternative sizes of the commune will have to be considered.

(iv) Members of the commune will behave non-selfishly to some degree.

The method now employed is similar to that outlined in Chapter 4 and used in the chapter on voluntary wage restraint. Once again two strategies are open to each member. He may work (an alpha strategy) or slack (a beta strategy). For simplicity I rule out intermediate positions. To make this more convincing imagine that specific tasks are allocated and either are or are not carried out. Let every member be sufficiently well motivated to prefer a properly working commune to the outside world; the game is then worth playing. Once again we need to know how unselfish people have to be to ensure that alpha will be played. For it is certain that if everyone tries to play beta no one will work and the whole thing will collapse. Let me attach a weight of v_1 to the goods I receive and $(1 - v_1)$ to those received by everybody else.[6]

It will be a great simplification to work in terms of a single unit so it is assumed that the trouble and bother of working (or its disutility) may be expressed in units of goods. The most catastrophic result for me would be if I worked but everybody else slacked. My output would be divided among everyone (including me), but I would be doing all the work. Mine would be a sucker's pay-off *par excellence*. This sucker's pay-off is the worst thing that could happen, and our joint anxieties to avoid it are the roots of a standard prisoner's dilemma lock-in. I would have to be very unselfish indeed not to mind being a sucker. In fact, the extent to which I would have to be unselfish may be seen from the following expression:

$$v_1 < \frac{1}{rN},$$

where v_1 has already been defined, N is the number of members in the commune, and r is the ratio, c/X_1, where, in turn, c is the disutility of effort and X_1 is total output when only one member is working.

The formidable nature of this restriction becomes clear if pseudo-realistic illustrations are considered. Let r be 2/3. Then a commune of three requires (for feasibility) that I attach a weight of no more that 1/2 to myself. It will ease discussion to consider 1/2 as a reasonable lower bound to v_1. The perfect altruist would, of course, give a weight of $1/N$ to everyone, including himself. He would be prepared to work even if everyone else slacked.[7] It is worth observing that, if the effort of working is slight so that r is small, I shall be prepared to behave co-operatively even when membership is quite high.

Now take the opposite case. Suppose that I am credibly assured of the co-operation of others. A similar condition for my co-operation emerges.

$$v_1 < X'(N)/cN$$

where $X'(N)$ is the additional output consequent upon the co-operation of an extra man or the *marginal product*. At this stage of the analysis some assumption has to be made about technology before anything more concrete can be said. Everything hinges on the behaviour of marginal product as commune size increases. To

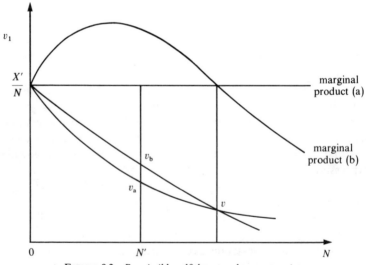

FIGURE 9.2 *Permissible selfishness and commune size*

see this consider Figure 9.2. The figure plots $X'(N)/cN$ as N increases. The curves are a resultant of the marginal product itself and the downward thrust of higher values of N. Only two cases are depicted,[8] (a) constant marginal returns and (b) rising and then falling marginal returns. In both cases larger communes are feasible only if the individual is prepared to be less selfish. With a prescribed degree of selfishness, v_1, it is a simple matter to read off the largest feasible commune. On the other hand, the larger the marginal product, the more selfishness is permissible. Thus at the arbitrary N', $v_b > v_a$. But when the marginal products are equal so are the permissible v's. Both the curves have been drawn as downward-sloping, as indeed they must be unless marginal products are rising very sharply.

An alternative technological assumption is a constant elasticity of output with respect to labour. Let the production function be

$$X = X_1 \cdot N^\rho$$

where ρ is the constant elasticity. It is easy to show that the general requirement on v_1 is that

$$v_1 < \frac{1 + \pi \left(\rho N^{\rho - 1} - 1\right)}{rN}$$

where π is the probability that others, taken as a whole, will play α and $(1 - \pi)$ that they will play β.

This obviously reduces to the 'sucker' case where $\pi = 0$; and where $\pi = 1$, the assurance case, it reduces to

$$v_1 < \rho N^{\rho - 2}/r.$$

Again, it is useful to put in some illustrative numbers just to get the feel of the thing. Impose the previous 'reasonable' constraint that v_1 should not be less than half and also that $r = \frac{1}{2}$; then the largest feasible commune is four when $\rho = 1$, sixteen when $\rho = 1.5$ and without limit when $\rho = 2$. It hardly needs to be pointed out that values of ρ in the region of 2 are barely credible.

Enough has been said, I think, to establish that with plausible assumptions about production and unselfishness only relatively small communes will be feasible. There remains the usual question of whether or not the game has a *positive assurance tilt*: is co-operative behaviour more or less likely when one trusts others to co-operate? If marginal product is constant the game is assurance-neutral: it doesn't matter whether one trusts others to co-operate or not. If marginal product is decreasing it is assurance-negative and if increasing it is assurance-positive. Given the degree of selfishness, trust will aid co-operative behaviour if there is, in some sense, increasing returns.

This link between increasing returns and the efficacy of trust is confirmed by referring back to the voluntary restraint example of the previous chapter. The analogous assumption there was that a given percentage change in money wages led to a constant percentage change in prices. It was for this reason that the game turned out to be assurance-neutral until the introduction of a contingent grant. Though I have not seen the link discussed recently it was treated very clearly in Harrod's (1936) attempt to incorporate the Kantian into the Utilitarian view.[9]

Large successful communes are very rare for the reasons suggested in this analysis. But some communities based on sharing have been rather larger than one might have expected. Noyes's community reached a peak of about 300 around 1840. The Shakers, also reaching their peak at about the same time, averaged 330 per community, while the three communities of the Bruderhof much more recently averaged just below 300. For communities of this size to be sustainable either they must be *extremely* productive, or their members must be extremely unselfish. The first two were certainly cemented by charismatic religious leadership. It may be that religious or quasi-religious leadership is indispensible to any but the smallest commune.

But another possibility, unsympathetic to the Utilitarian view, should also be noticed. Perhaps members perceive the illusory nature of the sucker and free-rider pay-offs, realising that the game is truly between $\alpha\alpha$ and $\beta\beta$. They would then behave *as though* very altruistic: it is indeed in their group and wider individual interest to do so. As was remarked at the end of Chapter 4, Kantian behaviour and non-selfish Utilitarian behaviour come to much the same thing.

Summary

(i) Few communal experiments have been long-lived: most have been small in size and the more successful have benefited from ethical motives and/or charismatic power. Most blueprint utopias offer solutions to the economic problem based on plenty or upon satiation.

(ii) Closely related to the non-twisting theorem is the result that, unless 'social consciousness' is perfect, the rule for allocating according to need or ability is analogous to the competitive rule.

(iii) An application of the assurance game model to the feasibility of communes suggests that love certainly oils the communal wheels. The more of it there is, the more likely is a sharing society to work. But the demands made upon love are rather great if the community is large or if it is subject to diminishing returns over the relevant range.

10 Giving and Income

It has often been observed that altruism need not result in generosity. In this chapter I consider a general but simple formulation of the relationship between altruism and generosity. This is followed by a brief review of the evidence of the extent of voluntary transfers in three different contexts: transfers by individual households, by business and by countries.

TASTES AND TRANSFERS

Suppose an individuals' utility (u_i) is an increasing function of his own income (y_i) and of some other individual's income (y_j), where $y_i > y_j$. He will be prepared to transfer some income to the other up to the point where the marginal utility of keeping income for his own use equals the marginal utility of giving it to j. There is no need to speculate on i's inner reasons for wanting the transfer; so long as a ring fence may be drawn around what constituted i's possessions and what j's, a transfer from i to j may be talked about *as though* i were behaving altruistically. The trouble with this result, unexceptional though it is, is that it tells one only the 'first-order' or marginal conditions for the transfer. Unless it is possible to be a little more specific about the utility function, nothing may be said about the amount of the transfer itself. Once the utility function is given, however, it is possible to state the size of the transfer. Thus, in Figure 10.1 the optimal transfer from i's point of view is where his marginal valuation of his own income equals his marginal valuation of j's income and the amount of transfer is *T*. All it is possible to say in general is that the amount of transfer will be a non-decreasing function of i's income and a non-increasing function of j's income, *ceteris paribus*.

To go beyond this one needs to be slightly more specific about

90

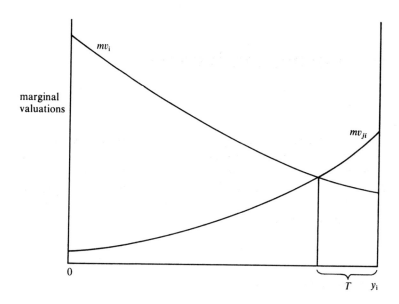

FIGURE 10.1   *Optimal transfer T from* i *to* j

the form of utility interdependence. One such function is selected in the chapter notes for illustration:[1] utility is a multiplicative function of the Cobb–Douglas type. In this case the *proportion* of income given away by individual i to individual j is indicated by the following equation:

$$t = v - (1 - v)\frac{1}{r}$$

where r is the proportion of i's income to j's and v is the power attaching to j's utility in i's utility function. The relationship is shown in Figure 10.2, which confirms what common sense would predict:

(i) the better off i is in relationship to j, the more he is prepared to give away to him;

(ii) the more altruistic i feels towards j, the more he is prepared to give away to him;

(iii) if i's income is actually less than j's he will be prepared to

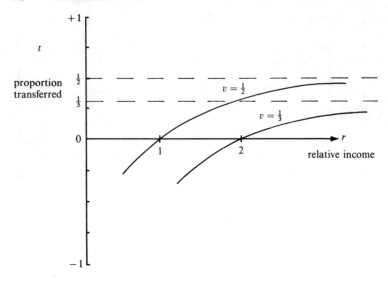

FIGURE 10.2   *Proportion of income transferred as relative income increases*

give away income only if v is greater than $\frac{1}{2}$ (i.e. if he weights j's utility more strongly than his own).

It is interesting to note that on these very special assumptions t increases with income though at a decreasing rate. In the limit the proportion an individual is prepared to give away will never exceed v even though his income becomes very large indeed. The empirical evidence on this is not at all strong and, for what it is worth, suggests that t will be pretty well constant over a wide range of incomes. Notice that if j's income is actually 0 (j is destitute) we have $t = v$ (see notes), so that the proportion of income given away is indeed constant. Certainly in the case of charity, as opposed to redistributive taxation as discussed in Chapter 11, it is reasonable to envisage the bulk of recipients as having very low incomes.

Enough has been said to show that, provided one is willing to make some assumption about relative incomes and about the forms of utility interdependence, it is quite possible to move beyond the mere statement of marginal conditions. Speculation about shapes of such functions is a fascinating but probably unrewarding business, and I now move on to consider some actual patterns of donation.

PERSONAL TRANSFERS

UK data in charitable contributions are highly treacherous but will be used (with caution) in this section. In the *Family Expenditure Survey* donations to charity are subsumed under 'subscriptions and donations, hotel and holiday expenses, and miscellaneous other services', which is clearly not good enough for the present purpose. However, 'charitable donations and subscriptions' are recorded separately though not published. Some very odd items are included under this heading (for example, pew rents and entrance fees to jumble sales), but the figure is probably the best obtainable short of carrying out a tailor-made large-scale survey. As will be seen in a moment, the American data are much more satisfactory.

The first point to strike one is that people seem to give away only very tiny fractions of their income, well under 1 percent for all income ranges. As the amounts involved are so tiny and their classificatory basis so weak, it is tempting to abandon them altogether. But I shall not do, for three more or less disreputable reasons: first, they are all we have; second, they are significant (the means are all several times the standard errors); third, they show a fairly systematic relation with income.

Table 10.1 shows 'charitable donations and subscriptions' (for short, 'donations') as against income for 1974. Using mid-points as means and making reasonable assumptions about the extremes of the distribution, the relationship between donations and income may be treated as linear or log-linear. As one is interested in elasticities, the log-linear regression is presented first:

$$\text{log donations} = -4.68 + 0.70 \text{ log income}$$

$$(0.11) \qquad R^2 = 0.75.$$

This suggests an expenditure elasticity of donations of the order of 0.7, a figure that agrees quite well with Feldstein's findings (based on a much more complex analysis) for the United States (see below). When expenditure, taken cross-sectionally, goes up by 1 per cent, donations go up only by 0.7 per cent. That is why one also finds a slight *negative* relationship between the *percentage* of income donated and income:

$$\text{donations} (\%) = 0.3493 - 0.0015 \text{ income}$$

$$(0.0006) \qquad R^2 = 0.37.$$

TABLE 10.1   *Charitable donations and subscriptions by income, 1974*

Income	Donations etc.
Under £12	6p
£12 and under £15	4p
£15 and under £20	5p
£20 and under £25	10p
£25 and under £30	9p
£30 and under £35	10p
£35 and under £40	12p
£40 and under £45	14p
£45 and under £50	9p
£50 and under £60	11p
£60 and under £70	15p
£70 and under £80	15p
£80 and under £100	24p
£100 and under £120	24p
£120 and above	62p

Notes
1. These figures were kindly provided by Mr. W. Le Grys of the Department of Employment based on the Family Expenditure Survey.
2. The item groups together such payments as donations and subscriptions to charitable organisations and benevolent funds, church collections, pew rents, entrance to bazaars or jumble sales, and payments to school charitable funds.
3. The sums involved are trivial, never rising to more than $\frac{1}{2}$ per cent, but they are always several times the standard error.
4. The proportion of recording households rises with income.

There is a slight tendency for the better-off to donate a smaller percentage of income but a scatter diagram suggests a 'curling up' at the edges, i.e. that both very poor and very well-off families donate rather larger percentages than those in the middle.

Useful as it is to have an elasticity measure, inspection suggests that the curvature is mainly due to the end observations. Retaining the end observations gives a linear regression with approximately the same R^2 as in the log-linear case, but if these are dropped one obtains:

$$\text{donations} = 0.0317 + 0.0019 \text{ income}$$

$$(0.0002) \qquad R^2 = 0.86.$$

This is, of course, consistent with the percentage of donations falling off slightly as income increases.

To summarise, the direct evidence on over-all donations is that:
(i)   the amounts given away are tiny (mean = £0.16 in 1974);
(ii) expenditure elasticity is around 0.7; but
(iii) the underlying data base is only moderately satisfactory.

Not a great deal can be said about different types of household. Most of the apparent variations in Table 10.2 are no doubt generated by characteristics that proxy for income (such as number of adults or whether or not the household is a pensioner one). Tentatively it does seem to be the case, however, that donations increase slightly (*ceteris paribus*) as the number of children in a

TABLE 10.2   *Charitable donations and subscriptions by composition of household and head of household, 1974*

Composition of household	Expenditure per week
1 adult with children	5p
1 man, 1 woman and 1 child	10p
1 man, 1 woman and 2 children	13p
1 man, 1 woman and 3 children	16p
2 adults and four or more children	19p
3 adults with children	29p
4 or more adults with children	29p
1 adult aged under 65	13p
1 man aged under 65	5p
1 woman aged under 65	20p
1 man, 1 woman aged under 65	17p
2 men or 2 women	25p
3 adults	24p
4 or more adults	32p
1 person pensioner	5p
2 person pensioner	9p
all pensioner	7p
all households	16p
Occupation of head of household	
Retired person	13p
Unoccupied person	12p
Occupied person	17p
All households	16p

Notes
1. Source as previous table.
2. Most of the large amounts arise in households with a large number of adults, presumably a reflection of income.
3. There is a slight suggestion that women are more 'generous' than men; alternatively may be they attend more jumble sales!

household increase and that women (especially non pensioner women) are more generous than men. On the latter I have no comment except that it seems to refute Adam Smith's observation that, 'the fair-sex, who have commonly much more tenderness than ours, have seldom so much generosity' (Smith, 1759). The fact that an incremental child seems to be associated with increased donations of a few pence per week may very well be related to contributions to 'school funds' or even with the pleasure young children find in pushing pennies into slots! The data are too meagre to bear much of a deductive superstructure.

THE US EVIDENCE

Dickinson (1970) put percentage private donations in the United States at between 2 and 3 per cent. This figure had not increased much since the 1930s – the generosity of the American people having, as he put it, manifested itself largely in public philanthropy. Comparisons with the lower British figure are not meaningful but one would expect the US figure to be higher (*ceteris paribus*) because US taxpayers are allowed to set charitable contributions against tax. Investigations have treated the price of giving as $(1 - m)$ where m is the marginal tax rate. The corresponding British device, whereby one covenants payments to charity, does not have the same effect:[2] in any case the necessary data would have to be specially collected for the purpose.

Feldstein and his associates have, in a series of papers,[3] estimated both price and income elasticities for US philanthropic contributions, almost invariably using a log-linear form. Schwartz had found rather low price (around -0.6) and income (around 0.3) elasticities, but Feldstein's estimates are substantially higher and based on larger sample sizes. Thus Feldstein and Clotfelter found income elasticities of around 0.8 and price elasticities of the order of -1.5. This latter elasticity implies that donees gain more from tax concessions than the US Treasury loses. Feldstein used (early) survey data as well as tax files. These higher elasticities were confirmed in a joint paper with Taylor, using some spendid tax file data.

The obvious objection to this method is that 'price' or $(1 - m)$ will depend on income and family composition. There seems to be little collinearity between price and income, but within narrow limits 'price' will be entirely determined by income and family composition (which, of course, determines tax allowances). Does having more children make a household more charitable *per se* or does it do so simply by virtue of reducing the 'price' of giving? The hypothesis that an extra child increases the area of 'engagement' of a family, and hence the field over which it might exercise its sympathies is equally plausible and is consistent with the UK data. A correct interpretation is important because if the alternative hypotheses holds one would not find the dramatic effects hoped for below.

On the basis of his elasticities Feldstein was able to estimate the effect of ten difficult possible US tax reforms – these all involve reducing the price of 'giving' to some or all households and, because of the size of the price elasticity, a larger increase in donations than loss of tax revenue. Feldstein found that, while eliminating the tax deduction altogether would reduce giving by about 26 per cent, the main groups of charities would be differentially affected. Removal would have a relatively small effect on religious donations because they tend to be concentrated among the poor, but would have dramatic effects on donations to hospitals and educational institutions. Boskin and Feldstein, using data collected in the 1974 National Study of Philanthropy, were similarly able to estimate price elasticity for the less well-off households. They found a considerably higher elasticity (around -2) than had previously been found for itemising higher-income families. They conclude that further tax incentives would substantially increase the flow of funds to charities.

The interesting question of whether giving depends on the incomes or giving of other (non-recipient) households as well as on one's own income must remain open. Schwartz had found that the inclusion of other incomes *lowered* own-income elasticities when own and other incomes were negatively correlated but *raised* own elasticities when the incomes were positively correlated: hence relative income seemed to be important. But Feldstein, using a variable that measured the giving of others *and* their economic proximity to the donor, failed to pick up evidence of interdependent giving.

Feldstein has extended his analysis to include bequests, but the results have to be treated with even more caution than usual, as the best fit for the whole sample gives a 'wrong' sign for price elasticity.

Fabricant (1962) noticed a feature of the American evidence that I would not have bothered to mention were it not for its appearance in the FES data too. It appears that, whereas the proportion of philanthropy to income was roughly constant in middle-income ranges, the proportion was rather higher for very poor (or old) families and for the very rich. He suggested that rising *per capita* incomes could probably not account for the increasing proportion of philanthropy over the decades 1929–59. A clue to a possible explanation of this is found in Feldstein's work in that the poor give disproportionately to religious institutions. A further clue may be found in our earlier discussion of the life support effect. In any community blindness, lameness, deafness and feebleness of mind arouse feelings of compassion and a desire to help – feelings by which the poor could be touched at least as strongly as the rich. If this is so one would expect a certain amount of giving even from the very poorest members of society. The widow's mite is, as it were, the intercept of a linear regression.

The upshot of the work done by Feldstein and others in the United States is that income elasticities are very broadly in line with that suggested by a simple cross-section study of UK expenditure. I have already expressed reservations about the basis for calculating price elasticities, but in so far as they are reliable they suggest quite substantial increases in charitable contributions would follow from more favourable tax treatment, *particularly* in the case of the less well-off.

GIVING BY BUSINESSES

The most striking thing about donations by business is that they too are quite tiny when compared with gross profits, roughly 0.7 per cent.[4] And, to compound the niggardly behaviour, a great many items are no doubt included under the heading '*identified contributions by companies to charities, which are non-profit-making bodies included in the personal sector*', which could not reasonably be interpreted as charitable in nature. When rough account is taken of this, proportionate company giving may be seen as running at about the same rate as private giving. It is of course, true that if companies reduced their contributions to zero and distributed the

money to shareholders instead, total charitable contributions would
fall quite drastically as shareholders would presumably increase
their private contribution by only a small percentage of extra share
income. However, this begs the more substantial question of
whether it would be better to have a company earn rather less
profit and consumers (or workers) higher real incomes.

One must return to first principles here, taking a hint from
Alfred Marshall (see Chapter 6). How should an altruistic
monopolist behave? I ask the reader to put out of his mind the
question of how our altruist came to be a monopolist in the first
place. The monopolist would surely wish to maximise the sum of
consumer's surplus and profit. But, as may be seen in Figure 10.3,
the sum of these is maximised at P^*, Q^* or at precisely the same

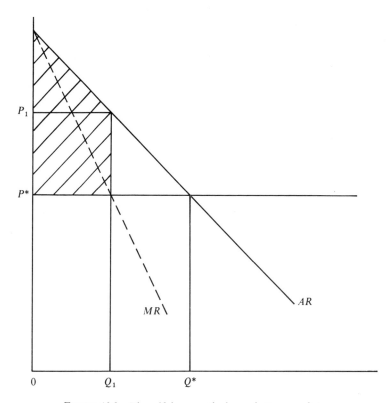

FIGURE 10.3 *The selfish versus the benevolent monopolist*

price–output combination that would have been achieved under the marginal cost pricing principle. Surplus here is clearly greater than at the profit-maximising output Q, where consumers' surplus together with profit is the shaded area. Thus the selfish monopolist sets marginal cost equal to marginal revenue and maximises profit in the usual way, whereas the altruistic monopolist adopts a public utility pricing principle. A partially altruistic monopolist would choose an output between the two.

The usual rule by which price is related to marginal cost under monopoly may be rewritten to take account of the weight (v) which the monopolist attaches to consumers' surplus.[5] It becomes

$$\text{price} = \text{marginal cost} \ \frac{e}{v + (e - 1)}$$

where e is price elasticity. The reader will recognise that this reduces to the usual case when $v = 0$ and the price equals marginal cost case when $v = 1$.

Suppose, though, the monopolist feels altruistic not towards his consumers or factors but towards some other group. The great business philanthropists have indeed not just been interested in redistribution of income from their customers to the 'poor' but have been anxious *not* to let the 'tastes' of their customers count as to how profits should be dispersed to the arts, education or whatever. My proposition about price–output rules therefore applies strictly only to the 'passive' altruistic monopolist: the active altruist may wish to fleece his customers so that part of the profit might go to some great cherished noble cause. While I (the philanthropist) would sponsor symphony concerts, you (the customer) would fritter away your extra real income on taped pop music.

This is one of those curious issues where Left and Right find themselves more or less at one against the soft-middle. Right-wingers tend to argue that the firm is in business to maximise profit which should then be handed to shareholders – if any philantropy is to be done it should be done by shareholders, not by managers. Firms should not, on this interpretation, be socially conscious except in so far as is implied in fair dealing, observing the law and so on. The 'soft-middle' argues that governments should prevent firms making excessive profits but that, if profits are earned, some of these should be used for socially responsible programmes of urban improvement, poverty relief, pollution reduction etc. The Left argues that such programmes tend to be window-dressing and that governments should instead by fully responsible for them.

The first two of these views are captured in the following quotations from *Social Audit*:[6]

industry cannot be expected to spend large sums of money of its own volition while its main obligation is to earn maximum profits for its owners, the shareholders. However conscious of its social responsibilities its actions will tend to be limited to its statutory requirements. [from *Tube Investments Magazine*]

and a statement by the CBI, which refers to

the functions, duties and moral obligations that go beyond the pursuit of profit and the specific requirements of legislation.

Part of the case against corporate 'altruism' is the well known point that corporate altruism is possible only because of monopoly profits (Manne and Wallich, 1972). Pressures for social responsibility are likely to be harmful for two reasons: first, giving might be seen as 'good in itself' with little incentive to check its effectiveness, and second, they imply an avoidance of competitive pressures. Cohn took a very jaundiced view of the conscience of the corporation in his 1971 book. There he traced the awakening of corporate interest in social programmes in reaction to racial urban crises and pressure from the Johnson administration. Such programmes are diversely motivated, from a genuine desire to do good to empty PR gestures. In any case, they tended to wane by about 1970 owing to the cessation of public pressure, the difficulty and high cost of social action and some adverse effects on profit. Cohn concludes that businessmen should not pursue urban programmes actively – rather, they should keep their own houses in order and provide tax revenue for the State; the donations route was simply an attractive way of expressing the corporate conscience.

One would pretty much expect to find this sort of thing on the basis of the free-rider analysis. The small town philanthropist might find it worth while to provide schooling, recreation or whatever for his workers and their children. But even quite a large firm would find it difficult to see any identifiable corporate pay-off from urban programmes, as its part in the over-all picture would be a minor one. Improvements tend to be public goods (at least locally), so it is difficult to mark off benefits that are essentially due to a particular firm's actions. Compounding this, firms have underestimated the amount of expertise and experience required to make a success of such programmes. Thus the free-rider and high cost aspects reinforce one another. As against this, if the pressure of public opinion favours these programmes, one may safely predict that firms will exaggerate their actual contributions.

OVERSEAS

The order of magnitude of overseas aid[7] will come as no surprise following the figures for private charity and for business giving shown in Table 10.3. Voluntary grants are simply one component

TABLE 10.3   *Overseas aid: private charity and business giving*

1974	Mean	Standard deviation
Official development assistance	0.40	0.19
Voluntary grants (as % of GNP of DAC members)	0.03	0.02

of total contributions to charity so one would expect them to be quite small. Indeed, given presuppositions about 'social distance', perhaps it is surprising that they are so great! Presumably this is because they include private response to various natural calamities. Even so there are widespread misgivings about overseas charities: Nightingale reports that they are most disliked by older people, the lower classes and people living outside the South of England. (Nightingale, 1973, p. 116).

As to official aid, Wall (1973) comments that

> voters in donor countries are frequently ignorant of the size, purpose and nature of the aid programmes their tax money supports. Most believe that the programmes are larger than they are, that aid is provided entirely in the form of outright grants, and that aid funds are usually corruptly embezzled by politicians in recipient countries. [Wall, 1973, p. 56]

For the UK in 1970 56 per cent favoured a $2\frac{1}{2}$ per cent level of aid but 79 per cent thought aid ought not to be increased! Explanations of official aid as the conscious outcome of voting processes should therefore be treated with suspicion. It is well known that overseas aid is based *not* merely on income and benevolence but to a major degree on the historical legacies of colonialism and on direct or indirect military interests. But attitudes must count to some extent: Norway and Sweden have the highest figures for both official and voluntary aid.

Dudley and Montmarquette (1974) put charitable motives as part of public interest (but only part) in the provision of the *public good* aid and attempted to measure its 'impact' as the volume of aid increased. It turned out that impact showed diminishing returns to volume, suggesting that the more aid a country gives, the greater should be the number of donee countries so as to prevent reduced impact on its own citizens, which is merely to say that the public's marginal valuation curve for aid to any one country is falling. But, as Wall showed, the public is badly informed about aid. All we can reasonably expect is a loose general relationship between the altruistic concern of the public and a government's development aid.

The free-rider problem comes up in a slightly different form than usual. When the purpose of aid is military or political there is a free-rider problem in that each ally will prefer its fellow allies to undertake the necessary expenditure. But if none of them undertakes it the 'enemy' will be able to gain control; hence alliances, with formal obligations and cost-sharing agreements. Ordinary bilateral aid (with strings) does not encounter the free-rider problem except in a mild form. But suppose the aid is on a purely charitable basis and is to be arranged multilaterally through an international agency (like the IDA). Smaller countries will feel that their impact on the total will be negligible and they would need to be very altruistic indeed to contribute as they might have done on a small-country-to-small-country basis. Larger countries may wish to encourage their participation in a voluntary scheme by leadership, example, exhortation, the setting of development targets and so on. Just as one found before with the free-rider problem, the difficulty is not so much a lack of 'altruism' as the lack of a sense of duty towards other similarly placed countries. Hence attempts at 'moral suasion' such as the 1 per cent target set in 1960. The only way a pooling of aid could lead to increases in its volume would be highly, and implausibly, successful moral suasion or through some international agency with power to levy an aid tax on potential donors.

Myrdal (1970) reminds us that politicians could well be wrong in placing the emphasis in aid policy so much on an often-spurious national interest: that people can be brought to act on the basis of compassion and solidarity. To disregard moral feelings indicates, he argues, the *absence* of realism, for 'it is unrealistic and self-defeating to distrust the moral forces in a nation' (p. 369). These are very major points. This mistaken reluctance to appeal to 'moral forces' may usefully be related to the 'contagion thesis'. The argument would then be that the moral sense atrophies if it is allowed to fall into disuse but revives and indeed strengthens if it is openly appealed to. That foreign aid is a duty rather than a matter of enlightened self-interest is more often said by liberal politicians to one another than to the public.

SUMMARY

(i) Three sorts of giving have been considered in this chapter – charitable giving by households, charitable giving by companies, and overseas aid. Their order of magnitude is quite small in relation to income or profits.

(ii) The relationship between income and giving depends on relative incomes and utility functions.

(iii) UK data suggest an income elasticity for charitable contributions of around 0.7, and this more or less accords with the more sophisticated results of Feldstein and others using American data.

(iv) The passive altruistic monopolist will adopt price–output rules similar to those of a public utility, but the active monopolist will wish to divert consumer real income to financial projects of his own. The costs of socially responsible programmes is large, and the free-rider problem important, so the 'socially conscious' corporation finds itself in a deeply paradoxical situation.

(v) Amounts given in foreign aid are not large in relation to GNP and are due to a variety of motives. Multilateral untied aid requires a higher degree of altruism than does bilateral tied aid, but all such aid is subject to aspects of the free-rider problem.

(vi) Generally speaking, the free-rider problem means that voluntary donations are an underestimate of people's willingness to make transfers. The relationship between voluntary and collective redistribution is therefore explored in the next chapter.

11 Taxation

The notion that any significant part of desirable redistribution could be 'voluntary' may seem faintly comic. Pigou (1920) put this rather well:

> Unfortunately it is quite certain that, in present conditions, voluntary transferences will fall very much below the aggregate of transferences from relatively well-to-do people which the general sense of the community demands.

Yet the literature stemming from Hochman and Rodgers (1969) on so-called 'Pareto-optimal' redistribution must be taken seriously if non-selfishness is to have a role in explaining the political economy of income redistribution. The underlying idea of that literature is that the rich will wish to transfer some of their income to the poor by an amount related to the difference between their incomes. A link is then forged between these private desires and redistribution through the tax system.

Optimality

The possibility of Pareto-optimal redistribution has already been noticed in Chapter 2, where, it will be remembered, neither party wished for allocations beyond his interior 'bliss-point'. Another way of putting this result is that some portions of the utility possibility curve will be *upward sloping*.[1] The utility possibility curve $k\hat{b}k^*\hat{a}$ is 'mapped' from the contract curve of the Edgeworth Box with $\hat{a}$ and $\hat{b}$ corresponding to bliss-points. Starting from some unequal allocation such as k, favourable to B, there will be a voluntary redistribution in A's favour from k to $\hat{b}$ (arrowed). However, I have added a social welfare isoquant W to take into account the point, made by Musgrave and others, that voluntary redistribution can have only a minor role. The policy-maker, armed with a Bergsonian

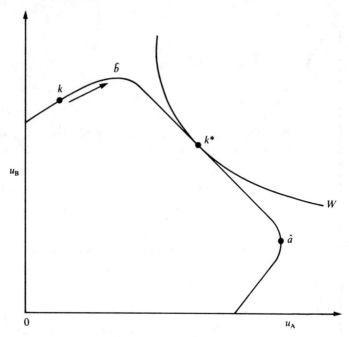

FIGURE 11.1   *Optimal and Pareto-optimal redistribution*

social welfare isoquant, chooses k^* as his optimum-optimorum so that, of the overall redistribution from k to k^*, only part is Pareto-optimal. This method of illustration makes it clear, I hope, that the Pareto-optimal approach in no way eliminates the well-known and valid distinction between matters of efficiency and matters of distribution, Musgrave, in attacking the Hochman–Rodgers view, remarks:

> Pareto-optimal redistribution constitutes a secondary redistribution which depends on the initial distribution of earnings. This distribution is determined by such factors as inheritance, earnings capacities, education and market structures. It may itself be changed through the political process. Such changes, referred to here as a *primary redistribution,* are not a matter of voluntary giving but of taking. [Musgrave, 1970]

Mishan (1972) has trenchantly attacked the whole notion on this and other grounds.

These points are well taken. But for the purposes of a positive

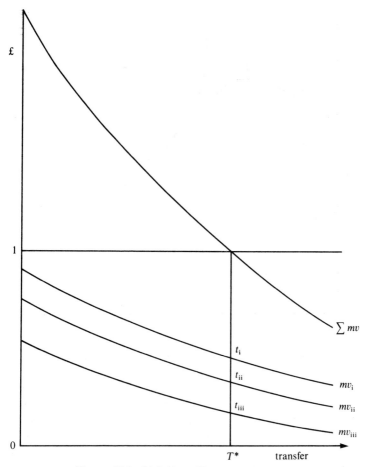

FIGURE 11.2 *Lindahl equilibrium transfer*

analysis it merely transforms the initial question into the different, though related, question: how much redistribution will people vote for in a democracy? It does this because our old friend the free-rider or non-Kantian altruist makes *voluntary* collective redistribution impossible.

THE FREE-RIDER

In the spirit of the public goods analysis of Chapter 3 a *redistributive Lindahl equilibrium* is conceivable. Starting from some initial distribution a transfer to the poor and a set of 'tax prices' could be calculated such that the transfer would be unanimously supported. See, for example, the analyses of Olsen (1969) and Thurow (1971).[2] The essence of the analysis is conveyed in Figure 11.2. The collective cost of transferring £1 to the poor, ignoring transfer costs, is of course, £1. How many pounds should be transferred and how should the cost be shared? Let the amount transferred to class iv, the poor, be T measured along the x-axis. The 'optimal' transfer is then T^* with the three classes contributing at rates t_i, t_{ii} and t_{iii} per £1 of transfer. I assume in this part of the discussion that the three classes are numerically equal. All that is then required is that the three classes declare their marginal valuations of transfer, that the three tax prices be calculated and announced and that individuals be then left to reach T^*. They are led, as it were, by a government assisted invisible hand.

If the analysis could be left here some simple comparative statics conclusions could be drawn. Consider first the 'demand' side. It seems reasonable to infer that transfer demand will increase:
  (i)   the more non-selfish are the three-better-off classes;
  (ii) the greater the disparity between their incomes and the income of the poorest class.

As for costs, anything that reduces the unit cost of transfers will, *ceteris paribus*, cause them to increase. Such a reduction could be effected by, say, favourable tax treatment. Both these sets of predictions are confirmed by common sense.

However, the disruptive role of the free-rider in this context is obvious. Unless the community is very small, even the charitable rich will find it tempting to report low valuations in order to pay low tax prices. In this situation the obvious alternative is collective action.

The gains from collective action and the strong temptation to have a free ride are illustrated in Table 11.1. As is usual, α represents the co-operative strategy (contribute) and β the non-co-operative strategy. It is assumed that private giving to particular individuals is already exhausted so the question is whether further, collective, giving will be worthwhile. Would it be attractive for a rich man (i) to contribute £1 on the understanding that others will also do so? R 'rich' individuals and P 'poor' individuals are assumed.

Following the analysis of Chapter 4, i will be prepared to join in collective action so long the weight he attaches to the income

TABLE 11.1 *Co-operative and non-co-operative charity*

other i's	α		β	
i's	i	each j	i	each j
α	-1	$+\dfrac{R}{P}$	-1	$+\dfrac{1}{P}$
β	0	$+\dfrac{(R-1)}{P}$	0	0
δ	-1	$\dfrac{1}{P}$	-1	$\dfrac{1}{P}$

of a poor man is at least P/R. Each rich man's contribution is in effect multiplied up by R but deflated by P, so the rich do not need to be as unselfish when the poor are few and far between. The degree of non-selfishness required to avoid the free-rider type of outcome is, of course, very high. To see this, consider row δ which shows the marginal effect of i's co-operation. This effect $(-1, 1/P)$ is the same *regardless* of whether he expects other i's to co-operate. In either case he would not choose voluntarily to contribute to a collective scheme unless he valued the poor person's transfer at at least P times his own contribution. Note that assurance makes no difference to the outcome.

Collective charity is likely to be attractive provided the better-off are moderately altruistic, but this will have to be based on compulsion (collectively agreed upon) rather than on voluntary contributions to a pool. One looks, therefore, to a tax system determined by some form of majority rule, rather than to a redistributive Lindahl equilibrium.

Von Furstenberg and Mueller (1971) have adopted a similar approach, using both hypothetical and actual US data. Again they initially assume three classes such that each takes into account the incomes of the classes below it.[3] Income is to be redistributed from the top two classes to the bottom class and these classes are to bear shares c and $1 - c$ of the cost.

A common feature of these models is unanimity. Collective transfers can be optimal only if altruistic preferences are the same *within income classes*. This is a convenient but unrealistic simplification, for, within any one group, there will be some altruistic people and some selfish ones. The selfish would presumably veto *any* redistributive tax structure favouring others. In principle one could get over this by taxing non-selfish people at a higher rate than others (i.e. pursue the benefit principle to its extremes). But this would offend another principle, that people with indentical taxable incomes should be taxed at the same rate. Once the assumption of homogeneity of tastes within income classes is abandoned (and abandoned it has to be), *compulsion* or involuntary redistribution is required and a gaping hole appears in the Pareto-optimal case.

Hochman and Rodgers (1969) postulated that the amount an individual wished to transfer to another depended on the difference between their incomes. They were thus able to make use of the notion of a *transfer elasticity* of demand.[4] By making assumptions about initial income distribution and transfer elasticity, it was possible to compare predicted transfers with actual US transfers. None of the predictions fitted terribly well, but even so the authors claimed that 'progressivity may be interpreted as a matter of revealed preference, which does not require inter-personal utility comparisons for its justification' (Hochman and Rodgers, 1969, p. 554).

This is quite a claim and must engage in battle with other explanations of actual distribution – explanations based perhaps on power, majority voting, pressure groups and so on.

Under both the transfer elasticities adopted, the amounts of transfer decreased monotonically with income. Hochman and Rodgers hazarded several possible explanations for the failure of this relationship to show up in actual US data: that many of the recorded poor were rural poor whose real incomes are understated by the statistics; that the poor have inadequate political power; that the result is attributable to statistical quirks of various sorts. A further possible explanation is that the very pooorest category over-represents single persons while the categories immediately above over-represent larger families. It is interesting that people at around median income (about $5,000) did rather badly while those around the lower quartile (about $2,750) did quite well (see Table 11.2).

The novelty of the Hochman and Rodgers approach should not be overstated in that similar conclusions had already been reached by Duesenberry (1949). This aspect of his work has been rather neglected compared with the more famous relative income

TABLE 11.2   *Amounts of transfer as related to income*

Income ($)	Transfer
800	+441
2,500	+1,110
3,500	+648
4,500	−58
6,250	−131
8,750	+148
15,500	−2.046

Source: Hochman and Rodgers, 1969, p. 555

hypothesis. That hypothesis is, however, an application of the more general notion of interdependent preferences, there being, he argued, 'strong psychological and sociological reasons for supposing that preferences are, in fact interdependent' (Duesenberry, 1949, Ch. 6). Consider a society divided into three classes, each of which takes into account the utilities of the classes below, but not vice-versa. Duesenberry shows that 'if for allocational reasons wage rates are equal to marginal productivities, it is clear that an income tax is required. Moreover the tax would have to be progressive' (p. 101). It is relatively easy to derive marginal tax rates given the utility functions.[5] Progressivity arises in his model because external concern at top income levels accumulates, as it were, the external concern of those below.

APPLICATION TO UK DATA

In this section I present a reworking of the Hochman–Rodgers calculations with UK data. The object of the exercise is to compare the actual pattern of transfers with predicted patterns based on Pareto-optimal redistribution. I have anchored the Pareto-optimal transfers on the amounts actually transferred to the poorest groups so the base transfers remain roughly the same for the actual and the two hypothetical transfers. Following Hochman and Rodgers, I

TABLE 11.3

Mean income	% of households	Actual cash transfer	P.O. cash transfer $E = 0$	P.O. cash transfer $E = 1$	Actual cash-and-kind transfer	P.O. cash-and-kind transfer $E = 0$	P.O. cash-and-kind transfer $E = 1$
104	16.6	+726	+726	+735	+877	+878	+867
422	1.4	+679	+569	+647	+785	+688	+763
505	1.3	+698	+545	+621	+694	+659	+733
612	1.5	+564	+521	+584	+607	+630	+689
739	1.7	+545	+493	+556	+605	+597	+656
903	1.6	+486	+464	+510	+547	+561	+602
1,088	2.3	+374	+430	+454	+392	+520	+536
1,319	3.1	+272	+383	+392	+361	+463	+463
1,606	4.4	+30	+318	+308	+65	+385	+363
1,946	7.1	−72	+218	+215	−87	+264	+254
2,346	9.5	−242	+73	+102	−235	+88	+120
2,816	11.6	−324	−109	−27	−379	−132	−32
3,411	12.0	−504	−315	−194	−609	−381	−229
4,108	10.2	−675	−508	−385	−844	−615	−454
4,956	7.4	−902	−661	−627	−1,204	−800	−740
7,639	8.3	−1568	−798	−1,376	−2,012	−966	−1,624
			transfer 8.7	$k = 0.0028$		transfer 10.52	$k = 0.0033$

Source: Own calculations and *Economic Trends* (February 1976)

have postulated two transfer elasticities, $E = 0$ and $E = 1$. The method used is first to calculate a matrix of income differences, second to derive appropriate basic transfers by anchoring on the poorest groups, third to calculate how much each group receives from each of the others and fourth to calculate how much it pays to each of the others. The net transfers[6] are then as reported in Table 11.3. Notice that the basic amounts or proportions transferred are reported at the foot of the appropriate column. In the case of $E = 1$ the anchored transfers are only approximately equal as greater precision would require an inconvenient number of decimal places in k, the proportion of income differences transferred.

Unlike the reported position in the United States, it may be seen from Figures 11.3 and 11.4 that amounts transferred do decrease monotonically with income as predicted by the Pareto-optimality assumption. The pattern of transfers, though not the actual amounts, is more in accord with a unit than a zero elasticity the latter greatly understating the amounts transferred by the more prosperous groups. Neither is there any suspicious 'peak' in net transfers at any income range; in particular, there is no evidence

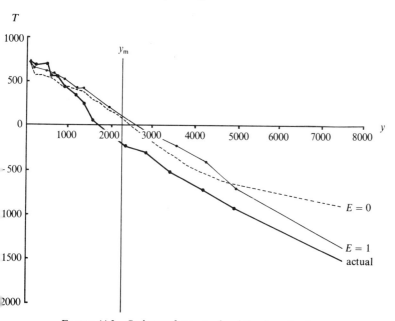

FIGURE 11.3 *Cash transfers: actual and Pareto-optimal*

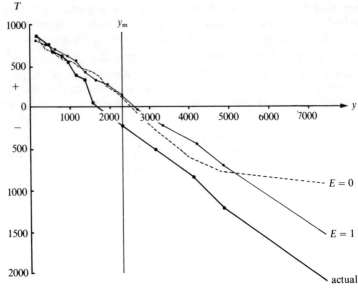

FIGURE 11.4   *Cash and kind transfers: actual and Pareto-optimal*

that median income groups do especially well out of the system (median income is denoted by y_m). This is consistent with many hypotheses but not the double one that

   (i) redistribution is the result of simple majority voting and

   (ii) that voters behave entirely selfishly.

It is certainly consistent with effective voting control being exercised by any higher (benevolent) quantile group. Hochman and Rodgers's suggestion that perhaps elasticity increases at the higher income ranges is interesting. It must be seen in the light of evidence of charitable giving, however, which seems to show a less than unit elasticity of transfer over most ranges of income with a mere hint of a higher elasticity at higher incomes.

    Figures 11.3 and 11.4 both indicate that the effective net tax structure is very approximately linear. The structure predicted by the Pareto-optimality approach depends both upon transfer elasticity and the pre-tax distribution of income. For example, the more very poor people there are and the smaller the number of those in the third quartile, the more altruistic will those in the upper quartile need to be to sustain a given set of transfers to the poor.

A SIMPLE CASE OF NON-SELFISH VOTING

Let each individual be purely selfish, his attitude to taxation depending entirely on his place in the income distribution. Also assume that taxation is purely redistributive (at zero transfer cost) and that redistribution from poor to rich and disincentive effects may be ruled out. Consider any individual with income r times mean income. Then all those individuals with $r > 1$ will vote for a zero tax, all those with $r = 1$ will be indifferent and all those with $r < 1$ will vote for a tax rate of unity with the tax receipts distributed equally. But the actual distribution of pre-tax incomes in this country and elsewhere is approximately log-normal with the median income below the mean. Under all these assumptions and majority voting the outcome would be a unit tax rate (Figure 11.5).

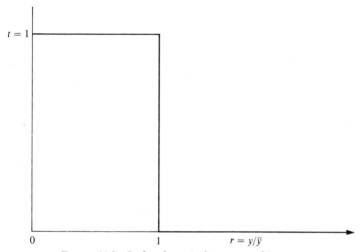

FIGURE 11.5   *Preferred marginal tax rate and income*

Non-selfishness may now be introduced into this very simple framework. Let each individual's income be given by:

$$Y_i = S + (1 - t)\hat{Y}_i$$

where S is a lump-sum 'social dividend' paid to everyone, t the marginal tax rate and $\hat{Y}_i$ pre-tax income. On the assumption of purely redistributive taxation $S = t\,\bar{Y}$ where $\bar{Y}$ is mean income. If he is purely selfish he will prefer a unit or zero tax depending on whether $r \gtrless 1$. Now introduce non-selfishness by letting each individual attach a weight a to the social dividend and $(1 - a)$ to his own income. His psychic income is then given by

$$W_i = \text{a t } \bar{Y} + (1 - a)[t \ \bar{Y} + (1 - t)\hat{Y}].$$

Obviously, if $t = 0$, psychic income is $(1 - a)\hat{Y}$, and if $t = 1$, psychic income is $\bar{Y}$; and he will be indifferent between zero and unit tax rates when

$$r = \frac{1}{1 - a}.$$

The greater is a, the higher is break-even income. For example, if $a = \frac{1}{2}$ all those up to *twice* mean income $(r = 2)$ would vote for a unit tax rate. One effect of non-selfishness is therefore to increase the likelihood of the better-off voting for steeply redistributive taxation.

Several necessary concessions to realism cry out for attention. Primarily these are to do with the very high tax rate desired by those below mean income and with the very sharp step function. If the poor suspect that tax disincentive effects are important in that $\bar{Y}$ might eventually *fall* (or be lower than it might otherwise have been) they will press for a high but not *very* high marginal tax rate. *A fortiori*, the better off will be aware not merely of this effect but of disincentive effects on their own incomes. Hence the preferred tax function is likely to start below $t = 1$ and fall more gradually than the step function in the figure.

Related questions about 'preferred' tax rates have been treated in a much more sophisticated fashion in the literature on optimal taxation, a brief review of which follows.

OPTIMAL INCOME TAX

The first point to be made is that no account is taken in the optimal tax literature of non-selfishness. Thus Mirrlees:

> it is not probable that work decisions are entirely, or even, in the long run, mainly, determined by social convention, psychological need, or the imperatives of cooperative behaviour. [1971]

And Atkinson:

> no account has been taken of inter-dependencies (the possibility that a person's welfare may depend on the income of others). If such interdependencies exist, raising the tax rate . . . may still be Pareto-optimal in terms of individual utilities. [1973]

Thus the literature, as it stands, is based on self-interested behaviour. Feldstein (1976) has similarly noticed

> the significance of ignoring externalities in consumption. In particular this precludes incorporating either the effects of altruism or envy. This exclusion may explain why all of the studies of the optimal progressivity of the income tax have implied surprisingly little redistribution through the tax transfer process. [p. 81]

The object of the optimal tax exercise is to determine the income tax schedule, given the following.

(i) A social welfare function incorporating some preference for equality. The tax schedule is selected so as to maximise social welfare, given the further information below. The function represents a value judgement, of course, but may be varied so as to display the sensitivity of the generated tax schedule to the value judgements made. Other things being equal, the greater the preference for equality the higher will be the marginal tax rate. The most egalitarian of the assumptions made (see Atkinson, Broome) is the Rawlsian one of maximising the utility of the least well-off.

(ii) The distribution of abilities. Unlike the social welfare function, the distribution of abilities is an empirical matter: unfortunately one knows little or nothing about it. It is customary, in the face of ignorance, to assume a log-normal or Pareto distribution, and all the results obtained depend heavily on the assumption that high ability is relatively scarce and is linked closely to high earnings.

(iii) Preferences over goods and leisure. These are important because they determine the disincentive effects (if any) of income taxation. For example, Sheshinski (1972) showed that the elasticity of the labour supply function sets an upper bound to the optimal marginal tax rate. Thus, if the elasticity is 0.4 the upper bound is 63 per cent.[7] Referring back to the limited case just discussed, if there is zero elasticity of labour supply the upper bound to the tax rate is unity.

The optimal tax rate is, of course, sensitive to the assumptions made under these heads. Generally speaking the tax rates emerging from the literature have been rather lower than one might have expected given its built-in egalitarian assumptions. The reason for this is the uneven distribution of abilities and the presence of disincentive effects. Broome was able to produce a high rate only by using a Rawlsian social welfare function and setting a limit on low ability.

The optimal tax rates so calculated will be optimal with respect to a social welfare function. Of more interest to us, however, is that each *individual* will have a view (albeit rough) about the optimal tax structure. How would non-selfishness affect these individual views?

Atkinson (1973) has already linked the optimal tax literature with majority voting. Itsumi (1974) has gone further than this, calculating preferred (linear) tax rates for individuals at each point on the income distribution. As would be expected, the more able individuals vote for low and the less able individuals for high marginal tax rates. The crucial preference under simple majority voting will be

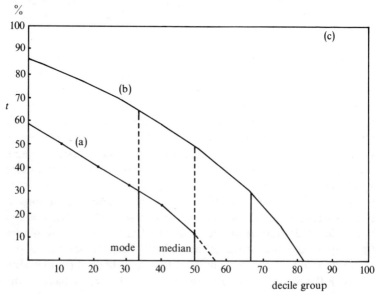

FIGURE 11.6   *Preferred tax rates by decile group. Curve (a) is based on Itsumi (1974), assuming log-normal ability distribution with $\sigma = 0.39$, following Mirrlees, and $a = 1.0$*

the *maxi-median*, the tax rate giving the greatest utility to the (selfish) person of median ability. At the lower end, the maxi-min rate is that preferred by the least able and should be chosen if one is interested (after Rawls and Broome) in maximising the welfare of the least well-off. As already remarked, this rate will be less than unity because of the poor's appreciation of disincentive effects. In addition to the maxi-min and maxi-median, Itsumi has calculated preferred tax rates for other decile groups (Figure 11.6).

Curve (*a*) of the figure shows preferred tax rates by decile group on one particular set of assumptions. Unlike the simple step function discussed earlier, the maxi-min tax rate is *not* unity but well below it (just under 60 per cent),[8] and the favoured rate decreases to zero somewhere between the median and the mean (not shown). On the assumptions made by Itsumi, individual preferences on tax rates will be 'single-peaked': utility monotonically decreases on either side of the preferred tax rate. This is comforting if one wants to make use of simple voting theory:

> Single-peakedness not only makes it possible to say that the less able individual always has his maximum welfare level at a higher marginal tax rate, but also ensures the effectiveness of a majority voting political system for making a social choice on the marginal tax rate. [Itsumi, 1974]

Non-selfishness may now be expected to have two types of effect. First, as has already been noted, it will tend to move the tax function to the right. Decile groups who, if selfish, would vote for a zero tax are now prepared to vote for a positive tax. Second, it will tend to raise the function vertically because the better off attach a *positive weight* to the welfare of the beneficiaries of their tax payments. In the limit, if they attach the same weight to others taken together as to themselves, there will be no disincentive effects whatever. For a simple analysis of this second point see the notes to this chapter.[9] Taking these two points together there is a presumption that the 'non-selfish' tax function will lie wholly to the north-east of the selfish function – for example, the curve (*b*). Under (*b*) *some* positive redistributive tax would be favoured even by those at around the eightieth income percentile. Curve (*c*) shows the extreme limiting case where everyone is highly altruistic and a unit tax rate commands unanimous support.

Although the poor do well on the non-selfishness assumption, it does not follow that they themselves are behaving selfishly. All that has happened is that non-selfishness implies a willingness to redistribute in favour of *poorer* groups. Without this assumption the monotonicity of our results collapses: at the extreme the very benevolent poor might wish to transfer income to the only slightly benevolent rich. This would be inconsistent not merely with our assumption about transfers but, more importantly, with the empirical evidence on transfers. If it held, non-selfishness might upset single-peakedness, thereby undermining confidence in a unique majority voting outcome.

A NOTE ON ABILITY TAXES

It is commonly held that income taxes distort the work–leisure choice so it is not surprising to find that the 'non-twisting' theorem is relevant to Pareto-optimal redistribution. Just as the private contract curve coincided with the social contract curve under pure exchange when preferences were non-meddlesome, so will efficient *redistribution* require no 'distortion' in the exchange between goods and leisure. The corresponding non-meddlesome assumption here is that one is interested in the utilities of others, not merely in their command over goods. But if redistribution of income is inefficient this seems only to leave 'ability', which is rather difficult to redistribute *per se*. However, ability may be regarded as generating a pure rent in the Ricardian sense and therefore able to bear a tax without creating any allocative distortions. Admittedly, no effective ability tax is in sight, but the foregoing remarks on optimal income tax must be regarded as being of a second-best nature.

SUMMARY

The extent of non-selfishness is most important to any positive explanation of how much income redistribution takes place in a society, though the possibility of 'Pareto-optimal' or voluntary redistribution in no way diminishes the role of a social welfare function in settling upon a normative optimum. In this chapter the link between theoretical willingness to make collective transfers and actual transfers was explored and an extension of the Hochman–Rodgers type of analysis made to UK data. A further link between studies on voluntary transfers and those on optimal income taxation was attempted and it was suggested that (with certain provisos) the introduction of non-selfishness will cause each decile group to vote for a higher linear tax rate than before. This point is particularly important in communities where decisions are effectively made by groups in the upper quantiles rather than around the median of the ability distribution.

12 Redistribution in Kind

Redistribution in cash seems to be easier, more effective and morally more attractive than redistribution in kind. Each individual is free to decide on his own commodity bundle at market prices within his new budget constraint. As well as offering freedom of choice it has the attraction of being neat and tidy; it implies the abolition of subsidies and earmarked vouchers and, in its simplest form, requires the one instrument of redistributive income taxation. It is buttressed by the ethical proposition that, even if one's preferences in respect of others *are* 'meddlesome' or 'paternalistic', they *ought not* to be. Their preferences are their business, not mine.

A healthy mistrust of paternalism ought not to blind one, however, to cases where it is surely permissible; children, drunks, the mentally handicapped, the badly informed, etc. In the case of normal adults a useful rule for the 'rightness' of paternalism might be to test for its reversibility.[1] Would I, upon reflection, have others behave towards me in a similarly paternalistic way? Obvious examples come to mind like taking car keys from a drunk or giving first aid. Individual freedom versus paternalism, especially the paternalism of bureaucrats, is an exciting, but not compelling, clarion call.

Yet the question here is not whether goods externalities as opposed to utility externalities are morally permissible but whether they are empirically strong. If so a positive analysis must give them due consideration. The overwhelming weight of impressionistic evidence is that people are concerned less with other people's incomes or utilities than with their consumption of specific commodities. Any reader who believes himself to be entirely non-paternalistic in his concern is asked to perform the following mental experiment. I notice that my neighbour is badly fed and badly clothed so I give him some money which he then spends on beer and tobacco. Do I feel entirely happy about this or do I somehow feel that my intentions have been thwarted?

The history of charities suggests that concern is highly specific or even wilfully and eccentrically meddlesome.

> There are charities to give foul-weather jackets to the poor of Appleton, Berkshire; cloaks and bonnets to widows and spinsters at Wolverhampton, Buckinghamshire; soap and candles to eight poor people at Lydney, Gloucestershire, on All Souls Day; bread and fish to the poor of Dronfield, Derbyshire; spiced bread to the poor of Broughton, Lincolnshire; gowns to 'ancient maids' at Britwell Salome, Oxfordshire. [Nightingale, 1973, p. 12]

Buchanan puts the point forcibly:

> What libertarian backers of such proposals [like negative income tax] do not fully appreciate is the lack of interest on the part of the public in real income distribution as such. One must search diligently to find much 'social' concern expressed for the prudent poor whose lives are well-ordered and stable. The evidence seems to indicate that general redistribution of purchasing power, or even general change in relative levels of well-being, is not generally desired. Instead members of the public want, and express through their behaviour, relief for specific spending patterns. [Buchanan, 1968].

Tullock (1970), though calling for more research, takes a similar view, and Arrow comments that

> the subsidies or other governmental help go to those who are disadvantaged in life by events the incidence of which is popularly regarded as unpredictable: the blind, dependent children, the medically indigent ..., virtually nowhere is there a system of subsidies that has as its aim simply an equalisation of incomes. [Arrow, 1971]

One is on good ground, therefore, and in good company, in assuming that specific concern is an important and widespread phenomenon.

Hochman and Rodgers (1970) have argued, convincingly in my view, that the delineation of so-called merit goods may be regarded as endogenous once specific concern is allowed for. Merit goods are simply those goods that generate sufficient external concern to justify transfers in kind. They point to the very large part of effective US redistribution that seems to be made up of transfers in kind (42 per cent). About 50 per cent of those UK benefits reasonably allocable to individuals are made up of benefits in kind and a further 8 per cent of subsidies: cash redistribution is apparently less important than implicit grants made up of specific goods.[2]

I am not, of course, arguing that in-kind redistributions are entirely due to paternalistic altruism. For the present discussion one need note only that both private and public redistributions seem to have a highly important in-kind, specific, meddlesome or paternalistic component. This tiresome property leads to all sorts of difficulty and dominates the rest of this chapter.

TWISTING

In the case of utility externalities it has been shown (Chapter 2) that a non-twisting theorem holds such that the conditions for Pareto optimality remain unaffected. The same contract locus applies as in the ordinary selfish case but there is scope for Pareto-optimal redistribution. The only departure from *laissez-faire* is the need for collective organisation arising from the free-rider problem in voluntary redistribution. On the other hand, with meddlesome preferences, the efficiency conditions will not remain unaltered (except by chance) and the contract curve will have twisted.

This is a most important result. Pareto-optimal allocations will now lie on the twisted contract locus, *not* on the private or selfish contract locus. If so, competitive prices will no longer be appropriate and a set of taxes (subsidies) must be calculated such as to bring everyone to the social contract locus. The nature of this solution has been well described by Shapley and Shubick (1969), who postulate an imaginary economy Γ' which is just like the actual economy Γ except that all externalities are marketable and carry price tags. It is worth quoting them at length.

> Let each normal good in Γ be assigned the same price as in Γ'. Let each person in Γ who benefits from an external good be taxed, i.e. made to pay for it, at the price of the correspondingly 'labelled' good in Γ'. Finally let each producer of an external economy in Γ be subsidised, i.e. paid for the product, at a rate equal to the sum of the prices of its n 'labelled' counterparts in Γ', ... each individual is required to take his tax and subsidy payments into account in balancing his budget. Because of the direct relationship between Γ and Γ', the above prescription of prices, taxes and subsidies constitutes a kind of generalised

competitive equilibrium for Γ. Among its virtues is that it is in the core.... Among its drawbacks ... is the fact that *each beneficiary of an external economy would have to be taxed differently.* [my italics]

Why can we not simply leave the parties to find their own way to the social contract curve? In the two-person case this should be possible. Take the simple case of one selfish individual (B) and a paternalistic altruist (A) whose preferences are indicated by a U-shaped set of indifference curves. All that is necessary is for A to transfer goods to B. The only difficulty to arise is that B will have an incentive to misrepresent his preferences to A, thus inducing his unfortunate benefactor to transfer more than the Pareto-optimal amount. This shameful behaviour was discussed by Johnson: 'the donee will outwardly emit signs of distaste for the good, while the donor will play the role of a perfect classical economic man' (1968, p. 95). Strategic conduct of this sort will be particularly important when numbers are small and there is a face-to-face contact; an experienced donee will easily be able to gauge whether or not the donor is a 'soft-touch'. Potential donees must however be cautious in playing this strategy, which could very well become counter-productive as donors perceive that the price of inducing their favoured consumption patterns is rising.

Once one moves away from the two-person case a difficult version of the free-rider problem makes itself felt. I, as an individual A, may be prepared to exchange a merit good on favourable terms to B's. But I must be sure that other A's are behaving similarly, otherwise my intentions towards the B's will be thwarted. For a two-person solution, *writ large*, to emerge spontaneously the A's must behave Kantianly. Unless they do so there will be no hope of a voluntary solution and a tax (subsidy) regime of the kind described by Shapley and Shubick will have to adopted collectively.

Unfortunately, nearly all enforcement mechanisms must *either* frustrate the paternalist's intention *or* require unattractive policing.

THE TAX SUBSIDY SOLUTION

(a) Let the A's be meddlesomely altruistic in respect of X and the B's be entirely selfish (Figure 12.1). The initial allocation is at k_0 on the private or selfish contract curve such that the indifference

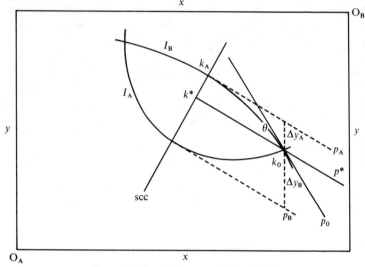

FIGURE 12.1   *A Pareto-optimal 'subsidy'*

curves I_A and I_B pass through k_0: p_0 is the supporting competitive price. (A's selfish indifference curve passing through k_0 is not shown, in the interest of diagrammatical clarity.) Retaining the convention that agents behave *as though* in a competitive regime, a new Pareto-optimum k^* may be supported by a new price line p^* also passing through k_0. It is as though the A's had decided to exchange X for Y at the favourable price p^* with an implied subsidy indicated by θ in the diagram.

Notice that at k^* the B's are not only holding more X than initially but have higher real incomes (they are on higher indifference curves). In the scenario I have outlined the A's have all the bargaining power, apart from dissimulation. Hence they are likely to be able to select a point like k_A along with a redistribution *away from* the B's equal to Δy. A collective decision to impose a maximum price on X so as to bring the price ratio to p^* would be an effective way of securing k^*. A collective decision to tax each B by Δy and then impose a price ratio P_A would be an effective way of securing k_A. Whether such conduct by the A's may in any way be described as 'altruistic' is a moot point. For completeness I also show the outcome k_B such that the B's manage to squeeze maximum advantage out of the situation. An amount Δy is then transferred to the B's and a price p_B enforced.

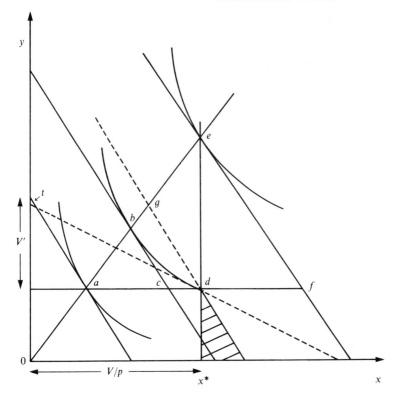

FIGURE 12.2   *Alternative schemes for inducing a specific consumption pattern* (*d*)

(b) Figure 12.2 illustrates the position of a donee who is initially in equilibrium at point *a*. Consider first the case of the nonmeddlesome altruist who wants to enable the donee to reach the indifference curve *bd*. This may easily be achieved by an income transfer equal to *ac* when measured in terms of commodity *X*.

The meddlesome altruist, however, while happy about the donee's consumption of *Y*, would much prefer him to choose *X** of *X* at position *d*. Several methods are available:

   (i)   Marketable redistribution in kind or marketable vouchers. The recipient would simply exchange these for goods until reaching a private equilibrium at *g*, thus frustrating the donor's intentions.

  (ii)   Non-marketable redistribution in kind. The recipient would be handed *ad* extra units of *X* and that would be the end of the matter. Extra X would be both compulsory and free. This covers a very important class of cases (e.g. elementary education, health care).

(iii) Sufficient income redistribution. One could transfer sufficient extra income, *af*, to allow *e* to be chosen, But this would also entail much higher consumption of Y in which the donor is not at all interested. From his point of view it would be a very expensive solution. Notice that this feature of the solution arises solely from donor meddlesomeness, for had he been interested only in utility an efficient transfer could have been arranged much more cheaply.

(iv) Subsidised vouchers. Donees would be permitted to buy vouchers (redeemable in X) at less than their face value. The vouchers would cost V' and be exchangeable for V/p of X where p is the price of X in terms of Y. Effectively, the new budget constraint is the shaded triangle. Should the recipient wish to purchase more X than his voucher allows, this is certainly permitted but may be taken by the donor as a signal to charge more for the voucher. The solution is based on costless reinforcement. As Olsen concedes in his very useful discussion, costs are, in fact, likely to be rather large and, if so, the argument for cash transfers *even in the meddlesome case* is strengthened. That this is possible may be seen from the elaborateness of his voucher procedure:

> For each eligible family we must determine the optimal quantity of each good, set the face value of the voucher equal to the optimal quantity of the subsidised good times its market price, and set the charge for the voucher so that the family has just enough disposable income to purchase the optimal quantities of all other goods. [Olsen, 1971]

(v) Subsidies plus transfers. Donees (but only donees) would receive a transfer (t) and be permitted to buy at the subsidised price shown by the dotted line tangential to the indifference curve at d. The transfer is negative in the case illustrated but may be negative, zero or positive depending on the generosity of donors. The cost of the scheme to donors (per recipient) is ad, measured in x, the same as in the non-marketable voucher case. Paraphrasing, Olsen one might prescribe:

> For each individual family we must determine the optimal

quantity of each good and select that combination of transfer and subsidy which induces the family to make these optimal purchases.

In terms of complexity this is no less forbidding than the voucher system. It is sometimes argued that a voucher system is superior in that purchasers are able to choose commodity bundles at non-distorted market prices. But the price ratio is *not* equal to the marginal rate of substitution for recipients (except by a fluke), so first-order conditions are in any case violated. The rate of subsidy here corresponds, of course, to the rate of subsidy indicated in the Edgeworth Box analysis.

OTHER DERIVATIONS

Green (1971) derived a formula for differential prices in a two-good, two-person economy with mutual specific concern in one commodity. Modifying his formula[3] to the case where concern is one-sided, one finds, for example, that if A's utility, at the margin, from B's consumption of X is only a quarter of his own, then A should pay a third as much again as B. The more concern A has the more he should pay relative to B. If, in the limiting case, he gives no weight at all to B, the formula reduces to the ordinary case where both pay the same. One has to be careful, of course, about the meaning of differential prices in a two-person (or two-class) exchange economy. The bench mark is always the hypothetical competitive price.

It is also possible to derive[4] equilibrium conditions for an explicit subsidy. The individual i will choose that rate of subsidy to individuals j on X such that: i's marginal utility from j's consumption of X equals i's share in the cost of the subsidy *times* the number of individuals in class j relative to other classes, *divided by* j's price elasticity of demand for X.

The standard result that the rate of subsidy depends upon the reciprocal of the price elasticity demand is preserved but is now seen as merely one side of an equilibrium condition. It is easily shown that the formula corresponds to Green's condition in the two-person case.

The following comparative statics propositions seem to follow from this derivation. The rate of subsidy will tend to rise if,

(i)   the i's' specific altruism increases;
(ii) the relative number of potential recipients decreases;
(iii) the i's' share of subsidy cost decreases;
(iv) the j's' price elasticity falls.

A simple numerical example may be of help. Let i be one decile group and let the subsidy go to the lowest decile groups. Then the relative size of group j is $\frac{1}{4}$. Let the numerical value of price elasticity be 1.5 and let i bear its proportionate share in the subsidy. Then the required rate of subsidy is $\frac{2}{3}$ and the implied marginal utility to i from j's consumption is $\frac{1}{6}$. For simplicity I have been assuming identical preferences *within* classes. Without such an assumption it would be necessary to calculate $m(m-1)(k-1)$ different rates of subsidy, one from each person to each other person in respect of each good except for the *numéraire*.

One of the difficulties highlighted by Figures 12.1 and 12.2 and by the preceding discussion is the ambiguous nature of *paternalistic* altruism. Indeed, it is very simple to generate cases where the paternalistic altruist will wish both to subsidise a specific good *and* at the same time to reduce the recipient's disposable income. In principle the dividing line between paternalistic altruism and pure meddlesomeness is the recipient's original indifference curve. If I wish him to have a different commodity composition but to remain on the same indifference curve I am being purely meddlesome and I shall certainly want to reduce his real disposable income on other goods. If I want to change his commodity composition *and* raise him to a higher indifference curve I am being altruistically meddlesome, even though I might contrive some reduction in his other disposable income.

Several writers have expressed grave reservations about where this sort of intervention is taking us (see, for example, Robbins, 1976, and Tullock, 1971). Meddlesome preferences can certainly lead to messy and meddlesome interventions. Such interventions are doubly unattractive when the 'poor' play a purely passive role, merely responding to policies devised by the paternalistic altruist. Archibald and Donaldson (1976) have very appropriately labelled as 'Dog and Master' models those analyses based on Pareto-optimal redistribution.

TAKE-UP AND ENFORCEMENT

The trouble both with cash and with fully marketable vouchers is that they enable the recipient to frustrate the intentions of the paternalist. Even where open trading is not permitted, recipients will find all sorts of ways of improving their allocations. If issued with rent certificates, for example, they could come to an arrangement with landlords to rent for less than certificate values and obtain a refund (Tullock, 1971). The more efficient the set of subterranean markets of this sort, the more true will be Pauly's remark that

> it really makes no difference whether the individual is given x dollars' worth of the externality generating good, a voucher redeemable only for x dollars' worth of the good or simply x dollars in money, . . . one may as well give the poor cigarettes as warm clothes. [Pauly, 1970].

Olsen concedes that heavy enforcement costs could make cash transfers more attractive than vouchers but proposes rent certificates because

> I believe that there are many paternalistic altruists in this country and that housing is one of the goods that these people think the poor value too lightly. My belief stems from the casual observation that most governmental and non-governmental transfers to the poor are in kind (e.g. housing, food stamps and medicare). If this sort of consumption externality proves to be unimportant, then I will withdraw my rent certificate proposal. [Olsen, 1971]

Two quite separate practical problems may be distinguished in making in-kind transfers: the *take-up* problem and the *enforcement* problem.

Consider first the problem of take-up, a problem not confined to redistribution in kind but also associated with cash redistribution. It is well-known (see, e.g. Collard, 1971) that the marginal cost of raising take-up rates increases with the present rate of take-up. Even quite expensive 'campaigns' to persuade the poor of their rights fail to raise take-up rates to anything like 100 per cent. Moreover, the *pattern* of take-up rates is rather disturbing: take-up is very high indeed for student grants and direct grant school fees but very low for rent allowances in the furnished sector.[5]

Another worrying feature is that the multiplicity of forms and

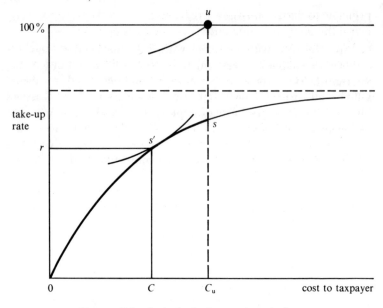

FIGURE 12.3   *Optimal selective or universal scheme*

paying authorities imposes heavy burdens on people least able to cope with complicated procedures. To a significant extent the costs of operating the system are borne by its clients.

Altruism is relevant to the choice between a completely universal and a means-tested system of benefits as is illustrated in Figure 12.3. Along the horizontal axis is measured the share of an individual (let us call him a representative taxpayer) in total provision costs. The rate of take-up is measured on the vertical axis. A universal scheme is indicated at U where take-up is 100 per cent and cost is c_u. Alternative selective or means-tested schemes (differing by publicity or presentation) are indicated along $os's$, which becomes asymptotic to some high rate of take-up. The heavy part of this line and the point u constitute a discontinuous *efficient frontier* from which the taxpayer selects. One possible set of preferences is indicated by the indifference curves which show that *if* a selective system is to be adopted the best system will have a take-up rate r and a cost C. But it would be better still to adopt the purely universal scheme. I leave to the reader an examination of various outcomes with different taxpayer preferences.[6] It is possible in principle to derive 'most preferred' systems by taxpayer group and hence the likely outcome under specified voting rules.

Assuming that the take-up decision has somehow been made, a problem of 'enforcement' remains whenever redistribution is not in money, e.g. vouchers, subsidies to individuals or direct benefits in kind. Tullock (1971) has described the problem in some detail. Suppose the poor are paying $60 a month for housing. Let there be introduced a $100 rent certificate but suppose that, had a poor person been given $40 extra, he would have spent $10 on housing and $30 on other things. He could arrange with his landlord to rent a $70 apartment with $100 certificate and obtain a rebate of *up to* $30. A similar situation arose with vouchers for cheap beef for pensioners in the UK in 1975: they were sometimes traded for cash and sometimes traded in for other types of meat. Tullock's point is that to declare this kind of behaviour illegal creates a new 'crime without a victim'. For this reason redistribution in cash will be 'better' than attempted redistribution in kind.

This enforcement problem is not as acute in practice in the UK as it seems to be in principle, for many types of redistribution are relatively unmarketable. It is almost impossible to trade a subsidised prescription or course of dental treatment and quite difficult to trade a rent rebate or free school meal. Vouchers are much more subject to the enforcement difficulty than are subsidies paid on specific redistribution *in kind*. For this reason, method (ii) of those discussed earlier in this chapter is not to be despised.

On these grounds, medical care seems quite a good candidate for *universal provision in kind*. First there is hardly any enforcement problem – it would be very difficult for me to trade my free operation. Second, most people would favour a take-up of around 100 per cent. I therefore turn to a more detailed discussion of health care.

HEALTH CARE

Health care is perhaps the most widely discussed of all 'benefits in kind'. Economists have become particularly fascinated with the rationale of the British National Health Service, which does not sit at all easily with the standard conclusions of welfare economics.

For example, provision through the State eschews the advantages of price in guiding the behaviour of immediate supplies and the service is free (with some exceptions) at the point of provision. Indeed the 'free' nature of the system has come increasingly under attack by some branches of the medical profession.

Arrow's well-known discussion (1951/1963 p. 71) leaves the matter unsettled. It rests upon the special characteristics of medical care including:

(i)   its irregular and (for individuals) unpredictable occurrence;
(ii)   'ethical' motives among physicians and 'non-profit' provision;
(iii) uncertainty about the consequences of medical care;
(iv)   the strong effect of non-market forces (e.g. training subsidies) on quality and quantity;
(v)   the prevalence of 'non-market' price practices, (linked to (ii) above).

The implications of his discussion for state provision are ambiguous however. Uncertainty about the incidence of medical care requirements may be dealt with through private insurance, but the argument for compulsory insurance through the state rests upon:

(i)   enormous economies of state insurance;
(ii)   poor (or zero) insurance cover available to those with chronic health care problems;
(iii) poor differentiation of private premiums;
(iv)   poor coverage of the unemployed, the institutionalised and the aged.

Strong as these arguments are, they add up to a case for a gigantic and probably subsidised compulsory insurance scheme organised by, or at least underpinned by, the State. But they do not add up to a case for state provision of health care. The British National Health Service was set up in 1948 on the principle that health care should be absolutely free at the point of treatment; treatment would be contingent not upon adequate insurance cover or income but solely upon medical need.

Arrow notices such moral considerations:

> The concern of individuals for the health of others, ... the taste for improving the health of others appears to be stronger than for improving other aspects of their welfare. [1951/1963 p. 220]

As he warns, there is an identification problem here in that both market failure and 'altruism' are present and difficult to disentangle. Other writers have made use of the 'specific altruism' phenomenon to explain the emergence of NHS-type systems. Arrow does not do this. Instead he stresses ethical motives on the supply side in the spirit of (ii) or (iv) in the above list of special features and counts on general relationships of confidence and trust to *make up for* the inadequacies of insurance systems, particularly in respect of ineffective treatment. His argument here comes close to Titmuss's view of the *gift relationship* discussed in Chapter 13 and to Hirsch's (1975) 'collective intermediate goods'. He returns to the same theme in the related context of 'moral hazard':

> One of the characteristics of a successful economic system is that the relation of trust and confidence between principal and agent are sufficiently strong so that the agent will not cheat even though it may be 'rational economic behaviour' to do so. [Arrow, 1968]

Where markets fail, it appears, quasi-ethical forces may sometimes be relied upon to come to the rescue.

Others have gone further than this, making direct use of specific altruism to justify zero pricing of health care. Lindsay assumes that the degree of inequality of medical provision enters directly into utility functions.

> An aspect of demand ... which has received scant attention from economists [is] ... the apparently universal desire and willingness to share. [Lindsay, 1969]

But this desire to share must be organised collectively because of the 'free-rider' problem. People may be sharers but not Kantian sharers. The two sharing techniques that best survive Lindsay's analysis are the use of subsidies and 'abstention'.

> It is surprising how well the [NHS] seems tailored to the essential requirements derived from the analysis.... in communities and countries where egalitarian feeling is strong and a spirit of national sharing in general, a national health service may indeed be the most efficient means of satisfying these wants. [Lindsay, 1969]

Cuyler (1971b) and others have noticed that Lindsay's form of the externality relationship is a very special one, in that it is not the whole vector of medical care that enters into the individual utility function but simply one non-selfish element, an index of equality or inequality. Perhaps this is not altogether unreasonable, as individuals will never know the whole vector but, instead, will have to rely upon manifestations of shortage (such as waiting lists) for which some aggregate indicator will serve as a proxy.

I now make use of the Edgeworth Box to show how a concern for 'equality' may be incorporated into simple exchange. This is done by having U-shaped indifference curves such that, *given* an amount of Y, each would experience lower utility as his share of X rose above some level $\hat{X}$. It is assumed, in this part of the discussion,

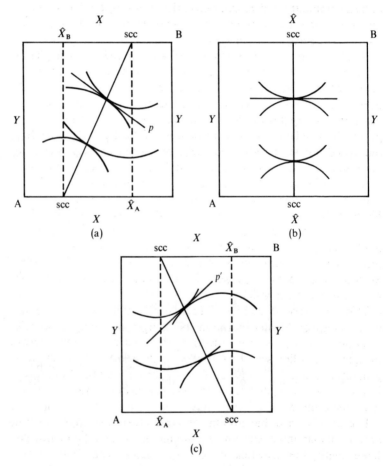

FIGURE 12.4　*Preferences for equality in x*

that concern is symmetric. The moral basis of this concern is slightly odd in that each could be bribed to take more than his 'fair' share by an offer of more Y. Even to the right of his $\hat{X}$ each would be on a higher indifference curve with more Y. Three cases are illustrated in Figure 12.4.

(a) $\hat{X} > \frac{1}{2}$. The social contract curve is compressed, and whoever has the larger holding of X is prepared to sell it to the other at a positive (but 'subsidised') price such as p in Figure 12.4(a). It would be a matter of practical convenience whether the (Pareto-better) move to the social contract curve was achieved entirely by subsidy or by a combination of a direct allocation and subsidy. The stronger the desire for equality, the more compressed does *scc* become and the lower the exchange price of X.

(b) $\hat{X} = \frac{1}{2}$. Here the desire for equality is complete – each prefers an equal share of X to any other (though, as in (a), every man has his price!). It is then Pareto-optimal[7] to make free transfers of X (health care) to whosoever has less. Clearly, a convenient way of institutionalising this would be to make an equal allocation to each person, for in a large community, because of the 'free-rider' problem one could not leave individuals who happened to have access to more than a 'fair' share of X to transfer it at zero cost to others. Not surprisingly, a strong desire for equality leads to equality.

(c) $\hat{X} < \frac{1}{2}$. Potentially there is an 'after-you' problem: each sees his own fair share as less than one-half. However, the problem is easily solved in terms of *negative prices* like p'. Suppose B already has his 'subjective' fair share X_B. Then he could be bribed to accept more than this share by A offering some Y as an inducement. Such a trade would be possible because each remained selfish in respect of the other good.

This symmetric treatment is qualitatively different from the so-called Dog-and-Master situation. No longer is one agent merely responding in a passive way to the other, but a common interest in equality sets limits to the tolerable distribution of the externality generating good. If it is granted, for the moment that this framework is more or less adequate, the prior question arises of how the limits $\hat{X}$ are determined.

It is at this stage that notions of 'need' must arise. Work in this area is similar in conception to (though as far as I know not yet linked with) the investigation of 'equivalence scales'[8] for family budgets. Just as in that field families of different composition are shown to need different levels of money income to bring them to some specified utility level, so, it can be argued, different people need quite different amounts of health care to bring them to some basic functional level. Moreover, the amounts of health care required are doubly uncertain. They are uncertain not just in the ordinary insurable way but also in terms of initial position. Some of the next generation will be born blind, lame, etc. We do not yet know which but we do know that their medical needs will be greater than the needs of others. In other words they are *entitled*, or have *rights*, to larger amounts of medical care. It is surely considerations such as these (rather than mere utility interdependence) that govern our notion of 'fair' or 'just' allocations of health care.

How does this relate to the diagrammatic treatment of the problem? It means that in principle there will be a consensus allocation (or at least a consensus range) of health care allocations based on an underlying notion of rights. There is no reason, of course, why this allocation should be equal – it will be so only if health needs are equal. The remaining question is whether subsidised health care or direct free provision in kind would be better in achieving the underlying just allocation. This, I am afraid, brings one back to paternalism. As I have already noted, direct provision in kind more or less eliminates the enforcement problem. Whether 'health care' should be merely subsidised or allocated directly depends almost entirely on the closeness of the underlying consensus. If it is not very close, the simplest thing is to guarantee some minimum level of health care for each and then allow trade to take place at a 'subsidised' price. If consensus is pretty close (as was assumed at the time the NHS was set up) one might as well adopt the consensus allocation straight away on a 'free' basis. The distinction made here is relevant to developments in Britain in that as medical technology becomes more complex and as more kinds of treatment are viewed as a matter of patient choice, the consensus becomes less tight. The less consensus or agreement there is, the more pressure there is to move from 'free' provision to market prices.

The search for an allocative principle prior to utility interdependence does not imply the abandonment of altruism. Indeed, an empathy for others is an essential part of the perception of their rights. It is, however, a common humanity towards unidentified and unknown others that is at stake, not merely benevolence towards particular individuals.

SUMMARY

Redistribution in kind is important in practice and reflects paternalistic altruism. Such altruism indicates a departure from competitive prices or a 'twisting' of the social contract curve.

There are various ways of achieving Pareto optimality including vouchers and subsidies, but devices to enforce preferred consumption preferences can be costly and meddlesome. The enforcement problem was considered together with the separate but related issue of 'take-up' to which altruism is shown to be relevant.

Finally, health care is treated as a special case in which prior consensus (or consensus range) is obtained, based on recognised health 'needs'. Where consensus is close the simplest procedure might be to allocate the consensus quantities on a free basis.

13 Blood and the Gift Relationship

Richard Titmuss in his important book, the *Gift Relationship*, wrote:

> In terms of the free gift of blood to strangers there is no formal contract, no legal bond, no situation of power, domination, constraint or compulsion, no sense of shame or guilt, no gratitude imperative, no need for penitence, no money and no guarantee of or wish for a reward or a return gift. They are acts of free will; of the exercise of choice; of conscience without shame. [Titmuss, 1970, p. 89]

Those remarks apply, strictly, only to Titmuss's type H donor, the 'voluntary community donor', but are evocative of the central importance he attaches to the gift relationship. His book has attracted much attention from economists, who have attempted to separate the Titmuss thesis into two quite separate propositions. The first is that voluntary donation, as in the UK, is more effective, in terms of both quantity and quality, than commercialised selling of blood, as in the USA. The second proposition, or 'grander theme', is that the discarding of a voluntary system will have unfavourable effects throughout society:

> Altruism in giving to a stranger does not begin and end with blood donations. It may touch every aspect of life.... It is likely that a decline in the spirit of altruism in one sphere of human activities will be accompanied by similar changes in attitudes, motives and relationships elsewhere. [Titmuss, 1970, p. 198].

Economists have been prepared to grant the substantial truth of the first proposition, certainly *vis-à-vis* the comparative systems of the UK and USA. They have, however, been openly sceptical of the second proposition, which seems implausible on both empirical and theoretical terms. In this chapter I wish to confront the theory of altruistic behaviour so far developed with the phenomenon of voluntary blood donation.

140

MOTIVES AND MODELS

Motives for blood donation are various but seem predominantly to be of a humanitarian type. The number of people giving blood is, in fact, relatively small (about 6 per cent of eligible donors) and many of them (16 per cent) drop out each year (see Oborne, 1975). Surveys are, of course, an unreliable way of getting at motivation, if only because people are often unconscious of it themselves, but to quote Titmuss again:

> Over two-fifths of the answers in the whole sample fell into the categories 'Altruism', 'Reciprocity', 'Replacement' and 'Duty'. Nearly a third represented voluntary responses to personal and general approaches for blood. A further 6% responded to an 'Awareness of Need'. These seven categories accounted for nearly 80% of the answers, suggesting a high sense of social responsibility towards the needs of the other members of society. [p. 236]

The motives of non-donors and ex-donors are just as interesting as those of donors themselves. Oborne (1975) reports that ex-donors gave primarily medical reasons for discontinuation and that non-donors frequently mentioned inconvenient times and location of blood doning sessions – though these could be rationalisations. He recommended that the Blood Transfusion Service should, in its advertising, emphasise humanitarian and 'insurance' reasons for giving and also pride (though this modestly). Attempts should also be made to reduce apprehension and tension and to provide convenient crèches, car parks, etc.

Possible egocentric explanations of voluntary donation include:

(i)   the belief of some donors that the occasional replenishment of their blood is good for them;

(ii) the obligation to replace blood transferred to themselves or to close relatives, balancing a moral profit and loss account, as it were;

(iii) a superstitious belief that the giving of blood now will bring the donor good luck;

(iv) a wish for the moral approbation of others – hence the use of medals, badges, stickers, etc.;

(v)   the moral self-approbation that follows a good act (though I would not wish to separate this from non-selfish motivation).

Granting all this, it surely cannot be denied (*vide* Titmuss) that the voluntary donor is moved primarily by non-selfish motives.

This is hardly surprising, for, the wish to give blood accords with our general proposition that the bonds of human sympathy are strongest in matters of life and death. To label this as an irrational exception must surely be embarrassing to a science that, like economics, concerns itself with human action.

The immediate task is to derive a plausible 'model' of voluntary donation that is:

(i) consistent with rational economic behaviour,

(ii) useful in speculating on the effects of a mixed voluntary and commercial system,

(iii) meaningful in terms of Titmuss's 'grander theme'.

Let the probability, π, of some randomly drawn individual, being able to obtain a blood transfusion if required, enter into my utility function. The randomly drawn individual could be an anonymous stranger, a relation, or even myself. If a transfusion is easily available then $\pi = 1$. If it is completely unobtainable then $\pi = 0$. Certainly, no individual donor will have precise information about π but he will have a crude proxy for it in that, whenever π is significantly below one, the transfusion service will intensify its advertising and recruitment. The individual donor must be satisfied that a need exists and he must wish to help meet it.

We are by now familiar with the notion that altruistic concern towards third parties may, owing to the free-rider problem, be a weak source of giving, especially in a large community. The *non-Kantian altruist* will perceive that π is negligibly affected by his own donation. But one is then back in the old familiar prisoners' dilemma. If everyone shared this perception there would be no voluntary donations and 'society' would be worse off than if all had behaved Kantianly. The only exception to this miserable outcome would be in the case of potential donors in rare blood groups whose actions would have direct repercussion on π. In the commoner blood groups a concern for π would not be a sufficient reason for donation.

One is driven back, therefore, to the notion that potential donors (or at any rate some of them) behave Kantianly. They reason that, although the effect of their own individual failure to donate would be negligible, the effect of 'everyone' behaving like this would cause π to fall towards zero. They have a duty or responsibility to give blood: in other words they act *as though* $d\pi/d\pi_i{}^1$ were not 0, but 1 (where π_i is the probability of i's donating blood). It is not part of my present case that the sense of duty is an overriding one, for many other things apart from π are taken to affect utility. Even for the Kantian, π is just one argument in the utility function and the marginal donor could well be discouraged by an increase in the 'time and trouble' costs of giving. His concern for π is traded-off with his concern for other things. It is important to make this point because economists fear that the Kantian categorial imperative replaces choice by duty, leaving no place for adjustments at the margin. It is introduced here merely to counter the free-rider aspect of just one element in the utility function.

An alternative route to the Kantian one is to assume *anonymous empathy*. Each donor then views his gift as a non-selfish transfer to some other unique but unknown individual to whom he is linked by sympathy and common humanity. I am anxious to maintain this as an alternative hypothesis, for it leads to slightly different predictions of the effect of introducing a mixed system.

PAYING FOR BLOOD

In their polemic *The Price of Blood*, Culyer and Cooper (1968) argued that the UK should introduce a mixed voluntary and commercial system in place of the present entirely voluntary system. The principal economic point here is that the optimal mix in a dual system will be where the marginal costs of collecting blood are equal for each method. Such a mixed system ensures that any stipulated quantity of blood (usually measured in bottles) is obtained at the least cost. The tone of their pamphlet was sympathetic to payment by the ultimate consumer but advocated payment simply by the collecting agency, which would then sell its blood to the National Health Service. Economists have tended to treat this as a rather limited technical question, separable from the grander theme.

The short answer[2] to the Culyer and Cooper argument is that the evidence of a shortage of blood in the UK is occasional and impressionistic. By contrast, in the United States, which has a rich mixture of voluntary and paid systems, there are acute shortages of blood as well as a serious problem of serum hepatitis. This is because the poor (or the addicted) have a financial incentive to deceive others and perhaps themselves about the quality of their blood; whereas in the UK, money-payment in no way enters into self-selection and donors are a pretty representative cross-section of the community: in the United States prisoners, the poor and the addicted are seriously over-represented.

It follows that the commercial system could be made greatly more effective if some simple method could be found for detecting infected blood. Salsbury (in Institute of Economic Affairs (1973)) cautiously suggests that recent advances in research have made important strides in this direction. Some economists, taking a rather doctrinaire free market stand, have turned Titmuss's argument on its head, suggesting not too much but *too little* commercialism in the American system.[3] If only patients were free to sue hospitals, which in turn were free to sue the blood collecting agencies where negligence could be proved, the bad agencies would be driven out of business. But until some cheap and effective method of detection is perfected, the coarse sieve of voluntary self-selection is better than the formidable combination of the market and the law suggested. After all, serum hepititis is pretty well negligible in the UK.

Titmuss is able to show that the UK system is superior to the North American system in respect both of meeting 'need' and of quality. But it is certainly conceivable that some dual system would be ideal. A difficulty is that one is involved in a comparative study of institutions and that the greatest care must be taken before transplanting one set of national institutions into the alien culture of another country. That it would be possible to increase supply by raising price from zero to some attractive level seems so unexceptionable as to be beyond question, but it is widely conceded that some voluntary donors would cease to give, once cash payments were introduced. This seems to have happened following the introduction of cash payments in Japan (see Singer, 1973).

How is one to reconcile this curious withdrawal of voluntary donors with altruistic motivation? It hardly seems consistent with non-selfishness that the donor should retire in a fit of pique once payments are introduced. The key to the mystery is that in a dual system the total supply of blood will be made up of two parts, the voluntary and the paid. The probability of obtaining blood is given by:

$$\pi = \frac{B_v + B_p}{B^*}$$

where B^* is the amount of blood 'needed', B_v is voluntary blood, and B_p is paid blood. Now, the individual voluntary donor has to consider $d\pi/d\pi_i$. We have already noticed that if potential donors are Kantians they will gauge the effects of their actions by asking what would happen if their behaviour were universalised. But in the present case they also have to consider the behaviour of the authorities in setting price. Consider the extreme case where the authorities so adjust price as to keep $\pi = 1$. The individual voluntary donor then knows that if he and others like him cease to give blood, π will be completely unaffected. The introduction of price then makes a Kantian altruist behave *as though* he were a non-Kantian altruist: it removes his sense of responsibility and his duty;

> the commercialisation of blood is discouraging and downgrading the voluntary principle. Both the sense of community and the expression of altruism are being silenced. [Titmuss, 1970, p. 157]

Things will not be quite as bad as this, as in practice the individual donor will not articulate his problem in the way described; neither could the authorities be relied upon to adjust price so as to equate supply and demand, but the general presupposition that at least some voluntary donors will withdraw is entirely consistent with the model being used here.

This problem of withdrawal may be so severe that the supply curve is actually backward-bending as price rises from zero.[4] Advocates of pricing are willing to concede this, but they argue that a higher price can always be found such that an adequate supply is forthcoming. Returning to the analysis of utility maximisation, recall that π was merely one argument in the utility function. Some individuals who have a low or even zero interest in π will be prepared to give blood so as to earn income. This positive effect is said to outweigh any opposite effects due to frustrated Kantians, as price becomes large. Even so, the required price could be very high indeed, especially if the incidence of infected blood increased – price would have to be set sufficiently high to enable an allowance for wastage or retreatment on this account. The marginal cost of obtaining blood of a given quality by this method could turn out to be very high – probably higher than an efficient use of extra money for publicity and recruitment by the Transfusion Service.

Indeed, these considerations lead one to speculate that the

optimum system might not be dual at all but might lie, as it were, at a corner: that the extreme monotechnical solutions,

(i) an entirely voluntary system and

(ii) a commercial system plus litigation,

may be more efficient than combinations of them. The Americans are, on this view, stuck with a rather unhappy system which combines the worst of all possible worlds. Further, if Titmuss is right, the Kantian habit may be lost (through atrophy) in moving away from (i) but cannot easily be rekindled in type (ii) systems. One should be most reluctant to move away from (i) if it seems to be working reasonably well.

Additionally, system (ii) implies an extension of the commercial principle beyond the mere collection of blood right through to the patient. Some of the repugnant features of this have been eloquently described by Solow in a critical review:

> Risky blood would, of course, sell at a lower price than safe blood. Poor people would buy cheap blood; rich people could afford safe blood.... Suppose that the introduction of a commercial market would in fact result in some marginal improvement in efficiency [though Titmuss's story suggests it wouldn't]. The judgement that such an improvement could justify the creation of differentials in quality of blood received by income class does strike me as morally obtuse. [Solow, 1971]

The evil effects of a commercial system on poor donors were also described by Titmuss. A press report[5] indicates that the problem is becoming an international one. The World Health Organisation has complained that US firms buy blood in the developing world at \$2 to \$4 a pint and sell it at home at ten times the price. It cites the death of a Filipino mother through excessive donation and the case of Spanish children giving without parental permission. The blood is often of poor quality. Perhaps even more serious is that commercial trafficking could reduce voluntary donations in the developing countries themselves, so making the introduction of a cash-nexus inevitable.

Finally in this section, one must ask how far these remarks about dual systems have to be modified when *anonymous empathy* rather than Kantianism is the rule. One would not expect the anonymous empathiser to react as negatively as the Kantian to the introduction of price. He could argue that his pint of blood was being used by *some* anonymous stranger with whose welfare he managed to identify. But he would also have to accept that if he ceased to be a donor the authorities would adjust price so as to ensure a supply of blood to that same stranger. There would, as before, be a weakened sense of responsibility towards the anonymous stranger.

THE GIFT RELATIONSHIP

As already mentioned, Titmuss's 'grander theme' has been greeted with much scepticism even by sympathetic economists. Is it really 'likely that a decline in the spirit of altruism in one sphere of human activities will be accompanied by similar changes in attitudes, motives and relationships elsewhere'? Arrow (1974) while welcoming a 'resonant evocation of central problems of social value ... [which] ... has greatly enhanced the quality of social-philosophical debate' and conceding that 'the categorial imperative and the price system are essential complements', is extremely doubtful of the thesis itself.

Some points from our discussion in this chapter so far add a little weight to the Titmuss view. The Kantian donor acts in the expectation that other potential donors (or at any rate a sufficient number of them) will also behave in a Kantian way. Failing this, the individual Kantian may see donation, though his moral duty, as ineffective utilitarianly. Second, the introduction of price into a previously gift-based relationship may reduce gifts even from Kantian altruists. Third, the introduction of price into an alien social and institutional context could permanently reduce willingness to give in that community (cf. the United States and developing countries). Fourth, it is probably difficult to introduce a Kantian spirit successfully when a cash relationship is already firmly established.

A convincing case may be made out therefore that the gift relationship is not only precious but is also efficient in the blood context and that it may be seriously damaged when commercial motives are introduced. But Titmuss's thesis is more ambitious than this. The first point to be established is that Kantian altruism is useful. Now it has been shown in Chapter 2 that, when altruistic concern is non-paternalistic, ordinary market exchange will be efficient within rather broad limits. Altruism is then important only *à propos* income redistribution. But would one wish to rely on the gift relationship to achieve the appropriate redistribution – as would occur under Kantian altruism? Titmuss would certainly argue not. He would wish to State to redistribute income, though the extent to which this is politically possible will depend on how altruistic people are in their voting behaviour. It was also shown in Chapter 12 that spontaneous redistribution in kind could in principle occur if people were meddlesome Kantian altruists, but that in practice a complex system of transfers in kind, subsidies and taxes would have to be organised by the State. Once again altruism would have to be harnessed through the ballot box rather than directly. The fostering of altruism remains important but gifts have become institutionalised through the State.

Indeed, direct reliance on the gift relationship to achieve social justice is no part of Titmuss's social philosophy, to which the apparatus of the welfare state is essential. Generalising from the blood example, the relatively small band of Kantian altruists would find themselves bearing the whole cost of the welfare state. The voluntary donation of blood works because donors see blood transfusions as part of essential life support, consider blood donation as a relatively low cost activity and trust that a sufficient number of other donors will come forward to meet requirements. But one would not expect to build hospitals on the scale required, or motorways, on the basis of voluntary contributions. The relevant gift relationship then becomes that implied in altruistic voting behaviour.

Titmuss has a separate chapter on truthfulness and the social costs involved in dishonesty. Truthfulness may here be seen as one of Hirsch's 'collective intermediate goods' (1975) that oil the wheels of society. The voluntary donor is truthful about the state of his health and medical history; the paid donor is tempted not to be. Truth, duty, responsibility, obligation are all important, it was argued earlier, in enabling society to move away from gamma traps. These qualities are in constant need of servicing and maintenance;

without use they atrophy. Hence Titmuss's fears that a reduction of Kantian conduct in one sphere could help to undermine the delicate but vital forces of social cohesion.

A similar argument may be put in terms of altruism itself. I have referred before to the Hume–Titmuss contagion thesis. Mere reminders of moral obligation seem to be insufficient to elicit helping behaviour. Children follow examples that establish co-operative norms (increasingly with age) but do not respond except in the most temporary fashion to exhortation (see Bryan and London, 1970). Doubt has already been cast on the liberal view that time and progress will lead to a gradual improvement in human nature and on the Marxian thesis that social consciousness will come into its own only after a prolonged post-revolutionary period. The contagion hypothesis, although it has an idealistic ring about it, is to do with the here-and-now or, at any rate, the near future. Hence the importance of the clues to co-operative behaviour in the prisoner's dilemma literature. The trust and confidence built up during a dynamic game may easily be destroyed by a run of non-co-operative moves. With this background Titmuss's notion that a weakening of altruistic behaviour in one sphere may damage it elsewhere becomes plausible.

It must also surely be conceded that the Robertsonian view, endorsed by Arrow, that the stock of altruism is scarce and must therefore be economised upon, is probably false. That view is in direct conflict, of course, with the Hume–Titmuss thesis. Singer, attacking Arrow's view, suggests that altruism may be rather more like sexual potency than a scarce resource in that it is developed and strengthened by use.

Marx's view (1844) that the market mechanism alienates true relationships between man is, on the face of it, rather similar to the Titmuss thesis. But Marx goes a great deal further: the distorting power of money forms the basis of an attack on the whole process of exchange. It enables man to feel god-like by having money command over articles he could not himself make. The similarity lies in the power of commerce to drive out love: a kind of moral Gresham's Law. The social democratic view is presumably that the market mechanism is reasonably acceptable except (as my late colleague H. D. Dickinson used to stay) for important goods.

SUMMARY

The behaviour of voluntary blood donors may usefully be described in terms of the theory of Kantian altruism. That theory also offers some clues as to why dual systems need not be more effective in blood provision than more extreme systems. Some support is found for the controversial thesis, due to Titmuss, that commercial motives may weaken some forms of altruistic behaviour.

14 Disasters

Though the study of disasters is in its infancy, it seems to be reasonably well established that non-selfishness is more prevalent in post-disaster situations than one might have expected. Quarantelli and Dynes (1976), on the basis of 100 natural disasters investigated by the Disaster Research Centre at Ohio State University, report little conflict in the early stages when, they argue, it would be 'dysfunctional'.[1] Indeed, looting and violence were rare and charity towards fellow victims common: it is also the case that the prices of 'necessities' do not rise to famine levels.[2]

Some controversy has arisen as to whether or not this behaviour is consistent with self-interest and *if not* whether a 'taste-change' takes place once disaster strikes. My own view is, of course, that post-disaster co-operation fits easily as a special case of the non-selfish model, whereas egotistical models have to be stretched beyond credulity. A purely selfish interpretation may be retained only by postulating the gene, rather than the individual, as the basic unit of analysis.

TRANSFERS

The first point to be noticed is that, following a disaster, large transfers typically take place from the rest of society to the stricken community *and* within that community. Drama and publicity are usually essential to this process. Major disasters produce very large sums, conflicting even with the general rule that appeals on behalf of distant nations get less than those on behalf of nearer ones.[3] Disasters seem to stimulate the imagination and sympathy of potential donors to a far greater extent than do ordinary everyday poverty and misery. Against this background it may be appreciated that income differences are one, but only one, consideration in charitable transfers. Not only must the potential donor perceive a need (hence the usefulness of publicity), but he must also acknowledge a legitimate moral claim on his aid. For these complex reasons people are more willing to contribute to appeals following major floods or earthquakes than to routine aid programmes.

Nevertheless, it is perfectly straightforward to show that, if donors are mildly altruistic and if 'transfers' are a normal good, a fall in recipients' income relative to donors' will, provided certain conditions are fulfilled, lead to (more) transfers. Figure 14.1 shows a simple two-person case. Initial incomes are equal at R and no transfers take place because donor, although mildly altruistic, would rather be at R^1.

Two assumptions are made about the income transfer curve. First, in Figure 14.1(a) it is shown as a straight line but in 14.1(b) it curves upwards, indicating a decreasing transfer elasticity. Now suppose that recipient's income falls dramatically as a result of natural disaster, along the line R, R'', R_0. Donor suffers no such income reduction. Notice that no transfers will take place up to R'',

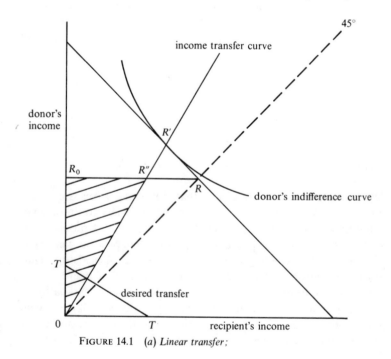

FIGURE 14.1   (a) *Linear transfer;*

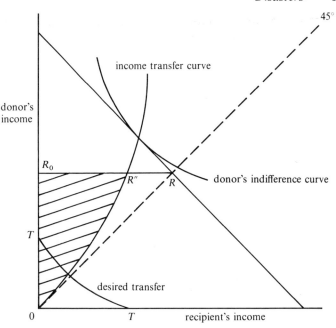

45°

income transfer curve

donor's
income

R_0

R'' R donor's indifference curve

T

desired transfer

0   T   recipient's income

FIGURE 14.1   (*b*) *non-linear transfer*

as recipient's income is only moderately reduced. However, to the left of R'' there is a positive derived transfer, plotted on the diagram as TT. (Construction: from any R draw a 45° line until it intersects with the income transfer curve; T is the vertical distance to the curve). Desired transfer increases steadily as recipient's income falls on assumption (a) but increases more rapidly on assumption (b) as recipient's income falls to really low levels.

So far I have been assuming that donor is not directly affected by the disaster. He may be thought of as living outside the stricken community. Now change this assumption by allowing both incomes to fall while retaining the assumption that donor escapes relatively lightly. Then as long as the new, disrupted, incomes lie within the shaded area, donor will wish to make a positive transfer, but outside this area changes in relative income will have no effect. For this case of transfer within the stricken community it seems reasonable to assume a curved TT as incomes become really low: life support systems are threatened and community subsistence and survival may depend on transfers from the badly-off to the starving.

It must be stressed that the preferences being discussed here are contingent upon recipients having some sort of legitimate moral claim. Not only must there be sympathy or societal ties, but their disastrous fall in incomes must be seen as in no way the 'fault' of the stricken.

SCARCITY PRICES

The second, narrowly economic, point about disasters is the alleged failure of the prices of necessities to rise by as much as might have been expected. This comes as no surprise to the theory of non-selfish exchange in which demand is (in general) a function not only of prices and incomes but also of the total available. Altruism is taken to be paternalistic or 'meddlesome' in that potential donors perceive some goods, necessities, to be more important than others. Liebenstein showed in a different context that:

> an increase in price will . . . result in price and bandwagon effects that are negative, and in Veblen and snob effects that are positive, provided that the price effect is greater than the Veblen effect; that is, if the net result is a decrease in the quantity demanded at the higher place. [Liebenstein, 1950]

However, the nearest Liebenstein gets to the disaster problem is the question of taboos. There is further discussion along the lines suggested by Liebenstein in Green (1971). The essential point is that, when supplies of necessities become low, consumers take the supply per head into account when making their decisions. In other words, they behave partially in a Kantian way. There is plenty of evidence that this happens: a recent example is voluntary restraint in UK water consumption.[4]

An easy way of modelling this is to let the normal demand curve hold as long as the mean quantity available, $\bar{x}$, is greater than or equal to some conventional minimum x_{min}. But in a situation of major scarcity it might happen that $\bar{x}/x_{min}$ enters the demand function. The case of constant elasticity is taken.

$$Xd = AP^{-a}(\bar{x}/x_{min})^b \qquad b = 0 \text{ when } \bar{x} \geq x_{min} \qquad (14.1)$$

$$Xd = X. \qquad (14.2)$$

Equation (14.1) is a demand function and (14.2) is the equilibrium condition that demand equals exogenous supply. The elasticity of *price* (in equilibrium) with respect to *supply* is:

$$e_p = \frac{b - 1}{a}.$$

Normally one expects the sign of e_p to be negative (the less the supply the greater the price), but it is clear that e_p is positive whenever b, the *co-operation elasticity* of demand, is greater than 1. The case I have taken is an excessively simple one. For one thing the reduction in supply will not be marginal so point elasticities do not apply. For another, b is less likely to be discontinuous at x_{min} than logistic with a steep portion in the region of x_{min}. In spite of these limitations the simple case does show that 'Kantian' behaviour can enter, in a relatively straightforward way, into the demand function. It also shows that when elasticity is estimated from a reduced form equation the apparent price elasticity of demand will badly estimate true price elasticity. The ratio of apparent to actual price elasticity is given by $1 - b$. As b moves from zero through 0.5 and 2.0 this ratio changes from unity, through 0.5 to -1.0. The contention is not that price elasticity itself changes but that a new 'Kantian' factor comes into play.

THE SOCIAL FABRIC

I now turn to the question of the preservation of the fabric of a post-disaster community. It has already been noticed that large transfers from outside the community are difficult to explain in terms of self-interest alone. Admittedly, the public's response is often curious and haphazard; and, indeed, the sending of inappropriate relief (like a surfeit of blankets) can be an embarrassment, but typically a major disaster strikes a nerve of common humanity. Even then, the positive response is marred by the ghoulish curiosity of sightseers (see Dacy and Kunreuther, 1969). The mysterious chemistry of disasters works more powerfully in the stricken community itself, which is often united by its hardships against the outside world.[5]

It does seem to be the case that some (though not all) societies are able to fall back on human solidarity in moments of great crisis. Even in Gorky's grim *Life of a Useless Man,*

> the people encouraged one another, praised each other's dexterity and strength, and abused one another in kindly jest . . . , it seemed as if in the presence of the fire everyone looked upon his neighbour kindly, and found pleasure in one another's company. [Gorky, 1971]

The free-rider problem is, of course, a major obstacle to any explanation of post-disaster co-operation. Douty (1972) attempted an explanation based almost entirely on self-interest and an informal insurance principle, considering that individuals own unwritten insurance policies which 'pay off' at moments of crisis. Apparent acts of altruism are then simple cases of social exchange which, in contrast to economic exchange,

> involve the principle that one person does another a favour, and while there is some general expectation of some future return, its exact nature is definitely *not* stipulated in advance. [Blau, 1964, p. 93]

While supporting a version of the insurance principle, de Alessi (1967, 1975) has, wisely in my view, rejected both Douty's self-interest and Dacy and Kunreuthers' function shift explanations. One difficulty with social exchange as a concept is that, as the implied exchanges become more complex and diffused, it becomes harder to find comprehensible patterns. In any case the egotist would surely find it tempting to take a free ride unless his acts of omission could easily be identified and remembered. Johnson (1968) suggests 'societal costs' as a limitation on the conduct of free-riders: costs such as disapproval by those whose respect one values.

In spite of Johnson's point that in a strictly formal sense societal costs increase with community size, I believe societal costs will be far more important in smaller communities. This reinforces the conclusion of our earlier discussion of games, that altruism may be sufficient to achieve co-operative behaviour when the community is small and when the actions of specific individuals are important to the community. Under such circumstances even moderately altruistic individuals may behave co-operatively. Further, there will be an element of increasing returns to co-operation in the rebuilding of a community's daily life so the game is quite likely to be *assurance-positive:* a community whose members 'trust' one another will be more resilient in the face of disaster than one where mistrust abounds. Take, by way of contrast, Banfield's backward Italian village[6] where his amoral familist observes the rule:

> maximise the material, short-term advantage of the nuclear family: assume that all others will do likewise. [Banfield, 1958]

Concerted action is almost impossible to achieve in such a community.

In large communities of anonymous individuals, altruism (and, *a fortiori*, egotism) cannot be relied upon to generate spontaneous co-operation. For most disasters this does not seem to be a major difficulty, as their full force is normally met by small communities or a network of such communities. Restoration of the social fabric is, of course, an elementary requirement so basic as to evoke, in all, feelings of duty and solidarity. These feelings are the social cement which bring together sympathy, assurance and enlightened self-interest to enable a successful outcome for the post-disaster co-operation game.

SUMMARY

This chapter considered three aspects of post-disaster behaviour, each implying some kind of altruistic behaviour.

(i) Transfers both to and within the stricken community may be treated as a particular manifestation of the general non-selfish assumption. Provided that potential recipients are seen as having a legitimate moral claim there is no need to scrape up an *ad hoc* explanation based on self-interest alone.

(ii) The generally reported failure of post-disaster prices to rise as much as might have been expected is consistent with available supply entering into the *demand* function. Perceived elasticity is then an amalgam of true price elasticity (which may be unaltered) and what I have called a 'co-operation' elasticity.

(iii) The social fabric is maintained successfully in post-disaster situations because all the conditions for a successful assurance game are present: relatively small members, increasing returns from co-operation, direct sympathy, trust and a perception that the 'true' game is alpha-alpha versus beta-beta.

15 Future Generations

On the general presumption that an altruistic generation will wish to take a responsible view towards future generations, I look in this chapter at several related questions.

   (i)   What should an altruistic generation's attitude be towards the discounting process and the rate of time preference?

   (ii) How much should an altruistic generation save?

   (iii) What should its attitude be towards resource depletion?

   (iv) Similarly, what should its attitude be towards environmental pollution?

   (v) Can altruism lead to a solution of the 'isolation paradox'?

A preliminary question is whether altruism need be invoked at all. In this, as in other areas, it is perfectly possible to devise selfish explanations for apparently non-selfish types of behaviour. One such explanation is that net saving over a lifetime is a 'mistake' in that people do not know for certain when they are to die and therefore find it impossible to arrange that their assets diminish to zero at the moment of death. Another explanation is based on uncertainty and implicit exchange with overlapping generations. In principle, if I fail to carry out my fair share of capital accumulation the next generation will be able to arrange that I am 'punished' for this by being denied adequate consumption in old age. To the extent that one remains in the game after a savings decision there may be a dynamic game with positive saving (see, e.g., Hammond, 1972).

Obviously there is altruism towards one's children and one's grandchildren. The more interesting question is whether this altruism may be considered as extending to one's contemporaries and their heirs as well – that is why it is important to consider the isolation paradox.

DISCOUNTING AND WEIGHTING

By way of contrast with their egocentric tradition in other matters, economic theorists have often taken a high moral line on discounting the future. Thus:

> It is assumed that we do not discount future enjoyments in comparison with earlier ones, a practice which is *ethically indefensible* (my italics) and arises merely from the weakness of the imagination. [Ramsey, 1928, p. 545]

Pigou (1920) had similarly complained of our 'defective telescopic faculty'.[1]

But a strict adherence to this view would make the benefits of investment appear indefinitely large, leaving the present generation to save everything in excess of subsistence income. Ramsey avoided this outcome by the rather special assumption of 'bliss' or the notion that enjoyment would increase asymptotically to a finite limit. The so-called Ramsey–Keynes formula expresses the optimum amount of saving solely in terms of the shortfall from bliss and the marginal utility of consumption.

It is more usual to allow discounting, with an implicit weight of unity for each and every generation.[2] There is a real sense, therefore, in which the 'discounted Ramsey policy' is *perfectly altruistic*, for future consumption is discounted only in respect of its date, regardless of whether it is 'our' consumption or 'theirs'. A paradox concerning this altruistic interpretation of discounting will be discussed in a moment. Nevertheless, on this interpretation, one's altruism over time is simply measured by the inverse of the discount rate: the more altruistic the society, the lower its rate of time preference.

Phelps and Pollack (1968) contrast this 'perfectly altruistic' assumption with the case where we not only discount by date but attach a somewhat lower (but uniform) weight to future generations.[3]

The question arises of whether *any* of these assumptions adequately captures the notion of altruism between generations. Cost–benefit analysts frequently employ the perfectly altruistic assumption – that one discounts only in respect of date. On the face of it this is very generous towards future generations. But it remains true that the great arithmetical power of discounting has the *effect* of giving very little weight to them. And this is quite apart from considerations such as uncertainty, probable relative affluence and so on. When discounting it makes very little difference whether the benefits flowing from an act of investment last 100 years or 200 years – even though there is no conscious discrimination against future generations. It does seem unsatisfactory that society is pretty well indifferent between creating something which will last for 100 years and something which will last for ever.[4]

One source of difficulty is that we insist on doing the next generation's discounting for them. Consider the perspective of members of the next generation. They will derive a lifetime's benefit from our current act of investment but it must be discounted to *our* present date: it will count for little more than if the benefits had completely dried up at the death of the current generation. A possible alternative approach may be illustrated in terms of a project that yields a benefit of one unit *for ever*. The standard approach values this at $1/i$ where i is the rate of discount. But, alternatively, one could allow each generation to discount its own lifetime benefits to present value and repeat the exercise for each subsequent generation, attaching appropriate altruistic weights.

Consider the simple case of unit benefits for ever with an interest rate of 10 per cent. Their present value is 10 units. The alternative approach asks what the present value is *over a lifetime* only. Say this is 8 units. Then the alternative approach gives a higher present value whenever the weight given to the next generation is greater than 0.2. Indeed, it gives a higher value than the conventional approach whenever

$$v > 1 - r$$

where v is the altruistic weight and r the ratio of lifetime to indefinite present value.[5] This approach has the advantage of (as it were) allowing future generations to do their own discounting.

I would therefore challenge the view that equal treatment plus discounting is an adequate way of dealing with non-selfishness at project evaluation level and have suggested a method of separating discounting and altruistic weighting so as automatically to give an advantage to longer-life projects.

If, however, one is dealing with monolithic generations the important consideration is the weight to be given to each – whether it arises from discounting or from limited altruism is of secondary importance.

OPTIMUM SAVINGS

The discussion that follows has the very limited aim of showing that the more altruistic generation will undertake greater saving but that there are rational limits to such saving. The technique employed is a very simple two-period diagram.

One difficulty to be settled is the question of whether or not future generations can be relied upon to behave in the same way as we do. We certainly cannot force them to. Phelps has considered this question in some detail:

> The marginal utility for the present generation of the capital it bequeaths depends upon the value the present generation assigns to future consumptions and the *disposition of capital for consumption by future generations.* [Phelps, 1975, p. 90; my italics]

I shall assume, in the discussion that follows, that the next generation may be relied upon to save the same proportion of income as the present generation. As I say, we can have no guarantee of this. Phelps speculates on the sociological nature of taboos that inhibit societies from irresponsible behaviour towards future generations and upon the ethical nature of rules that might anchor a game-theoretic solution of the savings problem. If we know that future generations will not choose that rate that we would wish them to choose, the rate we settle upon will be only a second-best, constrained by the expected behaviour of future generations.

The model that follows (see Arrow, 1973; Dasgupta, 1974) assumes that capital may be either consumed or saved and that the next generation may be relied upon to save at the same ratio, s, selected by the present generation. Figure 15.1 shows the consumption possibilities (C_1, C_2) for the two generations given an initial capital (K_1) and its productivity (λ). (The figure also shows C_3; see below.)

Notice particularly the dotted portion of the consumption possibility curve, which provides a very important safeguard against 'excessive' altruism. No generation giving positive weights to con-

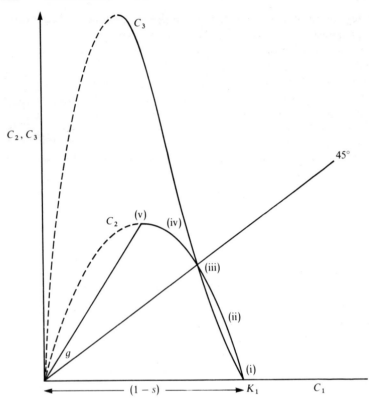

FIGURE 15.1   *Consumption possibilities with a sustained savings ratio*

sumption could possibly choose $s > 0.5$. This is because it is reluctant to impose heavy sacrifices upon the next generation which has to match its savings rate. At any point on the dotted line it will be possible to find a 'Pareto-better' s such that both generations will have higher consumption. I turn, in a moment, to the possibility of excessively high rates of saving.

The degree of altruism felt towards the next generation is indicated by the slope of a straight line supporting the consumption possibility curve – the less the slope, the greater the altruistic weight. A simple relationship may be derived linking the savings ratio explicitly to the degree of altruism.[6] All that remains is to rotate this line and see what happens.

(i) The degree of altruism (v) is inadequate to generate any savings at all: it is less than $1/(1 + \lambda)$. For example if $\lambda = 3$, v must be greater than $1/4$, otherwise this generation, just like a purely egotistical generation, would gobble everything up, leaving nothing for its successors.

(ii) The degree of altruism is sufficient to generate gross but not net saving. Most moralists would take rather a poor view of this behaviour. After all, capital investment is productive, so it is not 'unreasonable' to expect the present generation to arrange a level of consumption at least as high as its own, for others.

(iii) The degree of altruism is just sufficient to generate a constant stream of consumption. For this it is required that $s = 1/\lambda$ and $v = 1/(\lambda - 1)$. This case has attracted much attention in the literature as it seems to follow from a strict application of Rawl's maxi-min criterion: that a just distribution maximises the welfare of the least advantaged. Interpreting this rule in inter-generational terms the present generation may be presumed the least advantaged so *its* welfare is to be maximised. But this does not entitle it to run down its capital, for if it does so some future generation will replace it as the least advantaged. A constant consumption stream $\bar{c}$ seems therefore to be indicated. Given that investment is productive, this does seem rather an unsatisfactory conclusion, for it would take very little sacrifice now to make things a great deal better in the future. On this interpretation of Rawls mankind seems to be 'imprisoned in perpetual poverty if it begins in poverty' (Dasgupta, 1974).

(iv) The degree of altruism generates positive net savings as one would expect in an analysis that takes altruism into account. There is scope here for the weights to be equal or for them to be unequal *in either direction* (i.e., one might give more weight or less weight to the next generation than to oneself). The criticisms that follow are based on less weight being given.

Conscious of the difficulty mentioned above, Rawls himself modified his hostility towards altruistic motivation to the extent of allowing each generation some concern for the next generation's welfare:

> Since it is assumed that a generation cares for its immediate descendants, as fathers, say, care for their sons, a just savings principle, or more accurately, certain limits on such principles, would be acknowledged. [Rawls, 1972, p. 288]

Unfortunately, Arrow and Dasgupta have shown that, if Rawls

is thus interpreted and the maxi-min principle applied, the resulting savings pattern is 'saw-toothed' from one generation to the next: a very odd just savings pattern indeed. Extending concern for future generations up to some horizon has the effect of periodic repetition with the period equal to the horizon. Arrow also shows that:

> under altruism towards future generations forever the difference between the maxi-min criterion and the utilitarian disappears. [Arrow, 1973]

If each generation strictly keeps to the 'optimal ratio', s, the future course of consumption is easily traced out. The consumption of any future generation (n) is given by:

$$C_{t+n} = (1 - s)\lambda^n s^n K_t.$$

To take an extreme example, if the Rawlsian generation felt altruistic towards generation 3 but had no interest in generation 2 it might be prepared to arrange for generation 2 to make heavy sacrifices. More moderately, if the Rawlsian generation attempts to strike a balance between future generations it is likely, in effect, to be behaving utilitarianly.

(v) The degree of altruism is such as to maximise the next generation's consumption *consistent with* an obligation for it to continue the same savings behaviour. Subject to this condition, the *rate of growth* is maximised at this savings ratio and is indicated by g. Any extra saving is 'excessive' in the sense already discussed.

Suppose now that the 'target' generation is not the next but a more distant generation. Then it is easy to show that, where generation 1 is concerned solely with generation n's welfare and not at all with its own, the utility maximising savings ratio becomes:

$$s = \frac{n}{n + 1}$$

so that, as n becomes large (the target generation becomes more distance), s approximates to unity and the whole of income is saved.

The absurdity of excessive savings has been well-drawn by Meade:

> The result would be that everyone was always saving the whole of his income in order to leave property to children to enable them to leave property to grandchildren – and so on down the generations – in order that some day (which would never arrive) some generation (which would never be born) should have a

tremendous blow-out of consumption (which would never occur).
[Meade, 1968, p. 236]

To recapitulate:

(i)   Altruism can exist without being sufficiently strong even for
      the present generation to maintain capital intact.
(ii) The more altruistic the present generation is, the more saving
      it will undertake.
(iii) The amount of saving undertaken will be modified by the
      obligations that it imposes upon future generations.

RESOURCE DEPLETION

The altruistic generation will presumably take a different attitude
towards conservation and the environment than will a selfish
generation. However, the issues are not quite as straightforward as
they seem, and I confine my treatment in this section to the spectres
of Doomsday and of resource depletion.

If a 'resource' is absolutely *essential* to the continuance of life –
that is to say, if no substitute is available – then it is legitimate to
refer to a Doomsday. Let there be 1,000 million tons left and let
the minimum used each year be 20 million tons. By simple arithmetic
Doomsday will arrive in fifty years from now at most. If, in the
interim, we are slightly more greedy (say we use 25 million tons),
Doomsday will be forty years from now, and so on. I put this
simple point in its stark form to emphasise that if a truly essential
resource is running out the choices are rather harsh. Would it really
be worth tremendous sacrifices on the part of the present generation
to reduce its own standards very much below the conventional
minimum (to say 15 million tons) in order to put off Doomsday
for another sixteen years or so? Possibly, because our children
and grandchildren will still be here. But how about reducing our
usage to 10 million or even 5 million? The choice is between a
few generations living in comfort and many more generations living
in misery. Obviously the process of discounting will bring the
Doomsday forward – the higher the discount rate, the nearer the
Doomsday, (see Koopmans, 1974). It is by no means clear, however,
that an altruistic generation would wish to eke out the resource for

as long as possible. In the limit a very altruistic generation would consume only a tiny slice of resources so as to enable more generations to survive. But even such an altruistic generation as this would surely want to put some lower limit on the levels of future consumption which it would regard as acceptable: it would have to trade-off 'number of generations' against 'living standard per generation'.

Should any depletable resource be truly essential in this way there is little more to be said except that some fairly grim choices will have to be made sooner or later and that it is not clear which rate of depletion the altruist should favour.

Recent work on the economics of non-essential resource depletion has suggested a simple rule for the pricing of such a resource depending upon whether or not it is close to exhaustion. If it is nowhere near exhaustion then the correct price is the marginal cost of extraction and transportation. If, on the other hand it is close to exhaustion, the price should, in addition, include a *royalty* payable on the resource not yet extracted. This royalty should rise at the rate of interest[7] 'because [the owner] has the option (at the margin) of lending at interest i instead of keeping the resource in stock' (Kay and Mirrlees, 1975).

Figure 15.2 attempts to capture this relationship for a simple but instructive case. I have left extraction and transportation costs

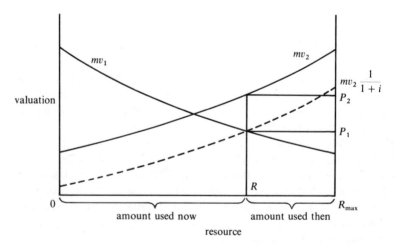

FIGURE 15.2   *Pricing and allocation of a depletable resource*

out of account and assumed identical marginal valuation curves for the exhaustible resource in the two periods. (There is no difficulty in relaxing these assumptions which are made in the interests of clear exposition).

Two things are immediately clear from the diagram. First, the greater the interest rate, the greater the amount of resource used 'now' rather than then: with zero discounting, use of the resource is split 50:50. Second, with prices equal to marginal valuations, $p_2 = (1 + i)p_1$; i.e., price is rising at the rate of interest. As the altruistic generation has a lower rate of time preference it is reasonable to hazard that the more altruistic any one generation is the less it will wish to use a depletable resource and the less rapidly will price rise over time.

A valid point, frequently made by environmental economists against conservationists, is that sauce for the goose is sauce for the gander: that is, if resources are to be depleted less rapidly owing to a lower discount rate, the same sort of argument leads to advocating greater investment now and faster capital accumulation – more growth in fact, but of a less resource-intensive kind.

> In general we believe that the interests of future generations will be better served if we leave them equipment rather than resources in the ground. [Kay and Mirrlees, 1975]

There is nothing paradoxical about this (cf. Krutilla and Fisher, 1975). The altruistic generation is simply making two sorts of sacrifice: it is holding back both on its use of depletable resources (and paying a higher price for them) *and* on its current consumption. If its self-discipline with respect to depletable resources stems from a lower rate of time preference, then this same discipline has to spill over into consumption behaviour. Admittedly, the argument rests on price expectations being more or less correct, but the same caveat applies to all the decisions to be made, not merely those concerning depletable resources.

To take a different view, to argue the inherent importance of the resource in question is to adopt what I have earlier called a 'meddlesome' attitude towards the preferences of the next generation. Rather than hand on to them a bundle of (malleable?) resources, we would wish to hand them relatively more minerals in the ground than our price predictions suggest they would choose. It would then be necessary to impose an extra resources tax on ourselves, i.e., to 'distort' the structure of relative prices.

The assumption in this part of the discussion is that the resource is not 'essential'. As it approaches exhaustion two sorts of things may be expected to happen. First, there will be substitution in favour of resources that are still relatively plentiful. Second, there will be an induced bias in technical progress so as to encourage the development of new techniques of production less intensive in the use of that resource. Altruistic restraint in resource depletion will, of course, slow up these processes.

Recapitulating, altruism in the use of a limited but truly essential resource can postpone the Doomsday, but only at the cost of lower living standards for all generations. It may lead to restraint in the use of depletable resources but it will also lead to a faster rate of capital accumulation.

POLLUTION

The altruistic monopolist will, as was noted in Chapter 10, set price equal to marginal *social* cost. The competitive producer cannot pursue such a policy unless all his competitors do so at the same time. Unless entrepreneurs are Kantian altruists (which not even I would suggest as reasonable), they will have to be forced either by pollution taxes or by legislation backed by suitable fines to take marginal social cost into account.

Much the same thing has to be said about those pollution costs that will be borne by future generations. Entrepreneurs will have to be led to put price equal to *discounted marginal social cost*. Once again, the sheer power of discounting will ensure that very little weight is attached to pollution costs falling on distant generations. For that reason the weighting adjustment described earlier should preferably be used.

Additionally there is a legitimate paternalistic preference here. Suppose that our great-grandchildren get used to wearing anti-smog masks pretty well all the time and even come to prefer filtered dirty air to fresh air which they find rather unpleasant. They would, if asked, certainly reply that they prefer dirty air and an abundance of material goods to fresh air and fewer goods. We, of the current generation, might very well believe that it would be *better* not to pollute the atmosphere in this way and for our great grandchildren not to prefer dirty air to clean. If so, the situation calls for strategic decisions affecting taste formation itself. It could certainly be argued that strategic preference formation stems not so much from a pejorative 'meddlesomeness' but from an underlying empathy which is at the basis of all selfless acts.

Apart from this it is doubtful whether a conventional treatment of uncertainty is adequate here. One approach would be to estimate the probability of some major ecological disaster (very large oil spillages or escape of radioactive materials) and put *discounted expected* marginal social costs into the calculation. Not only is it difficult to make reasonable guesses about these eventualities, but the damage following a really major disaster would be so horrendous as to put it beyond the marginal calculations one is used to making. If an uncertain disaster would be so appalling as to dwarf all other outcomes, a sensible maxi-min policy would be to avoid all possibility of it. Yet even this 'obvious' result hinges on an important assumption about the degree of altruism. To make this clear take a simple example.

Two sorts of technology are available, a non-polluting technology alpha and a polluting technology beta. If alpha is adopted there is no risk of environmental disaster but pay-off to the present generation is rather low. If beta is adopted, pay-off to the current generation is much higher and, if all goes well, things will be no worse for the next generation than had a non-polluting technology been adopted. But there is a risk, to which no firm probability may be attached, of an environmental disaster such that the next generation will incur very heavy costs. With the particular illustrative figures given, alpha will be the maxi-min strategy *provided that* that the present generation attaches a weight of more than about 0.001 to the pay-off of the next generation.[8] Obviously, the more

TABLE 15.1 *Pay-offs under alternative technologies*

	No environmental disaster		Environmental disaster	
	Generation 1	Generation 2	Generation 1	Generation 2
Non-polluting technology (α)	+ 1	0		
Polluting technology (β)	+ 10	0	+ 10	− 1000

major the possible disaster and the less the pay-off of a polluting technology to the current generation, the more likely is alpha to be maxi-min. As a limiting case, let the disaster be more or less total (set the pay-off at $-\infty$); then alpha will be maxi-min as long as the current generation has any concern at all (no matter how small) for the next.

Whether it is appropriate to make use of probabilities (e.g. the probability of sealed radioactive blocks on the sea bed deteriorating within t years and destroying marine life) or to regard the exercise as a wholly uncertain game against nature is partly a question of technical knowledge and partly a matter of attitude to risk aversion. A moral question arises of which attitudes to risk are appropriate when the risks are to be borne by later generations. The maxi-min strategy will always be the more cautious and will, in this context, always lead to a less polluting technology given the degree of altruism.

The Isolation Paradox

So far I have ignored any possible divergence between the savings wishes of individuals and those of the community as a whole. Sen and others have suggested that individuals could well find themselves 'locked into' an n-person prisoner's dilemma game such that they would wish, if it were possible, to save more collectively than they do as individuals. The context is a proposal that each individual shall save an extra pound, matched by everyone else, over and above his private saving.

Under certain simplifying assumptions,[9] it may be shown that co-operative saving will be superior provided that:

$$\frac{1}{v} > \frac{u}{w} \qquad (15.1)$$

where 1 is the weight I attach to my own consumption, v is the weight I attach to my heir's consumption, u is the weight I attach to consumption by my contemporaries and w is the weight I attach to consumption by future non-heirs. Using the notation used earlier in this book, collective saving ($\alpha\alpha$) is Pareto-better than purely private saving ($\beta\beta$) whenever the above condition holds.

The curious case where collective *disinvestment* would be optimal cannot be dismissed out of hand (Tullock, 1964; Lecomber, 1977). It hinges on a very low regard for future non-heirs relative to contemporaries (I would not wish my friends to make sacrifices for their children!). Sen has characterised his condition (15.1) as a balancing condition where:

> My relative evaluation of your heir's consumption (w) and your consumption (u) exactly corresponds to your relative valuation of your heir's consumption (v) relative to your own (1). [Sen, 1967]

Now, it should be clear from the earlier discussion of the *non-twisting* theorem that Sen's balancing condition is not merely an arbitrary and unlikely divide. It incorporates, in an important way, a non-meddlesomeness, a willingness to accept *other's* relative valuations of their own and their heirs' consumption. If this non-meddlesome condition seems reasonable, then there is no need to worry about the isolation paradox and the possibility that collective saving would be *better* (in either direction) than individual saving.

I now turn to the question of whether the paradox (if it exists) might not be resolved voluntarily – would each individual be prepared to carry out a socially desirable act of investment if he were to receive an *assurance* that others would do the same? In other words, when is the game converted from a prisoner's dilemma into an assurance game?

The simplified condition[9] for an assurance game is that $w > v$, i.e. that I as prepared to give a greater weight to other people's heirs' consumption than to my own heirs' consumption. This is, of course, a very improbable condition indeed. A more complex condition depends upon k and upon N as well:

$$w > \frac{N - vk}{k(N - 1)} \tag{15.2}$$

where k is the productivity of investment and N the population. As N becomes large (15.2) approximates to $1/k$; i.e., everything turns on whether the weight I attach to non-heirs exceeds the reciprocal of the productivity of investment. Notice that this more complex assurance condition depends on community size and is less stringent in a large than in a small community.

Finally, it should be noticed that the game is *assurance neutral*. The spontaneous co-operation condition is precisely the same whether or not I expect others to behave co-operatively. By now the reason for this should be familiar: the productivity of investment has been assumed constant at k – there are no increasing or decreasing returns to scale. With increasing returns to investment the game would have been assurance-positive and with decreasing returns assurance-neutral. An implication of this for policy is that where there are enormous gains to be made from acts of collective investment, and where planners believe that others have insufficient regard for their heirs, something may be gained from generating an atmosphere of exhortation and trust.

SUMMARY

(i) Discounting is difficult to defend on moral grounds as it effectively gives a low weighting to future generations. This may be obviated to some extent by combining a system of weighting and discounting.

(ii) Optimum saving was discussed in terms of weighting given to the next generation on the assumption that it continued with the same savings rate. Extremely high rates of saving are ruled out as Pareto-worse for both generations unless the 'target' generation is a distant one. Weak altruism is consistent with a failure to maintain capital intact. Within these extremes the planned savings rates (for all generations) will be greater the more altruistic the current generation.

(iii) Discounting may hasten the Doomsday in the case of an 'essential' resource but it is not clear how this is to be interpreted in terms of altruism. An altruistic generation will deplete a non-renewable but substitutable resource at a slower rate than a selfish generation, *ceteris paribus*; but by virtue of a lower discount rate will also grow faster.

(iv) An altruistic generation will leave fewer pollution problems for future generations and, if it takes a maxi-min view, will avoid pollution-generating technologies.

(v) The 'isolation paradox' does not arise when my preferences are non-meddlesome as to your valuation of your own and your heirs' consumption. If my valuation of your heirs' consumption is sufficiently high, the n-person prisoner's dilemma may be turned into a co-operative but assurance-neutral game.

16 Altruism, Duty and Socialism

In this chapter I set out the main characteristics of the 'good society'. It is a socialist society of a social democratic kind and is based in some quite fundamental way on fraternity which, of course, has to do more with the nature of man than with institutions. Whether or not such a society is possible hinges on the view one takes of the 'nature of man', various views of which are discussed. Finally, I argue that the possibility of the good society depends not only upon the prevalence of altruism but also upon a dynamic relationship between sympathy and political action.

The Good Society

Before doing so it is necessary to say what one means by the good society. I fear that my own version will be condemned as merely pale pink, though I believe its implications are quite radical. Four features may be distinguished.

(i) The first is *egalitarianism*, implying a substantial degree of equality in purchasing power, duly modified to allow for different 'needs'. It will be equitable, *ceteris paribus*, to allow higher incomes (or goods in kind) to those having particular needs – for example large families in respect of food and clothing, old people in respect of fuel, the ill in respect of health care and the disabled in respect of supportive services. There is a general presumption in favour of providing for such needs on a universal rather than a selective basis, for in a socialist community a 100 per cent take-up would be more important than implied real income transfers (see Chapter 12). In my 'good society' there would be a rough and ready 'needs-adjusted' equality.

(ii) The second feature is *efficiency*. Historically, great stress has been placed on the efficiency of a socialist community (More,

St Simon, Owen, Marx, Stalin), both in the production of goods and in capital accumulation. Even in capitalist Britain the Labour Party made great electoral gains in the early 1960s on the promise of a National Plan to increase the rate of economic growth. Almost nowhere has a political party offered egalitarianism *as an alternative* to efficiency. Yet there is a central dilemma here. How is one to manage the trade-off, if trade-off there has to be, between egalitarianism on the one hand and efficiency on the other? What is one to do if the more able will not give of their best unless they obtain high rewards?

(iii) One way of achieving this is direction of labour which, however, conflicts with the third characteristic of my socialist state, *economic freedom*. That within reasonably broad limits people should be allowed to choose (once everyone's 'needs' have been met) how to allocate general purchasing power among commodities, to choose their jobs or careers or training programmes, to choose how hard or how long they will work and to choose where they and their families will live. This third requirement complicates matters a great deal as it removes the one obvious and simple way of reconciling the first two requirements of egalitarianism and efficiency.

(iv) The fourth requirement, *democracy*, is necessary, for it would, in principle, be possible to obtain something like the first three under anarchism or a benevolent dictatorship. The society of which I speak is, therefore, a social democracy with a strong dash of egalitarianism.

CONCEPTS OF MAN AND MORAL PROGRESS

I now consider four views of man and society that I regard as irreconcilable with my own, and characterise them according to their spokesmen, the cynic, the elitist, the meliorist and the revolutionary.

(i) *The Cynic*

The cynic holds that human nature is basically selfish: that apparently altruistic acts may nearly always be explained in terms of implied reciprocity, threat or simply error. He is prepared to concede no doubt that the absence of a powerful or dominating envy is probably necessary so as to avoid destructive or Pareto-inferior dog-in-the-manger consequences. He will, perhaps, also concede that (if not altruism) a curious mixture of shared ideology, language and trust is a necessary precondition of moving from gamma to beta strategies (see Chapter 1). But more than this he will not allow.

The cynic is fortified in his beliefs by the non-twisting theorem, which holds that (within certain limits) altruism makes no difference to the conditions for efficient exchange. He extends his cynicism to politicians who are as selfish as the rest of us, pursuing their political careers for the fruits of office or, failing that, to satisfy their suspect psychological needs. When confronted with the altruistic act – whether blood donation, disaster relief or charitable gifts – he looks for enlightened self-interest, for reciprocity, for power, and usually finds them. The cynic does not necessarily take a gloomy view of all this. If he has read his Adam Smith he knows that everything will work out reasonably well when each pursues his own interest. He probably doubts that human nature will ever 'improve' but is not depressed by the prospect. He regards himself as a hard-headed realist and those who talk of altruism as utopian idealists.

I do not attack the cynic. Of the views I shall be considering I consider his to be the most cogent alternative to the one I adopt.

(ii) *The Élitist*

My élitist is a benevolent élitist and may or may not be a socialist. On the whole he believes in 'doing good by stealth'. If only he can persuade the electorate to put him into power he will be able to carry out 'good' policies. But the electorate must not be fully aware of what he is doing because his own views are more advanced or more altruistic than their own. If they really knew what he was up to they would throw him out of power. Like Sir Dennis Robertson's (1956) economist, he economises on the scarce resource, 'love'.

The benevolent élitist is a good man, no doubt, but his position is in the longer run untenable for it essentially depends on hood-winking the electorate into voting for policies that are more altruistic than it would really wish to choose. This is to say nothing of his arrogance. Consider the example of redistributive taxation. There is no point in a socialist finance minister taxing the average wage-earner to provide an income for those unable to work if the average worker is deeply egotistical and objects to having his income redistributed in this way: after a lag to allow for learning, the minister would be dismissed from power and a new minister appointed whose policies were more congenial to the mass of voters.

One must not be too pessimistic, however, about the survival power of the benevolent élitist in a country (like Britain) where the upper reaches of the civil service are an élite drawn from a restricted class and where a bi-cameral legislature blurs the link between outcomes and median preferences. Even so, the benevolent élitist has to be dismissed as a permanent engine of human betterment.

(iii) *The Meliorist*

The meliorist, encouraged by the process of education, believes in the amelioration of man as civilisation progresses, and is almost inevitably a gradualist as these things take time. The classical liberal view of progress, as envisaged by J. S. Mill, for example, puts the élitist and the educator in harness. Most serious writers who have considered this question put 'duty' above altruism, in the spirit of Proudhon's quotation at the front of this book. On this crucial distinction it is worth quoting both Kant and Rousseau:

> Teachers and moralists must . . . concentrate as far as possible upon showing that charity is a duty which we owe to mankind and that in the last analysis it is a question of right.

> Inclination goes its own secret way; indeed it can do no other, because it has no principle.

> Commencing good from obligation through habit we can end by doing it from inclination, and to this extent love can be commanded. [Kant, 1930, pp. 195–6]

Altruism might come in the end but its path is duty. Rousseau, too, in his education of Emile, is anxious lest the pupil should attempt to act in favour of specific other individuals, 'for each man is part of his species and not of another individual'.

> The essential point is . . . that the only way in which the individual can both maintain the original principle of his nature and exist for others is by undervaluing his identity and good and by having as his concern the common identity and common good. *Education if skillfully carried through ensures* [*this*]. [Charvet, 1974, p. 889]

Mill's pupil comes in the end to act utilitarianly, Kant's to act Kantianly and Rousseau's to pursue the general will. Each achieves a partial submerging of the individual in the general.

As a practical proposition educational programmes can hardly comprise one-to-one tutorials with great philosophers. Children do seem to learn a 'norm' of helping others but this has more to do with example than with reminders of moral obligation or with exhortation. Krebs (1970), in a general (and rather breathless) review of the psychological literature, mentions that 'models' who behaved charitably were more effective than 'models' who preached. But one must beware that example and information are in joint supply so it is difficult to separate them out.[1] The link between education and amelioration of man's character is a tenuous one. Indeed, a major effect of education systems open to all is that the more able obtain the top jobs and the best salaries. This is no bad thing, either in terms of social justice or in terms of economic efficiency, but it has little or nothing to do with the improvement of moral qualities.

The meliorist looks not merely to education but also to the general rise in well-being and living standards for a softening in competitive attitudes – as in Mill's stationary state where pushing and shoving have ceased. But again, the evidence offers little support for this view. I do not claim that people become more selfish as nations become richer, only that they do not become noticeably less so.

The annoying thing about the meliorist is his gradualism: his horizon can always be extended for a century or so without any change in his basic position. He neither promises nor expects quick results.

(iv) *The Revolutionary*

On the face of it the same cannot be said of the revolutionary, for he wants immediate results. Now not all revolutionaries are especially interested in the post-revolutionary nature of man. The objective might simply be to overthrow a corrupt regime or to redistribute property. But a socialist must, I think, believe that *eventually* as a result of the revolution a change in the human condition will come about. Marx (see Chapter 6) certainly believed this would be so; for if it were not, the achievement of the revolution would have been superficial.

Marx's own view was similar to the meliorist's in that a change in social consciousness would take quite a long time, even after the revolution. Indeed, the revolution plays the same role in Marx's scheme as education does in Rousseau's: in this respect Marx was a gradualist. Having observed the Soviet experience, with the dictatorship of the proletariat continuing for at least half a century, Mao sought to harness the social consciousness of the revolution itself by making the revolution permanent. In that way the individual could certainly be restimulated into searching for the social rather than his private good. Castro has tried to force the pace of social consciousness in Cuba. In Vietnam and Cambodia the communists have sought sudden (and often brutal) change by applying a cold douche to existing Western habits. Whether these methods work or not, they underline that the revolution, even after the establishment of an effective post-revolutionary regime, is not a sufficient condition for socialist social change. Neither do I believe it to be a necessary condition.

Of these spokesmen – the cynic, the élitist, the meliorist and the revolutionary – the cynic seems to me to have adopted the most consistently honest view, though I shudder at his notion of society and man. The non-selfish élitist in the selfish society cannot in the end attain his objects, the meliorist's dream has to be postponed indefinitely and the revolutionary cannot be relied upon to produce the good society afterwards. The cynic is concerned with the here-and-now and how to make it work. But his view cannot be acceptable to the socialist idealist who believes that, *if only* the distorting influences of capitalism were removed, man would reveal his true nature. I believe that socialists are mistaken in this, that the absence of environmental distortions is not sufficient to achieve the change they wish. Neither was the scorn poured by 'scientific socialists' on 'utopian socialists' justified.

THE SOCIAL DYNAMICS OF ALTRUISM

If long-run moral improvement is a chimera, are we then delivered into the arms of the cynic? Not quite. The clue to all this surely lies in a greater understanding of the social dynamics of altruism and duty. It seems to me that something of this has been captured in what I have earlier called the 'contagion' thesis. Hume and Titmuss have already been cited as proponents of the view that, by example and by exercise of that faculty, altruism could spread throughout the community. Of course, there is little direct evidence for it. Hume believed the same to be true of the 'passions' generally. Titmuss used the argument to emphasise that a diminution of the opportunity for altruism in one area (blood donation) would weaken it in others. Both were emphasising the *dynamic* relationship between action and human nature. But in spite of the lack of direct evidence, the dynamics of the relationship are attractive to the modern eye: preferences, selfish or otherwise, cannot on this view be taken as static but are subject to interaction with events. There is, moreover, some indirect evidence in favour of the contagion thesis: it may plausibly be said to have been holding, though in a downward direction, in Nazi Germany. At a more humdrum level economists have found it convenient to explain consumer durable purchases in terms of pioneers, taste learning and epidemics.

An important part of this dynamic process is the relationship between inclination and duty. In the analysis of consumption externalities one assumes that either the goods or the utilities of other people enter into one's own utility function; that they do so is entirely a matter of taste, for, as Kant says, inclination has no principle. But benevolent preferences (tastes) may be seen, in Frances Hutcheson's terminology, as creating 'imperfect rights'. These are based partly on 'taste' and partly on 'need'. Perceptions of need vary from one individual to another but it is clear that in *an objective sense* some goods are more important than others. It is hard to better Tawney's list of those goods the access to which is a strategic factor in life-chances:

If the first use which a sensible society will make of its surplus is to raise the general standard of health, and the second to equalise educational opportunities, the third is not less obvious. It is to provide for the contingencies of life and thus to mitigate the insecurity which is the most characteristic of the wage-earner's disabilities. [Tawney, 1931, p. 147]

In a similar spirit Sen's 'weak equity axion' requires a redistribution in favour of those with greater needs (disability, age, etc.) (Sen, 1973a). More technically, recent work on 'equivalence scales'[2] is relevant. But a perception of 'need' cannot, of course, be purely technical: it requires sympathy and imagination.

Once one's perception is aroused, however, benevolence becomes a rational requirement on action. The rational individual sees that benevolent impulses felt towards particular others must be universalised – that benevolence towards one individual must be generalised and extended to unknown others in that same category. Starting from inclination, transfers became a matter of duty and rights.

In the dynamic process at which I have been hinting,[3] sympathy and duty, like hatred and duty, are mutually reinforcing. The role of politicians as entrepreneurs in this process is vital, for the universalisation of benevolent impulses has to be articulated as policy. Imperfect rights are consolidated by law and tend to be embodied deeply in the preference structure of the next generation. It is difficult to exaggerate the role of politicians in this connection. The possibility of the social dynamics of hatred working symmetrically with those of love surely makes Titmuss's fear of the dangers of eroding altruism less absurd than many commentators have found it. It adds to the force of Myrdal's complaint that politicians seem to be afraid of appealing to moral reasons for giving overseas aid. It also follows that politicians may do serious long-run damage when they seek to achieve progress in social provision by stealth instead of by appealing boldly to the moral sense of the electorate. Of the famous trio, liberty, equality and fraternity, it is the last and most neglected that makes the other two *simultaneously* possible.[4]

Finally, I do not accept the view associated with Proudhon, Kant, Rousseau and others that altruism enters the matter only at a rather low moral level. Kant's principle is, after all, of no use if contractors have no interest in third parties. Generous actions towards them will be possible only if there exists some bond of imagination and sympathy. Adam Smith's notion, which is based on a subtle interaction between individual preferences, approbation and sympathy, is certainly attractive here. For at the basis of duty lies 'sympathy – the one poor word which includes all our best insight and all our best love'.

17 Postscript

A great many issues have been discussed, all too briefly, in this book. A number of areas for future research work stand out very clearly; no doubt there are others.

(i) Some sharpening up of hypotheses is required so that the predictions of 'selfish' and 'non-selfish' preferences may be tested empirically. The shifting of the selfish assumption (whereby indirect exchange and long-term enlightened self-interest are invoked) makes this rather difficult.

(ii) More general relationships (by which, for example, taxpayers feel altruistically towards those on lower incomes but malevolently towards those on higher incomes) may be tried out on tax data.

(iii) Some survey evidence of the frequency distribution of non-selfishness in the population would be useful. Even if only rough indices were derived they would be better than nothing. One suspects that the distribution would be highly skewed.

(iv) It would be useful to have further evidence on what I have called the 'contagion hypothesis'.

Notes

CHAPTER 2

1. EXTENDED NOTE: FIRST-ORDER CONDITIONS

There are two standard ways of obtaining the 'first-order' or 'efficiency' conditions. The first is to postulate a social welfare function, which is then maximised subject to a production constraint (for an early and thorough use of this method in the externalities context see Tintner's excellent paper, 1946). The second method is to maximise each individual's utility function subject to prescribed utility levels for other individuals and to a production constraint. Both methods are discussed by de Graaff (1957). As he points out, the second method will pick out all points on the utility possibility frontier whereas the former will pick out only its downward sloping portion.

(i) *Maximising social welfare*

Let there be commodities $\qquad$ $1, 2, \ldots, r, s, \ldots m$
and individual's $\qquad$ $1, 2, \ldots, i, j, \ldots n.$
Each individual's utility function is $\quad u_j(\ldots x_{rj} \ldots x_{si})$
and social welfare is $\qquad$ $W(\ldots u_i, u_j \ldots).$
The production constraint is $\qquad$ $G(\ldots X_r, X_s \ldots) = 0$
$\qquad\qquad\qquad\qquad$ where $X_r = \sum_j x_{rj}.$

Write the Lagrangean

$$V = W[U(x)] - \lambda G(X)$$

from which

$$\frac{\partial V}{\partial x_{rj}} = \sum_i \frac{\partial w}{\partial u_i} \frac{\partial u_i}{\partial x_{rj}} - \lambda \frac{\partial G}{\partial X_r} = 0 \qquad (2.1)$$

and

$$\frac{\partial V}{\partial x_{sj}} = \sum_i \frac{\partial w}{\partial u_i} \frac{\partial u_i}{\partial x_{sj}} - \lambda \frac{\partial G}{\partial X_s} = 0 \qquad (2.2)$$

Given the utility of individual i and social welfare we have from (2.1) and (2.2)

$$\frac{\partial x_{sj}}{\partial x_{rj}} (w) = \frac{\partial x_s}{\partial x_r} (G) \qquad (2.3)$$

or, the social marginal rate of substitution of j's consumption of x_r and x_s equals their marginal rate of transformation in production. This has to be compared with the egotistical condition:

$$\frac{\partial x_{sj}}{\partial x_{rj}}(u_j) = \frac{\partial x_s}{\partial x_r}(G) \tag{2.4}$$

or, j's own private marginal rate of substitution between x_r and x_s equals their marginal rate of transformation in production. As in general (2.3) and (2.4) will not be equal, the standard prescription would appear to be to impose subsidies (taxes) equal to

$$\frac{1}{\lambda}\sum_{i \neq j} \frac{\partial w}{\partial u_i}\frac{\partial u_i}{\partial x_{rj}}$$

or to the marginal externalities, expressed in terms of cost.

It is clear from examination of (2.3) and (2.4) that these two conditions will be equivalent if society's 'concern' is proportionate to the individual's. *A sufficient condition for this is that only the utilities of others into one's utility function.* For if this is so we are able to rewrite

$$\frac{\partial u_i}{\partial x_{rj}} \quad \text{as} \quad \frac{\partial u_i}{\partial u_j}\cdot\frac{\partial u_j}{\partial x_{rj}}$$

and if this substitution is written into equations (2.1) and (2.2) it is easily seen that they reduce to (2.4) rather than (2.3).

(ii) *Maximising individual utility*

Continuing with the same notation, let individual j attempt to maximise utility subject to constrained (feasible) utilities of others as well as the resources constraint. Thus for each individual i,

$$[\bar{u}_i - u_i(\ldots x_{ri} \ldots x_{sj})] = 0$$

Write the Lagrangean

$$V = u_j(x) - \sum \mu_i[\bar{u}_i - u_i(x)] - \lambda G(X)$$

from which

$$\frac{\partial V}{\partial x_{rj}} = \frac{\partial u_j}{\partial x_{rj}} - \sum_{i \neq j} \mu_i \frac{\partial u_i}{\partial x_{rj}} - \lambda \frac{\partial G}{\partial X_r} = 0 \tag{2.5}$$

$$\frac{\partial v}{\partial x_{sj}} = \frac{\partial u_j}{\partial x_{sj}} - \sum_{i \neq j} \mu_i \frac{\partial u_i}{\partial x_{sj}} - \lambda \frac{\partial G}{\partial X_s} = 0. \tag{2.6}$$

As before, when $\partial u_i/\partial x_{rj}$ is rewritten

$$\frac{\partial u_i}{\partial u_j}\frac{\partial u_j}{\partial x_{rj}}$$

(2.5) and (2.6) reduce to the usual first-order condition.

(iii) *The two-person exchange case*

In the discussion of the text, attention is concentrated upon the Edgeworth Box with two individuals and no production. As noted there, we have in that case

$dx_i/dx_j = -1$. Thus the efficiency condition for the maximising individual is

$$
\frac{\dfrac{\partial u_i}{\partial x_{ri}} - \dfrac{\partial u_i}{\partial x_{rj}}}{\dfrac{\partial u_i}{\partial x_{si}} - \dfrac{\partial u_i}{\partial x_{sj}}} = \frac{\dfrac{\partial u_j}{\partial x_{rj}} - \dfrac{\partial u_j}{\partial x_{ri}}}{\dfrac{\partial u_j}{\partial x_{sj}} - \dfrac{\partial u_j}{\partial x_{si}}},
$$

an equation that holds at every point on the social contract curve. As in the more general cases, this condition reduces to the more familiar egotistical condition when $\partial u_i / \partial x_{rj}$ is rewritten as

$$
\frac{\partial u_i}{\partial u_j}\frac{\partial u_j}{\partial x_{rj}} \text{ etc.}
$$

One then has

$$
\frac{\partial x_{sj}}{\partial x_{rj}}(u_j) = \frac{\partial x_{si}}{\partial x_{ri}}(u_i)
$$

or the equation of the private contract curve. As Archibald and Donaldson (1976) point out, separability of the utility function is a sufficient condition for what I have called 'non-twisting'.

2. Frisch's (1971) discussion is particularly thorough and treats of particular forms of interdependent utility functions. See also Schall (1972, 1975) and Danielson (1975). Apart from Boulding, Walsh (1970) gives a good introduction to closed indifference curves and, furthermore, duly acknowledges Edgeworth's treatment.

3. See, for example, Archibald and Donaldson (1975, 1976) and Daly and Giertz (1972, 1976).

4. The relevant pages in Arrow and Hahn (1971) are 132-6 which refer back to earlier chapters. There are several minor slips in their numbering of assumptions but the correct numbering becomes clear on working one's way through.

5. See especially the discussion between Osana (1972) and Ledyard (1971) on the role of limitedness of information in reaching Pareto optimality. Osana argues that the second optimality theorem emerges relatively unscathed as long as agents' judgements are convex and there is a 'fair-limitedness' of information.

6. This reminds one of the potlatch of the Tlingit and Haida tribes of north-west America, a system of 'agonistic total presentation' in which relative wealth is established by, as it were, a process of repeated subtraction and destruction (an expensive, but decisive way of doing arithmetic). See Mauss (1925).

CHAPTER 3

1. Adam Smith (1759) comments: 'There is many an honest Englishman, who, in his private station, would be more seriously disturbed by the loss of a guinea, than the loss of Minorca, who yet, had it been in his power to defend that fortress, would have sacrificed his life a thousand times' (p. 332).

2. Let there be $m + 1$ goods $\quad 1, 2, \ldots \ldots r, s, \ldots . m, Z$
   and n individuals $\quad\quad\quad 1, 2, \ldots \ldots i, j, \ldots . n$
   Where Z is a public good.

Each individual's utility function is,

$$u_j[\cdots x_{rj}, x_{si} \cdots Z_j(Z), Z_i(Z)]$$

and social welfare is

$$W(\cdots u_i, u_j \cdots).$$

The production constraint is

$$G(\cdots X_r, X_s \cdots Z) = 0$$

where

$$X_r = \sum_j x_{rj}.$$

The appropriate Lagrangean expression is

$$V = W[u(x, Z)] - \lambda G(X, Z).$$

One is interested in the formulation of $\partial V/\partial Z$.

(i) self-interest:

$$\frac{\partial V}{\partial Z} = \sum_i \frac{\partial W}{\partial u_i} \frac{\partial u_i}{\partial Z_i} \frac{\partial Z_i}{\partial Z} - \lambda \frac{\partial G}{\partial Z} = 0$$

where it is assumed that Z yields an identifiable service $Z_i(Z)$ to individual i. If this is not so one writes the usual

$$\frac{\partial V}{\partial Z} = \sum_i \frac{\partial W}{\partial u_i} \frac{\partial u_i}{\partial Z} - \lambda \frac{\partial G}{\partial Z} = 0$$

(ii) meddlesomeness:

$$\frac{\partial V}{\partial Z} = \sum_i \frac{\partial W}{\partial u_i} \sum_j \frac{\partial u_i}{\partial Z_j} \cdot \frac{\partial Z_j}{\partial Z} - \lambda \frac{\partial G}{\partial Z} = 0$$

(iii) altruistic neutrality:

$$\frac{\partial V}{\partial Z} = \sum_i \frac{\partial W}{\partial u_i} \sum_j \frac{\partial u_i}{\partial u_j} \cdot \frac{\partial u_j}{\partial Z_j} \cdot \frac{\partial Z_j}{\partial Z} - \lambda \frac{\partial G}{\partial Z} = 0$$

It is this last case that corresponds to 'non-twisting'.

3. One has to be very careful when translating a general equilibrium into a partial equilibrium rule. At Z^* we have,

$$\sum_i \frac{mu_i}{\lambda_i} = \sum_i mv_i = \sum_i t_i = mc$$

i.e., the sum of (own weighted) marginal utilities in money terms equals the sum of marginal valuations, equals the sum of individual tax prices, equals marginal cost. Given the initial income distribution there is unanimous support for Z^*. The 'weights' attached to marginal utilities are the reciprocal of λ_i, the marginal utility of money, and will therefore be increasing with income on the assumption of diminishing marginal utility of money.

Under non-selfishness there has to be a 'double-adding' rule whereby each individual's social marginal valuations are added up. But under non-twisting the same non-selfish weights are attached to all goods, not just public goods.

4. Olson's rule for optimal *private* provision of the public good (if any) has to be modified to:

$$\frac{dG}{dT_i} = \frac{1}{F_1 + V_i(1 - F_i)} \frac{dC}{dT_i}$$

when individual i is unselfish. G is group gain, T is the level of i's help to the organisation, C is total cost of provision and F_i the individual's share in group benefit. V_i is the weight i attaches to the benefit going to all the other individuals taken together. This reduces to Olson's purely private case when $V_i = 0$ and to his rule for collective provision when $V_i = 1$ (cf. Olson, 1965, p. 24).

5. Hammond (1976) has shown that the only decentralisable mechanism with competitive budget constraints is a 'Lindahl' mechanism for which each consumer is allowed the same net expenditure on private goods.

6. Let the most preferred amount of public good Z at specified tax prices for each individual be indexed on a scale 0 to 1. The median amount will be that selected by a simple majority as a movement to it could always command greater than 50 per cent support. With a two-thirds rule the outcome would not be at the median (except by chance). If it started off between the 33rd and 67th percentile it would stay there. If it started out at less than 33 per cent it would move up, and if at more than 67 per cent it would move down, to those levels.

CHAPTER 4

1. For an account of the prisoner's dilemma see, for example, Rapoport (1960). The famous 'isolation paradox' is an *n*-person prisoner's dilemma.

2. See Sen (1973a) for stimulating comments on the assurance class of games and my review (Collard, 1974).

3. For an assurance game, $\alpha\alpha > \beta\alpha$

$$(1 - v) + v > 2(1 - v) - 2v$$
$$v > \tfrac{1}{4}.$$

At the higher weight $v = \tfrac{1}{2}$ the game would become wholly co-operative as α would be played each time.

4. The condition is

$$(1) \,.\, (1 - v)\pi + (1)v\pi - (2) \,.\, (1 - v)(1 - \pi) + 2(v)(1 - \pi) > (2) \,.\, (1 - v)\pi - (2)v \,.\, \pi.$$

5.

	(π)		$(1 - \pi)$	
	α		β	
α	$x_1{}^{\alpha\alpha}$	$x_j{}^{\alpha\alpha}$	$x_1{}^{\alpha\beta}$	$x_j{}^{\alpha\beta}$
β	$x_1{}^{\beta\alpha}$	$x_j{}^{\beta\alpha}$	$x_1{}^{\beta\beta}$	$x_j{}^{\beta\beta}$

In each case the difference between my playing α and β is

$$\delta_1{}^{\alpha}, \delta_j{}^{\alpha}, \delta_1{}^{\beta}, \delta_j{}^{\beta}$$

e.g., $\delta_j{}^{\alpha}$ is the difference made to each other person's pay-off by my co-operation if he himself is co-operating. For my co-operation:

$$\pi \sum v_i \delta_i{}^{\alpha} + (1 - \pi) \sum v_i \delta_i{}^{\beta} > 0$$

where $\sum v_i = 1$.

6. Too frequently the players are students and the pay-offs trivial so the 'realism' of the experiment is in doubt.

CHAPTER 5

1. To this extent Spencer had noticed the role of altruism at the stage of establishing a species but not at the later stage of the potential destruction of the habitat.

2. Notice also Briffault's remarks about the family, which was in his view 'not the foundation but the negation of society'. Human society, on the contrary, owed its rise to 'instincts which obliterated individualistic instincts . . . sentiments of inter-dependence, loyalty, solidarity and a devotion to a group larger than the patriarchal family'.

3. Consider a Mendelian dominant – recessive pair B, b. Social co-operation between two bb individuals is highly effective, but failure to link with a second bb is fatal. A survival probability σ is postulated such that $0 > \sigma < 1$ where σ attaches to non-bb's and 1 to bb's. B has a frequency $1 - \beta$ and b a frequency β. A function $F(\beta)$ is then derived with the general properties indicated in Figure 5-1 where there is a fixed point of the mapping $\beta \rightarrow F(\beta)$. The basic qualitative form of $F(\beta)$ is apparently quite stable and, indeed, β crit would fall as a result of assortative mating.

This whole line of argument is predicated upon the presence of the 'altruist' gene and one would want some evidence of its existence and frequency before taking this kind of model too seriously. I am grateful to Dr Peter Flood for discussion of this point.

CHAPTER 6

1. See for example MacFie (1967), Campbell (1971, 1975) and Coase (1976). Most modern writers are rather dismissive of *Das Adam Smith Problem*. Coase argues against the usual interpretation of *Moral Sentiments*, making the case that Smith's view of man in that book was both unflattering and modern.

2. A view put more recently by the novelist John Fowles: 'charity, kindness to others, actions against injustice and inequality should be acts of hygiene, not of pleasure' and 'not doing good when you usefully could is not immoral, it is going about with excrement on the hands' (1968, pp. 82, 84).

3. According to Sayers, Empedocles taught that the universe was held together by discord but that from time to time motions of heaven brought harmony or love.

When this happened, like matter flew to like, and the Universe was once more resolved into its original elements and so reduced to chaos.

4. See the discussion of alpha, beta and gamma strategies in Chapter 2 and the article by Bush and Mayer (1974) in which it is shown that the Orderly Anarchy solution is better than the Hobbesian Jungle solution.

5. The properly educated *Emile* would pursue the common good, but if a child behaves altruistically through a desire to please his parents then this motive is at the root of *amour-propre*; see Charvet (1974). Such esteem by others is, of course, at the basis of Smith's view.

6. See, for example, Duncan's *Marx and Mill*: 'Is the radical dream in one sense a return to the liberalism previously dismissed as hollow?' (1973, pp. 298, 299).

7. See Collard (1975) for an evaluation of Edgeworth's contribution.

8. This paragraph is worth quoting in full, though not in the main text:

> If k be the fraction of importance that I attach to a pound in the hands of my heirs compared with myself, and $\phi(t)$ the probability that I shall be alive t years from now, a certain pound *to me or my heirs* then attracts me now equally with a certain pound multiplied by $\{\phi(t) + k[1 - \phi(t)]\}$ *to me* then. This is obviously increased by anything that increases either $\phi(t)$ or k. If, through an anticipated change of fortune or temperament, one pound after t years is expected to be equivalent to $(1 - \alpha)$ times one pound now, a certain $\{\phi(t) + k[1 - (t)]\}$ pounds of the then prevailing sort attracts me equally with $(1 - \alpha) \{\phi(t) + k[1 - \phi(t)]\}$ pounds, of the prevailing sort to me then. Therefore a certain pound to my heir will be as persuasive to call out investment now as the above sum would be if I were certain to live for ever and always to be equally well off and the same in temperament. [Pigou, 1920, p. 26, n. 1.]

CHAPTER 8

1. An earlier version of this and the following chapter was presented to a Bristol – Oxford – Reading seminar in the spring of 1975.

2. EXTENDED NOTE: THE BASIC PAY-OFF MATRIX

	Strategy Probability Number	α π			β $1 - \pi$		
		N_1	N_2	N_3	N_1	N_3	N_3
.ion 1							
	α	0	0	0	$-(1 - l)rm,$	$m[1 - (1 - l)r],$	$-(1 - l)rm$
	β	$m(1 - rl),$	$-rlm,$	$-rlm$	$m(1 - r),$	$m(1 - r),$	$-mr$
fference	δ	$m(rl - 1),$	$rlm,$	rlm	$m(rl - 1),$	$rlm,$	rlm

The strategies are α and β with subjective probabilities of π and $(1 - \pi)$. Each trio of pay-offs represents the pay-off to union 1, to each other union and to 'pensioners' in that order. It is assumed that with $\alpha\alpha$ there would be no change in real income for anyone, though this anchoring is arbitrary and not essential to the argument. With $\beta\beta$ there would be increases in real income for the unions but decreases for pensioners. There are N_1 members of union 1, N_2 members of other unions and N_3 pensioners. The final row, δ, is the important row in considering union 1's adoption of an α strategy. Notice that δ is the same whether the others play α or β.

(i) *For collective co-operation*

$$0 > uNm(1 - r) - u_3 N_3 mr$$

where u is the weight that unionists attach to their own real incomes and u_3 the weight they attach to pensioners. N is the total of N_1 and N_2. Substituting $u_3 = 1 - u$ and writing $N_3/N = R_3$, we calculate the critical value of u_3 as in expression (8.1) of the text.

ii(a) *and* ii(b). *For individual union co-operation,*

we need

$$u_1 N_1 m(rl - 1) + u_2 N_2 rlm + u_3 N_3 rlm > 0$$

where

$$u_1 + u_2 + u_3 = 1.$$

For ii(a) assume $u_2 = 0$. For ii(b) assume $u_1 = u_2 = (1 - u_3)/2$. Whether or not co-operation would be forthcoming in the more general case may be discovered by inserting assumed values into the inequality.

The conditional grant pay-off matrix. It is necessary to rewrite only the left-hand-side of the matrix as the right-hand-side stays as it was.

		α	
α	0,	0,	g
β	$m(1 - rl)$,	$-rlm$	$-rlm$
δ	$m(rl - 1)$,	rlm	$rlm + g$

(iii) *For collective co-operation*

$$u_3 N_3 g > uNm(1 - r) - u_3 N_3 mr.$$

Making the same substitutions as before, the critical value of u_3 is as in expression (8.3) in the text.

(iv) *For individual co-operation*

For this it is necessary that the weighted row of δ's be positive.

$$\pi[N_1 u_1 m(rl - 1) + N_2 u_2 rlm + N_3 u_3(rlm + g)]$$
$$+ (1 - \pi)[N_1 u_1 m(rl - 1) + N_2 u_2 rlm + N_3 u_3 rlm] > 0.$$

This reduces easily to:

$$u_1 m(rl - 1) + n_2' u_2 rlm + n_3' u_3 rlm + \pi n_3' u_3 g > 0.$$

Direct substitution into the inequality is possible in the general case. Expression (8.4) gives the crucial value of u_3 for the specially simple case where $u_2 = 0$.

Notice that the *size* of the money wage increase under free collective bargaining is now relevant in so far as it appears in the ratio g/m. Inspection of the above inequality indicates that the greater is π the more likely the left-hand-side is to be positive.

3. The tax/wage restraint package of spring 1976 was similar in spirit to the tactic. But it was brought to bear only on the first part of the problem, the collective choice of alpha-alpha over beta-beta. It was not seriously believed that the tax package would be withdrawn if individual unions adopted beta. In any case the whole of that package was underpinned by the threat of a statutory policy and no such threat has been assumed in this chapter. The unions effectively called the Chancellor's bluff following a similar package in spring 1977. As this final draft is being written (summer 1977) the 'social contract' has collapsed to be replaced by free collective bargaining constrained by strict cash limits in the public sector.

CHAPTER 9

1. A world, no doubt, of Lytton Stratcheys and David Garnetts.

2. In this connection Armytage tells the following anecdote of the Earl of Pembroke and Charles II. Pembroke, kneeling, told His Majesty that he had a message 'to deliver him, and that was, the end of the world would be this year, and therefore desired his majesty to prepare for it'. 'Well,' said the King, 'if it be so, yet notwithstanding, I will give you seven years' purchase for your manor of Wilton' (Armytage, 1961, p. 33).

3. Ruskin, of course, fumed against both political economy and industrialisation and extolled the virtues of what would now be called intermediate technology: 'by hand-labour, therefore, and that alone, we are to till the ground. By hand-labour also to plough the sea; both for food, and in commerce and in war: not with floating kettles there neither, but with hempen bridle, and the winds of heaven in harness' (Ruskin, 1898, p. 377). For a more detailed account of Ruskin's views on social and economic matters see Sherburne (1972).

4. Birrell's account seems more pessimistic than many but, as he himself remarks, the communes he investigated were non-industrial and more likely to give rise to problems.

5. Unless social consciousness is complete the centralised and voluntary allocations of labour coincide only when

$$(1 - \alpha) = \frac{\eta}{\beta}$$

which, slightly adapted, corresponds with the rule given in the text and in Figure 9.1. The notation here is Sen's and should not be confused with that in the main text. α is the proportion of income distributed according to need, β the ratio of income to total output and η the elasticity of output with respect to labour.

6. Notice that in this chapter v stands for the selfish and $(1 - v)$ for the unselfish weight. This reverses the similar notation of the previous chapter but is convenient for expositional purposes.

7. Like the horse, Boxer, in *Animal Farm*.

8. The curves will fall unless $X''(N) > X'(N)/N$, where $X''(N)$ is the second derivative of the production function. Should this happen to be the case over a range of commune size then one could easily have *minimum* and maximum feasible *commune* sizes.

9. 'There are certain acts which when performed on n similar occasions have consequences more than n times as great as those resulting from one performance' (Harrod, 1936, p. 148). He adds (p. 155) that 'altruism is essential to the ordinary notion of moral goodness'.

APPENDIX

Each 'other'

Strategy Probability Number	α π		β $1 - \pi$	
	1	$N - 1$	1	$N - 1$
α	$\dfrac{X(N)}{N} - c,$	$\dfrac{X(N)}{N} - c$	$\dfrac{X(1)}{N} - c,$	$\dfrac{X(1)}{N}$
β	$\dfrac{X(N)}{N},$	$\dfrac{X(N-1)}{N} - c$	$0,$	0
δ	$\dfrac{X'(N)}{N} - c,$	$\dfrac{X'(N)}{N}$	$\dfrac{X(1)}{N} - c,$	$\dfrac{X(1)}{N}$

α in the table represents 'work' and β 'slack'. In each case my pay-off is given first and each other's second. The difference made to each player's pay-off by my co-operation is indicated in row δ. If no one works there is no output and no effort.

Is it worth being in the commune? I shall suppose that potential members compare the $\alpha\alpha$ pay-off with their position outside the commune. This requires a comparison of the attractions of being in a commune (fraternity, etc.) with the advantages and disadvantages of remaining in the outside world. Such comparisons are avoided when considering work behaviour *within* the commune itself. I shall assume that $\beta\beta$ is definitely worse than being outside so once members get themselves locked in to $\beta\beta$ the commune breaks up.

If a member, is it worth co-operating or pulling one's weight? The general condition on v_1 follows easily from row δ.

$$\pi\left[v_1\left(\frac{X'(N)}{N} - c\right) + (1 - v_1)\left(\frac{X'(N)}{N}\right)\right]$$

$$+ (1 - \pi)\left[v_1\left(\frac{X(1)}{N} - c\right) + (1 - v_1)\frac{X(1)}{N}\right] > 0.$$

This simplifies to

$$v_1 < \frac{\pi X'(N) - (1 - \pi)X(1)}{cN}$$

of which the various versions in the text are special cases or rearrangements.

CHAPTER 10

1. Let i's utility function be given by:

$$U_i = A(y^i)^{(1 - v)}(y^j)^v$$

where A is a constant and the y's are incomes. Consider a transfer T and let pre-transfer incomes be indicated by y_0. The utility function then becomes:

$$U_1 = A(y_0{}^i - T)^{(1 - v)}(y_0{}^j + T)^{(v)}.$$

Differentiating,

$$T = vy_0{}^i - (i - v)y_0{}^j$$

or, putting

$$\frac{T}{y_0{}^i} = t \quad \text{and} \quad \frac{y_0{}^i}{y_0{}^j} = r,$$

$$t = v - (1 - v)\frac{1}{r}$$

as in the text. Clearly, if $y_0{}^j$ is 0 the equation reduces to

$$T = vy_0{}^i \quad \text{or} \quad t = v.$$

A slightly different version would take the *ratio* of incomes into account:

$$U_1 = (1 - v)\log Y_i - v \log \frac{Y_j}{Y_i}.$$

One merit of this function is, of course, that it differentiates very easily. There are numerous variations on this theme, making use of $|Y_i - Y_j|$ or its logarithm.

2. Under the British system, the price of giving an effective pound is £$1/(1 + m)$ when the gift is covenanted. In putting the effective contribution into the utility function one assumes the individual is interested in the amount the charity *receives*.

3. The various papers are listed in the bibliography: it would be cumbersome to make detailed reference to them in the text.

4. See *National Income and Expenditure 1965–75*, Table 5d.

5. Let the monopolist's objective function be:

$$p(x)x - c(x) + v\left[\int_0^x P(x)\,dx - px\right].$$

By simple manipulation this gives the rule stated in the text:

$$p = c'(x)\frac{e}{v + (e - 1)}$$

6. See *Social Audit* (1973–4), vol. 3, p. 60.

7. *British Aid Statistics* 1971–75, Ministry of Overseas Development HMSO (1975).

CHAPTER 11

1. The slope of the utility possibility frontier is given by:

$$\frac{\partial u_A}{\partial u_B} = -\frac{\dfrac{\partial u_A}{\partial x_A} - \dfrac{\partial u_A}{\partial x_B}}{\dfrac{\partial u_B}{\partial x_B} - \dfrac{\partial u_B}{\partial x_A}}$$

In the selfish case this reduces to

$$-\frac{\partial u_A}{\partial x_A}\frac{\partial x_B}{\partial u_B}$$

which is plainly negative. The parties are said to be 'malicious' if $\partial u_A/\partial x_B$ and $\partial u_B/\partial x_A$ are negative and non-selfish where

$$0 < \frac{\partial u_A}{\partial x_B} < 1 \quad\text{and}\quad 0 < \frac{\partial u_B}{\partial x_A} < 1.$$

De Graaff has noted (1957, appendix to Ch. 4) that the frontier can slope upwards only when external economies are marked and asymmetrical. This is *locally* true, but asymmetry should not be interpreted to mean that altruism is merely one-sided.

Polinsky (1971) has argued that the scope for Pareto-optimal redistribution is not limited to upward-rising parts of the utility possibility frontier, but it remains true that a positively weighted social welfare function would pick out only points on what he calls the 'true true welfare function'.

The utility possibility frontier can be considered as a mapping from the contract locus so that *a* and *b* have corresponding points on that curve.

2. On this approach see also Orr (1976), who considers transfers under the AFDC (Aid to Families with Dependent Children) programme. His outcome is, however, not 'voluntary' but based on majority voting and is entirely in the spirit of the later parts of this chapter. He shows that 'federal matching' increases the size of the transfer and that the transfer will be greater the more altruistic are taxpayers.

3. The utility function for person or class (i) was taken to be,

$$u_i = a \log Y_i + b \sum_{j=1}^{i-1} \log(Y_j/Y_i)$$

where $Y_j < Y_i$. The degree of altruism could then be indicated by b/a. For example with b/a at 11.1 per cent, $Y_1^* = 2,000$, $Y_2^* = 8,000$, $Y_3^* = 16,000$, the amount distributed to class (1) would be 889, one-third being paid for by class (2) and two-thirds by class (3). A basic ten groups are then derived from US tax tables. Various hypothetical values of b/a are then taken.

4. The transfer elasticity may be defined as:

$$\frac{\text{proportionate change in transfer}}{\text{proportionate change in income difference}}$$

or

$$\frac{dT}{d(Y_i - Y_j)} \frac{(Y_i - Y_j)}{T}$$

and is treated diagrammatically in Hochman and Rodgers (1969).

5. The tax rate on the highest group would be

$$1/[1 - (R_{21}/R_{22}) - (R_{31}/R_{33}) + (R_{21}/R_{22}) \cdot (R_{32}/R_{33})],$$

on the middle group

$$1/[1 - (R_{32}/R_{33})]$$

and on the lowest group zero where the R_{ij}'s are $\partial u_{ij}/\partial y_j$ etc.

6. Cash transfer is disposable income *minus* original income where the difference consists in cash benefits and direct taxes. Cash-and-kind transfer is 'income after all taxes and benefits' *minus* original income.

7. The limit is given by $1/(1 + e)$ where e is the (lowest) elasticity of labour supply.

8. The final segment of the curve is a crude extrapolation.

9. Let individual 1's utility be:

$$u = u(x_1, x_2, h)$$

where x_1 is his consumption, x_2 is 2's consumption and h is his working time. This may be written as

$$u = u[(1 - t)hw, m_2 + twh, h] \qquad (11.1)$$

where the price of x is unity, w is the wage rate, m_2 is 2's own income. Maximising with respect to h gives

$$\frac{du}{dh} = \frac{\partial u}{\partial x_1}(1 - t)w + \frac{\partial u}{\partial x_2} \cdot tw + \frac{\partial u}{\partial h} = 0. \qquad (11.2)$$

In the special case of no taxation, no externality this reduces to

$$\frac{\partial u}{\partial x_1} \cdot w + \frac{\partial u}{\partial h} = 0 \qquad (11.3)$$

or real wage equals marginal disutility of effort. It is easily seen that (11.2) reduces to (11.3) when

$$\frac{\partial u}{\partial x_1} = \frac{\partial u}{\partial x_2}$$

or, trivially, when $\partial u/\partial h$ is zero. For 'modest' non-selfishness

$$\frac{\partial u}{\partial x_1} > \frac{\partial u}{\partial x_2} > 0.$$

CHAPTER 12

1. For a useful discussion of this point see Archibald and Donaldson (1975). They refer to Rosemary Carter's MA thesis, *A Justification of Paternalism* (University of British Columbia, 1973).

2. See the CSO estimates regularly presented in *Economic Trends*. The reader is warned that their interpretation is a matter of some controversy. They almost certainly overstate the importance of in-kind redistribution to lower income groups as benefits from educational and health service spending are allocated (roughly) on a *per capita* basis. Benefits of a more strictly public good nature are properly excluded, e.g., defence, the law, public parks, etc. Generally speaking, the *ratio* of benefits in kind to total benefits *increases* with family size and with income (the reason for this latter effect being the decreased importance of cash transfers as income rises).

3. Let y be *numéaire* and let each pay the same price (unity) for it. Then the price of x to the two individuals A and B, where A has some concern for B's consumption of x, is given by (Green, 1971, pp. 290–2):

$$\frac{P_x^{\text{A}}}{P_x^{\text{B}}} = \frac{1}{1 - \dfrac{\partial u_\text{A}/\partial x_\text{B}}{\partial u_\text{A}/\partial x_\text{A}}}$$

Let there be 'classes' $1, \ldots i, j \ldots m$. The utility of an individual in class i is taken to depend on his own goods and upon the consumption of good x by a typical member of class j.

The subsidised price of x to class j is $p(1 - s_j)$ where s_j is the rate of subsidy.

The demand for x by an individual in j is a function of its price:

$$x_j = x_j[p(1 - s_j)].$$

There are n_i individuals in class i and n_j in class j. Class i bears α_i of its proportionate share of subsidy cost. Now write the Lagrangean

$$V = u_i\{x_i, y_i; x_1 \cdots x_j \cdots x_m\} - \lambda \left\{ m_i - px_i - y_i - \frac{\alpha_i}{n_i} \sum_{j \neq i} n_j s_j px_j[p(1 - s_j)] \right\},$$

then,

$$\frac{\partial V}{\partial x_i} = \frac{\partial u_i}{\partial x_i} + \lambda p = 0 \qquad (12.1)$$

$$\frac{\partial V}{\partial y_i} = \frac{\partial u_i}{\partial y_i} + \lambda = 0 \qquad (12.2)$$

$$\frac{\partial V}{\partial x_j} = \frac{\partial u_i}{\partial x_j} + \lambda \alpha_i n_{ji} s_j p = 0 \qquad (12.3)$$

where

$$n_{ji} = \frac{n_j}{n_i},$$

$$\frac{\partial V}{\partial s_j} = \lambda \alpha_i n_{ji} p \left[s_j \left(-p \frac{\partial x_i}{\partial p} \right) + x_j \right] = 0 \qquad (12.4)$$

From (12.1) and (12.3),

$$s_j = \frac{u_{ij}}{n_{ji}} \alpha_i \qquad (12.5)$$

where

$$u_{ij} = \frac{\partial u_i}{\partial x_j}$$

and from (12.4),

$$s_j = \frac{1}{e_j}. \qquad (12.6)$$

So, in equilibrium,

$$u_{ij} = \frac{\alpha_i n_{ji}}{e_j}. \qquad (12.7)$$

In the two-person case equation (12.5) has $\alpha_i n_j = 1$ so it coincides with Green's condition as:

$$\frac{p_i}{(1 - s_j)_i} \qquad \frac{1}{1 - u_{ij}}$$

The equilibrium condition (12.7) may be illustrated in terms of Figure 12.5 on the assumption that the demand curve for x has *decreasing elasticity* along its length.

5. A recent survey of the evidence, based largely upon Ruth Lister's work, was undertaken by the National Consumer Council in *Means Tested Benefits* (1976) (Table 12.1).

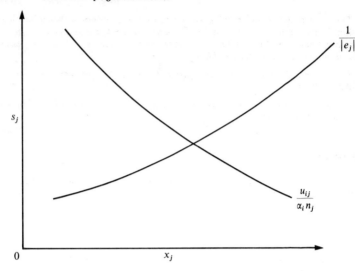

FIGURE 12.5   *Equilibrium condition for s_j*

TABLE 12.1   *Take-up rates*

Type	National %	Local %
Student grants	100	
Remission of direct grant school fees	95	
Free school meals	60	(64–78)
Family income supplement	75	(0–40)
Supplementary benefit	75	(48)
Rent rebates	70–75	(48–64)
Rent allowances (unfurnished)	30–35⎫	
Rent allowances (furnished)	10 ⎭	(0–25)
Milk and vitamins		(0–52)
Prescription charges		(4–48)
Dental, optical charges		(6–66)

6. A major advantage of this method is that the derivation of the efficient frontier is a purely technical operation and, although there are practical difficulties, it is possible to measure the marginal cost of raising take-up rates. Note in particular that some means tests will fail to generate more than a low rate of take-up (say, 30 per cent) even when a great deal of money is spent on publicity. Others (e.g. school meals) have a relatively high rate of take-up and quite a good information supply system via notes to parents. Derivation of these frontiers is an essential first step in a serious economic analysis of universal versus selective benefits. Altruistic (or other) preferences enter only at a later stage.

7. The free transfer is the analogue to competitive equilibrium. Other allocations within the core, reflecting different distributions of good *Y*, are also possible. But if Pareto-optimality is to be retained *X* must remain 'free' up to the consensus allocation once the distribution of Y is determined.

8. The notion of need and its relationship to demand is usefully discussed in Williams (1974).

9. For a review of recent work on equivalence scales and their relationship to demand analysis see Muellbauer (1977).

CHAPTER 13

1. Let *B** be the blood requirement, *n* the number of donors and π_i the probability that donor *i* will give blood this year. The possibility of someone being able to obtain blood is then

$$\pi = \frac{\sum_i^n \pi_i}{B^*}.$$

The non-Kantian potential donor sees $d\pi/d\pi_i$ as being zero in a large community of donors (though not in a small one), whereas the Kantian potential donor sees it as unity.

2. For an early comment on the *Price of Blood* paper see Collard (1968) pp. 12–13. The shortage thesis was questioned and some difficulties of a dual system considered.

3. See papers by D. B. Johnson and M. J. Ireland in *The Economics of Giving.* (Institute of Economic Affairs, 1973). Ireland cites Illinois as a state that enforces legal liability and argues that this will lead to improved quality. Johnson also claims, rather oddly, that the UK system is 'regressive' and makes captious remarks about Titmuss's 'unaudited questionnaires'.

4. It is almost impossible to obtain good evidence about this though Japan is frequently cited. An embarrassingly thin survey of a class of students is reported by Ireland and Koch (Institute of Economic Affairs, 1973): the number of individuals reporting a 'willingness' to give blood fell when the supposed price was raised from 0 to \$1 per pint but rose at \$5 and over. A show of hands at a conference of health economists at Bath in 1976 revealed that about half of current voluntary donors present would withdraw if the price were raised from 0 to £5.

5. See *The Guardian* (17 June 1975).

CHAPTER 14

1. For a brief report of the Centre's activities see the *Times Higher Educational Supplement* (24 January 1976). A full bibliography is published by the Centre but see, in particular, Quarantelli and Dynes (1976).

2. On this point and for a detailed analysis of particular disasters see Dacy and Kunreuther (1969). The authors attempt a stock-flow analysis of the price phenomenon but assume short run changes in utility functions (pp. 66–70).

3. See Nightingale (1973) for a discussion of differential response to appeals.

4. During the drought of 1976 water authorities reported voluntary reductions of well over 30 per cent.

5. For an early discussion of this and other points related to sympathy and antipathy see Tonnies (1887).

6. It should be remembered, however, that Banfield's book, although interesting, was based on impressionistic evidence only.

CHAPTER 15

1. More recently Solow, taking up Ramsey's point, has written:

> it does seem fundamentally implausible that there should be any *ex-post* right about the weight that is actually given to those who will not live for another 1,000 years. We have actually done quite well at the hands of *our* ancestors. Given how poor they were and how rich we are, they might properly have saved less and consumed more. [Solow, (1974b)]

2. One would maximise an expression of the following type:

$$W = \sum_{T=t}^{\infty} U(c_T)\, \delta^{-(T-t)} \quad \text{where} \quad \delta > 1.$$

Future utilities are discounted by the time preference rate $\delta - 1$. The rest of the notation is standard.

3. The preferences of the present generation are given by:

$$U = u(c_0) + \alpha\, \delta u(c_1) + \alpha^2\, \delta u(c_2) + \cdots$$

where $0 < \delta < 1$ and $0 < \alpha < 1$. α representing the discount factor and δu the degree of altruism. Perfect altruism occurs where $\delta u = 1$.

4. For an interesting paper on this point see Nash (1973), where the inappropriateness of discounting is discussed, particularly in respect of longer-term irreversible effects of investment decisions. However he does not offer a solution apart from that of keeping options open.

5. The present value of a unit stream over the life of the current generation is:

$$\sum_{t=0}^{t=T} \frac{1}{(1+i)^t} = y.$$

Repeating the exercise for each generation with a decreasing set of altruistic weights v, v^2 etc., the present value becomes:

$$y + vy + v^2 y \text{ etc.,}$$

or

$$\frac{y}{1-v}.$$

This exceeds the present value of the infinite unit stream whenever

$$\frac{y}{1-v} > \frac{1}{i}.$$

Now let r be the ratio of y to $1/i$. (In the example given in the text $r = 0.8$). Then the required condition becomes

$$\frac{r}{1-v} > 1.$$

Clearly r (in this simple case) depends solely on T, the horizon of the present generation.

6. Let there be two time periods such that consumption in period 2 is given by:

$$C_2 = (1 - s)\lambda K_1 s,$$

where s is the *common* proportion of gross income saved and K_1 is initial capital that may be saved or consumed. Let generation 1 attach a weight of v to the consumption of the next generation and $(1 - v)$ to its own. Then it wishes to maximise:

$$W = (1 - v)C_1 + vC_2.$$

After substituting, the welfare-maximising proportion s is found to be

$$s = \frac{v(1 + \lambda) - 1}{2v\lambda}.$$

Now consider a target generation n years ahead, whose consumption is given by:

$$C_{t+n} = (1 - s)\lambda^n s^n K_t.$$

If generation 1 is concerned only with generation n's welfare and not at all with its own, the welfare-maximising savings ratio would be:

$$s = \frac{n}{n + 1},$$

corresponding to the peaks in Figure 15.1.

7. The Kay–Mirrlees formula is:

$$p_t = c_x(x_t, t) + Qe^{it}$$

where p_t is expected price of resource at t, c_x is expected exploitation costs at t, x is the rate at which resources are then extracted, Q is the value to the owner of the resource (per unit) at time zero not yet extracted, and i is the interest rate.

8. If any weight at all is attached to the next generation's pay-off alpha will be the less attractive outcome as long as

$$9(1 - v) < 1000 v$$

where v is the altruistic weight.

9. In private equilibrium the gain from private saving equals 0 at the margin, i.e.,

$$[\lambda v + (1 - \lambda)w]k - 1 = 0 \qquad (15.3)$$

where λ is the share of future output going to my heirs. Assuming the gains from social saving to be distributed on a *per capita* basis, each individual will favour a social savings contract so long as:

$$k[v + (N - 1)w] > 1 + (N - 1)u. \qquad (15.4)$$

In other words, the gain to my heirs plus the gain to everybody else's heirs must exceed the current consumption losses of me and my contemporaries (suitably weighted).

Putting $k = 1/v$, (15.2) reduces to,

$$\frac{1}{v} > \frac{u}{w},\qquad (15.5)$$

the condition given in the text.

Now, setting the thing out as a simple game:

		Weight	No.	Contemporaries Social saving	Contemporaries Private saving
me		1	1	-1	-1
		u	$N-1$	-1	0
	Social saving	v	1	k	$\dfrac{k}{N}$
		w	$N-1$	k	$\dfrac{k}{N}$
		1	1	0	
		u	$N-1$	-1	
	Private saving	v	1	$\dfrac{N-1}{N}k$	$[\lambda v + (1-\lambda)w]k - 1 = 0$
		w	$N-1$	$\dfrac{N-1}{N}k$	
		1	1	-1	-1
		u	$N-1$	0	0
	Differences	v	1	$\dfrac{k}{N}$	$\dfrac{k}{N}$
		w	$N-1$	$\dfrac{k}{N}$	$\dfrac{k}{N}$

CHAPTER 16

1. Krebs also reports work on the personality traits of benefactors:

College-age male altruists tend to be socially oriented; they are free from neuroticism, and tend to think they control their fates. They are well-liked by

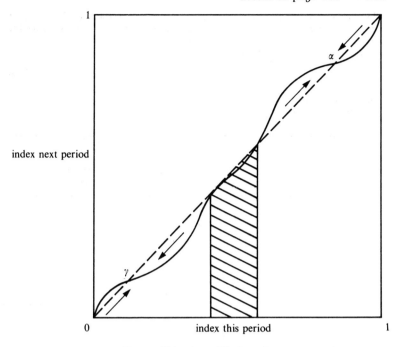

FIGURE 16.1   *A possible dynamics*

others, slightly on the conservative side, and may tend to be authoritarian. Although they are not more liable to be in the social sciences than business or engineering, they are more likely to train for the YMCA!

See also Friedrichs (1960) for an interesting list of commonly held personality hypotheses that were *not* supported.

2. See Muellbauer (1977), where equivalence scales are derived for families by age and number of children. No allowances were made for the more general sorts of 'need' mentioned in the text, though the analysis could clearly be extended to include more household characteristics.

3. Figure 16.1 is offered very tentatively and in the obscurity of a note, for it simplifies a complex social process and has a thin empirical base. But it is at least possible that something of the sort obtains. The index should be regarded as of 'revealed altruism' rather than of any inherent characteristic. Outside a stable central range a contagion process is assumed to take place which moves society either to a high (alpha) or a low (gamma) degree of co-operation. Extremely high and low indices are shown as unstable.

4. See Hobsbawm (1975). He considers the relative neglect of fraternity, 'which only emerged temporarily into daylight as an independent political slogan for a few decades after the French revolution. And yet . . . obstinately refused to disappear from sight'.

Only Cabet pinned his faith entirely on fraternity.

References and Bibliography

Most, though not all, of the following works used in the preparation of this book are referred to in the text. These abbreviations are used:

AER	*American Economic Review*
EJ	*Economic Journal*
JET	*Journal of Economic Theory*
JLE	*Journal of Law and Economics*
JPE	*Journal of Political Economy*
J Pub Ec	*Journal of Public Economics*
QJE	*Quarterly Journal of Economics*
R Ec Stats	*Review of Economics and Statistics*
R Ec Stud	*Review of Economic Studies*

G. C. ABBOTT 'Economic Aid as a Unilateral Transfer of Resources' *JPE* 78 (1970) pp. 1213–27.

L. DE ALESSI 'A Utility Analysis of Post-Disaster Cooperation' *Papers in Non-Market Decision Making* 3 (Fall 1967) pp. 85–90.

————— 'Toward an Analysis of Post-Disaster Cooperation' *AER* (March 1975) pp. 127–38.

A. ARBLASTER and S. LUKES (eds.) *The Good Society*, Methuen (1971).

G. C. ARCHIBALD and D. DONALDSON *Paternalism and Prices* Discussion Paper 75–18, Department of Economics, University of British Columbia (July 1975).

————— 'Non-Paternalism and the Basic Theorems of Welfare Economics' *Canadian Journal of Economics* IX (August, 1976) pp. 492–507.

ARISTOTLE, *Nichomachean Ethics*.

A. H. G. ARMYTAGE *Heavens Below: Utopian Experiments in England*, Routledge & Kegan Paul (1961).

K. J. ARROW *Social Choice and Individual Values*, Wiley (1951 reprinted 1963).

————— 'Uncertainty and Medical Care' in *Essays in the Theory of Risk Bearing*, North Holland (1971). Also in *AER* 53, (1963) pp. 941–73.

————— 'The Economics of Moral Hazard' *AER* 58 (1968) pp. 537–9.

————— 'Rawls's Principle of Just Saving' *Swedish Journal of Economics* (1973) pp. 323–35.

————— 'Gifts and Exchanges' *Philosophy and Public Affairs* 1 (1974) pp. 343–62. Reprinted in Phelps (1975).

————— and F. H. HAHN *General Competitive Analysis*, Holden Day (1971).

205

A. B. ATKINSON 'How Progressive Should Income Tax Be?' in M. Parkin (ed.) *Essays on Modern Economics*, Longman (1973). Reprinted in Phelps (1973).

———————— and J. E. STIGLITZ 'The Design of Tax Structure: Direct versus Indirect Taxation' *J Pub Ec* 6 (1976) pp. 55–75.

E. C. BANFIELD *The Moral Basis of a Backward Society*, Free Press (1958).

———————— *The Unheavenly City*, Little Brown (1968).

Z. BAUMAN *Socialism: The Active Utopia*, Allen & Unwin (1976).

W. J. BAUMOL, review article of Samuelson's *Foundations*, *Economica* (1949) pp. 159–68.

———————— 'On Taxation and the Control of Subsidies' *AER* 62, (1972) pp. 307–22.

———————— 'Business Responsibility and Economic Behavior' in Phelps (1975a) pp. 45–56.

———————— and W. E. OATES *The Theory of Environmental Policy*, Prentice-Hall (1975).

G. S. BECKER 'Altruism, Egoism and Genetic Fitness: Economics and Sociobiology' *Journal of Economic Literature* 14 (1976) pp. 817–26.

———————— 'A Theory of Social Interaction' *JPE* 82 (1974) pp. 1068–93.

M. J. BECKMAN 'A Note on the Optimal Rates of Resource Depletion' *R Ec Stud* Symposium (1974) pp. 121–2.

R. N. BELLAH *Emile Durkhein on Morality and Society*, University of Chicago Press (1973).

J. BENTHAM *Principles of Morals and Legislation* (1789), edited by J. H. Burns and H. L. A. Hart, London University (1970).

T. BERGSTROM 'A "Scandanavian Consensus" Solution for Efficient Income Distribution Among Non-Malevolent Consumers' *JET* 2 (1970) pp. 383–98.

R. J. BIRRELL 'The Centralised Control of the Communes in the Post "Great Leap Forward" Period' in A. D. Barnett (ed.) *Chinese Communist Politics in Action* Washington University (1969).

C. BLACKORBY, D. NISSEN, D. PRIMONT and R. R. RUSSELL 'Consistent Intertemporal Decision Making' *R Ec Stud* XL (1973) pp. 239–48.

P. M. BLAU *Exchange and Power in Social Life*, Wiley (1964).

S. A. BOORMAN and P. R. LEVITT 'A Frequency-Dependent Natural Selection Model for the Evolution of Social Cooperation Networks' *Proc Nat Acad of Sciences USA* 70 (1973) pp. 187–9.

GENERAL BOOTH *In Darkest England and the Way Out* (1890), cited by Armytage (1961).

A. BORGLIN 'Price Characteristics of Stable Allocations in Exchange Economies with Externalities' *JET* 6 (1973) pp. 483–94.

M. J. BOSKIN and M. S. FELDSTEIN *Effects of the Charitable Deduction on Contributions by Low Income and Middle Income Households: Evidence from the National Survey of Philanthropy* Discussion Paper 427, Harvard Institute of Economic Research (July 1975).

K. E. BOULDING 'Notes on a Theory of Philanthropy' in Dickinson (1962).

———————— *The Economy of Love and Fear: A Preface to Grants Economics*, Wadsworth (1973).

G. BRENNAN 'Pareto-optimal Redistribution: the Case of Malice and Envy' *J Pub Ec* 2 (1973) pp. 173–83.

R. BRIFFAULT *The Mothers: A Study of the Origins of Sentiments and Institutions*, vol. III, Allen & Unwin (1927).

S. BRITTAN *Capitalism and the Permissive Society*, Macmillan (1973).

J. BROOME *An Important Theorem on the Income Tax* Discussion Paper 18, Department of Economics, Birkbeck College, London (1974).

J. A. C. BROWN *Freud and the Post Freudians*, Penguin (1961).

E. A. BRUBAKER 'Free Ride, Free Revaluation or Golden Rule? *JLE* XVIII (1975) pp. 147–61.

J. H. BRYAN and P. LONDON, 'Altruistic Behaviour by Children' *Psychological Bulletin* 73 (1970) pp. 200–11.

J. M. BUCHANAN 'What Kind of Redistribution Do We Want?' *Economica* (1968) pp. 185–90.

————— *The Limits of Liberty* Chicago University Press (1974).

————— 'The Samaritan's Dilemma' in Phelps (1975) pp. 71–85.

————— 'Taxation in Fiscal Exchange' *J. Pub Ec* 6 (1976a) pp. 17–29.

————— 'The Rawlsian Difference Principle' *Kyklos* 29 (1976b) Fasc. 1, pp. 5–25.

————— and W. C. BUSH 'Political Constraints on Contractual Redistribution' *AER* (Papers and Proceedings) (May 1974), pp. 153–7.

————— and G. TULLOCK, *The Calculus of Consent*, University of Michigan Press (1962).

W. C. BUSH and L. S. MAYER 'Some Implications of Anarchy for the Distribution of Property' *JET* 8 (1974) pp. 401–12.

BISHOP BUTLER *Sermons and Dissertations Upon Virtue* (1726); reprinted in Selby-Bigge (1897).

————— *Sermons Upon Human Nature* (1729), (ed. W. Whewell, 1865).

T. D. CAMPBELL *Adam Smith's Science of Morals*, Allen & Unwin (1971).

————— 'Scientific Explanation and Ethical Justification in *Moral Sentiments*' in Skinner and Wilson (1975) pp. 68–81.

T. N. CARVER *Essays in Social Justice*, Harvard University Press (1915).

J. CHARVET *The Social Problem in the Philosophy of Rousseau*, Cambridge University Press (1974).

R. H. COASE 'Adam Smith's View of Man' *JLE* 78 (1976) pp. 529–46.

J. COHN *The Conscience of the Corporation: Business and Urban Affairs 1969–70* Johns Hopkins (1971).

D. A. COLLARD *The New Right: A Critique*, Fabian Society (1968).

————— 'The Case for Universal Benefits' in D. Bull (ed.) *Family Poverty*, Duckworth (1971) pp. 37–43.

————— 'Edgeworth's Propositions on Altruism' *EJ* (1975) pp. 355–60.

————— review of A. K. Sen *On Economic Inequality* in *EJ* (1974) pp. 398–9.

A. COMTE *Cours de Philosophie Positive* (1830–42), trans. S. ANDRESKI in *The Essential Comte* Croom Helm (1974).

J. CROPSEY 'Adam Smith and Political Philosophy' in Skinner and Wilson (1975) pp. 132–53.

A. J. CULYER 'Medical Care and the Economics of Giving' *Economica* (1971a) pp. 295–303.

————— 'The Nature of the Commodity "Health Care" and its Efficient Allocation' *Oxford Economic Papers* 23 (1971b) pp. 189–211.

————— *The Economics of Social Policy*, Martin Robertson (1973).

————— and M. COOPER *The Price of Blood*, Institute of Economic Affairs (1968).

D. C. DACY and H. KUNREUTHER *The Economics of Natural Disasters*, Free Press (1969).

G. DALY and F. GIERTZ 'Welfare Economics and Welfare Reform' *AER* 62 (1972) pp. 131–8.

208 References and Bibliography

————— 'Transfers and Pareto Optimality' *J. Pub Ec* 5 (1976) pp. 176–82.
T. E. DANIEL 'A Revised Concept of Distributional Equity' *JET* 11 (1975) pp. 94–109.
A. L. DANIELSON 'Interdependent Utilities, Charity and Pareto-Optimality: A Comment' *QJE* LXXIV (1975) pp. 477–81.
DANTE *The Divine Comedy;* (trans. by D. L. Sayers), Penguin (1949).
A. DASGUPTA *Conditions of Pareto-Optimality with Consumption Externalities in Goods and Leisure* Discussion Paper 23/75, Department of Economics, La Trobe, Australia (1975).
P. DUSGUPTA 'On Some Alternative Criteria for Justice Between Generations' *J Pub Ec* 3 (1974) pp. 405–23.
————— and G. HEAL 'The Optimal Depletion of Exhaustible Resources' *R Ec Stud* Symposium (1974) pp. 3–28.
R. DAWKINS *The Selfish Gene*, Oxford University Press (1976).

A. S. DEATON *Equity, Efficiency and the Structure of Indirect Taxation* Discussion Paper 50–76, Department of Economics, University of Bristol (1976).
M. DEUTSCH 'Trust and Suspicion' *Journal of Confflict Resolution* II (1958) pp. 265–79.
P. A. DIAMOND and J. A. MIRRLEES 'Optimal Taxation and Public Production I and II' *AER* (1971) pp. 8–27, 261–78.
————— 'Aggregate Production with Consumption Externalities' *QJE* LXXXVII (1973) pp. 1–24.
F. G. DICKINSON 'Philanthropy and Public Policy' *NBER* (1962).
————— 'The Changing Position of Philanthropy in the American Economy' *NBER* Occasional Paper 110 (1970).
A. DOWNS *An Economic Theory of Democracy*, Harper & Row (1951).
C. M. DOUTY 'Disasters and Charity: Some Aspects of Cooperative Economic Behaviour' *AER* (1972) pp. 580–90; reprinted in L. Wagner and N. Baltazzis (eds.) *Readings in Applied Microeconomics*, Oxford University Press for Open University (1973).
L. DUDLEY and C. MONTMARQUETTE *Foreign Aid as an Indirectly Consumed Public Good* Cahier 7401, Department des Sciences Economiques, Université de Montreal (January 1974).
J. S. DUESENBERRY *Income, Saving and the Theory of Consumer Behavior*, Harvard University Press (1949).
G. DUNCAN *Marx and Mill: Two Views of Social Conflict and Social Harmony*, Cambridge University Press (1973).

Economic Trends No. 259, HMSO (May 1975).
F. Y. EDGEWORTH *Mathematical Psychics* (1881); London School of Economics reprint (1932).
————— *The Pure Theory of Taxation*, Collected Economic Papers, (1897); reprinted in Phelps (1973).
J. R. EISER 'Cooperation and Conflict between Individuals (1975); to appear in H. Tajfel and C. Fraser (eds.) *Introducing Social Psychology*, Penguin (forthcoming).
T. S. ELIOT *The Idea of a Christian Society*, Faber (1939).
G. ELIOT *Adam Bede* (1859).

S. FABRICANT 'An Economist's View of Philanthropy' in F. G. Dickson (ed). *Philanthropy and Public Policy*, NBER (1962).
Family Expenditure, HMSO (1974).
M. FELDSTEIN *Charitable Bequests, Estate Taxation and Intergenerational Wealth Transfers* Discussion Paper 413, Harvard Institute of Economic Research (1975a).

——————— 'The Income Tax and Charitable Contributions: Pt II, The Impact on Religious, Educational and Other Organisations' *National Tax Journal* XXVIII (1975b) pp. 209–26.

——————— 'On the Theory of Tax Reform' *J Pub Ec* 6 (1976) pp. 77–104.

——————— and C. CLOTFELTER *Tax Incentives and Charitable Contributions in the United States: A Microeconomic Analysis* Discussion Paper 381, Harvard Institute of Economic Research (1974).

——————— and A. TAYLOR *The Income Tax and Charitable Contributions: Estimates and Simulations with the Treasury Tax Files* Discussion Paper 409, Harvard Institute of Economic Research (1975).

B. FINE *The Prisoner's Dilemma and Moral Philosophy* Discussion Paper 10, Birkbeck College, London (November 1973).

——————— *Interdependent Preferences and Liberalism in a Paretian Society* Discussion Paper 15, Birkbeck College, London (January 1974).

L. FOLDES 'Income Redistribution in Money and in Kind' *Economica* n.s. XXXIV (1967) pp. 30–41.

D. K. FOLEY 'Resource Allocation and the Public Sector' *Yale Economic Essays* 7 (1967) pp. 45–98.

——————— 'Lindahl's Solution and the Core of an Economy with Public Goods' *Econometrica* 38 (1970).

J. FOWLES *The Aristos* (revised ed.), Pan Books (1968).

A. FREUD *The Ego and the Mechanisms of Defence*, Hogarth Press (1937).

J. W. FRIEDMAN 'A Non-Cooperative Equilibrium for Supergames' *R Ec Stud* XXXVIII (1971) pp. 1–12.

R. W. FRIEDRICHS 'Alter versus Ego: An Exploratory Assessment of Altruism' *American Sociological Review* 25 (1960) pp. 496–508.

H. FRISCH 'Die Contraktkurve bei Interdependenzen im Konsum' *Kyklos* XXIV (1971) pp. 644–59.

N. FROLICH 'Self-Interest or Altruism, What Difference?' *Journal of Conflict Resolution* 18 (1974) pp. 55–73.

G. M. VON FURSTENBERG and D. C. MUELLER 'The Pareto-optimal Approach to Income Redistribution: A Fiscal Application' *AER* 61 (1971) pp. 628–37.

W. GODWIN *Enquiry Concerning Political Justice* (1793), ed. K. C. Carter, Oxford University Press (1971).

R. S. GOLDFARB 'Pareto-optimal Redistribution: Comment' *AER* 60, (1970) pp. 994–96.

MAXIM GORKY *The Life of a Useless Man;* trans. by M. Budberg, Penguin (1971).

A. W. GOULDNER 'The Norm of Reciprocity: A Preliminary Statement' *American Sociological Review* 25 (1960) pp. 161–78.

J. V. DE GRAAF *Theoretical Welfare Economics*, Cambridge University Press (1957).

H. A. J. GREEN *Consumer Theory*, Penguin (1971).

J. GREEN and E. SHESHINSKI 'Direct versus Indirect Remedies for Externalities' *JPE* 84 (1976) pp. 797–808.

P. GROUT 'A Rawlsian Intertemporal Consumption Rule' *R Ec Stud* XLIV (1977) pp. 377–46.

T. GROVES and J. LEDYARD 'Optimal Allocation of Public Goods: A Solution of the Free Rider Problem' *Econometrica* 45 (1977) pp. 783–810.

Guardian Guardian Report (17 May 1975).

P. J. Hammond *Charity: Altruism or Cooperative Egoism?* Department of Economics, University of Essex (1972); also in Phelps (1975).

——————— *Individual Incentive Compatability in Large Economies* Discussion Paper 88, University of Essex (1976).

R. F. HARROD 'Utilitarianism Revised' *Mind* XIV (April 1936) pp. 137–156.

J. C. HARSANYI 'Cardinal Welfare, Individualistic Ethics and Interpersonal Comparisons of Utility' *JPE* (1955); reprinted in Phelps (1973).

F. A. HAYEK *Individualism and the Economic Order*, Routledge & Kegan Paul (1949).

R. A. HINDE *Biological Bases of Human Social Behaviour*, McGraw-Hill (1974).

FRED HIRSCH *The Bagehot Problem* Warwick Economic Research Papers No. 65 (1975).

————— 'The Moral Re-entry' Ch. 4 of working draft of proposed book, (March 1974), subsequently *The Social Limit to Growth*, Routledge & Kegan Paul (1977).

E. J. HOBSBAWM 'Fraternity' *New Society* (27 November 1975).

H. M. HOCHMAN and J. D. RODGERS 'Pareto-optimal Redistribution' *AER* (1969) pp. 542–57.

————— 'Pareto-optimal Redistribution: A Reply' *AER* (1970) pp. 997–1002.

C. HOFFMAN *Work Incentive Practices and Policies in the Peoples Republic of China 1953–65*, State University of New York Press (1967).

S. HOOK (ed.) *Human Values and Economic Policy* New York University Press (1967).

E. M. HOWSE *Saints in Politics*, Allen & Unwin (1952).

D. HUME *Treatise of Human Nature* (1736); reprinted in Selby-Bigge (1897) Vol. 1.

F. HUTCHESON *On the Nature and Conduct of the Passions and Affections* (1725); reprinted in Selby-Bigge (1897) vol. 1.

————— *An Inquiry Concerning Moral Good and Evil* (1725), reprinted in Selby-Bigge (1897) vol. 1.

Institute of Economic Affairs *The Economics of Giving: Essays on the Comparative Economics and Ethics of Giving and Selling, with Applications to Blood* IEA (1973).

Y. ITSUMI 'Distributional Effects of Linear Income Tax Schedules' *R Ec Stud* XLI (1974) pp. 371–81.

D. B. JOHNSON *The Fundamental Economics of the Charity Market* Ph.D. thesis, University of Virginia (1968).

I. KANT *Lectures on Ethics*, Macmurray (1930).

A. S. KAUFMAN 'Wants, Needs and Liberalism' *Inquiry* 14 (1971) pp. 191–212.

J. A. KAY and J. A. MIRRLEES 'The Desirability of Natural Resource Depletion' in Pearce (1975) pp. 140–76.

J. M. KEYNES 'Economic Possibilities for Our Grandchildren' *Nation and Athenaeum* (11 and 18 October 1930); reprinted in *Collected Writings of J. M. Keynes* Vol. IX, Royal Economic Society (1972).

J. KLEINIG 'Good Samaritanism' *Philosophy and Public Affairs* 5 (1976) pp. 382–407.

E. KOHLBERG 'A Model of Economic Growth with Altruism between Generations' *JET* 13 (1976) pp. 1–13.

T. C. KOOPMANS 'Proof for a Case where Discounting Advances the Doomsday' *R Ec Stud* Symposium (1974) pp. 117–120.

S. KORNER 'Rational Choice' *Aristotelian Society Proceedings* supplementary vol. XLVII (1973) pp. 1–17.

D. L. KREBS 'Altruism – An Examination of the Concept and a Review of the Literature' *Psychological Bulletin* 73 (1970) pp. 258–302.

P. KROPOTKIN *Mutal Aid: A Factor of Evolution* (1902); Penguin reprint (1972).

J. V. KRUTILLA and A. C. FISHER *The Economics of Natural Environments*, Johns Hopkins (1975).

T. S. KUHN *The Structure of Scientific Revolutions*, University of Chicago Press (1972).

The Labour Party *Labour Party Manifesto* (October 1974).

J. J. LAFFONT 'Macroeconomic Constraints, Economic Efficiency and Ethics: an Introduction to Kantian Economics' *Economica* 42 (1975) pp. 430–7.

———— and G. LAROQUE 'Effets Externes et Theorie de l'Equilibre Général' *Cahier du Seminaire d'Econometric* 14 (1972) pp. 25–48.

J. R. C. LECOMBER *Economic Growth versus the Environment*, Macmillan (1975).

———— 'The Isolation Paradox' *QJE* (1977) pp. 495–504.

J. O. LEDYARD 'The Relation of Optima and Market Equilibria with Externalities' *JET* 3 (1971) pp. 54–65.

H. LIEBENSTEIN 'Bandwagon, Snob and Veblen Effects in the Theory of Consumers' Demand' *QJE* LXIV (1950) pp. 183–207.

C. M. LINDSAY 'Medical Care and the Economics of Sharing' *Economica* n.s. (1969) pp. 531–7.

D. LYONS *Forms and Limits of Utilitarianism*, Oxford University Press (1965).

J. MADDOX, W. HAMILTON and J. MAYNARD SMITH, two talks reprinted in *Listener*, (22 and 29 July 1976).

B. MANDEVILLE *The Fable of the Bees* (1714); ed. P. Harth, Pelican Classic (1970).

H. G. MANNE and H. C. WALLICH *The Modern Corporation and Social Responsibility* American Enterprise Institute for Public Policy Research, Washington, DC, (1972).

A MARSHALL 'Miscellaneous Notes on Economic Theory' in J. K. Whitaker (ed.) *Early Writings of Alfred Marshall* Vol. 2, Macmillan Royal Economic Society (1975).

———— *Principles of Economics*, Macmillan (1890).

KARL MARX *Economic and Social Manuscripts* (1844) in *Early Writings of Marx*, Pelican ed. (1975).

———— *Critique of the Gotha Programme* (1875), Moscow Foreign Language Publishing House (1959).

M. MAUSS *The Gift* (*Essai sur le don, forme archaique de l'échange*, 1925); trans. I. Cunnison, Cohen & West (1966).

J. E. MEADE 'Mr Lerner on "The Economics of Control"' *EJ* LV, (1945) pp. 47–69.

———— *The Growing Economy, Vol. II: Principles of Political Economy*, Allen & Unwin (1968).

———— *Theory of Economic Externalities: The Control of Environmental Pollution and Similar Social Costs*, Sijthoff-Leiden (1973).

K. MENGER 'An Exact Theory of Social Groups and Relations' *American Journal of Sociology* 43 (1938) pp. 790–8.

P. A. MEYER and J. J. SHIPLEY 'Pareto-optimal Redistribution: A Comment' *AER* 60 (1970) pp. 988–90.

J. S. MILL *Principles of Political Economy*, Parker (1848).

———— *Utilitarianism*, (1861); Dent (1972).

———— *Auguste Comte and Positivism*, Trübner (1865).

J. A. MIRRLEES 'An Exploration in the Theory of Optimum Income Taxation' *R Ec Stud* XXXVIII (1971) pp. 175–208.

———— *Optimal Tax Theory: A Synthesis* Working Paper 176, Massachusetts Institute of Technology (1976).

E. J. MISHAN 'A Survey of Welfare Economics' *EJ* (1960) pp. 197–265.

———— 'Redistribution in Money and in Kind: Some Notes' *Economica*, (1968) pp. 191–193.

———— 'The Futility of Pareto-Efficient Distribution' *AER* (1972) pp. 971–6.

H. MIZUTA 'Moral Philosophy and Civil Society' in Skinner and Wilson, (1975) pp. 114–31.

G. E. MOORE *Principia Ethica*, Cambridge University Press (1903).

THOMAS MORE *Utopia* (1516); Penguin Classic (1965).

O. MORGENSTERN 'Demand Theory Reconsidered' *QJE* (1948) pp. 165–201.

J. MOYLE and D. J. REID 'Private Non-profit-making Bodies' *Economic Trends* No. 259 (1975) p. 83.

J. MUELLBAUER 'Testing the Barten Model of Household Composition Effects and the Cost of Children' *EJ* (1977) pp. 460–87.

R. A. MUSGRAVE 'Pareto Optimal Redistribution: Comment' *AER* 60 (1970) pp. 991–3.

G. MYRDAL *The Challenge of World Poverty*, Allen Lane (1970).

A. L. MACFIE *The Individual in Society* ('Papers on Adam Smith'), Allen & Unwin (1967).

R. N. MCKEAN 'Economics of Trust, Altruism and Corporate Responsibility' in Phelps (1975) pp. 29–44.

E. F. MCLENNAN '"Comment on Buchanan"' in Phelps (1975) pp. 133–9.

L. W. MCKENZIE 'Competitive Equilibrium with Dependent Consumer Preferences in H. A. Antoziewicz (ed.) *Proceedings of the Second Symposium in Linear Programming*, Washington National Bureau of Standards (1955) pp. 277–94.

T. NAGEL *The Possibility of Altruism*, Oxford University Press (1970).

———————— 'Comment' in Phelps (1975) pp. 63–7.

A. C. NASH 'Future Generations and the Social Rate of Discount', *Environment and Planning* Vol. 5 (1973) pp. 611–17.

National Consumer Council *Means Tested Benefits*, Discussion Paper No. 3 (Jan. 1976).

National Income and Expenditure, 1965–75.

P. A. NEHER 'Democratic Exploitation of a Replenishable Resource' *J Pub Ec* 5 (1976) pp. 361–71.

O. NELL *Acting on Principle: An Essay in Kantian Ethics*, Columbia University Press (1975).

YEW-KWANG NG 'Income Distribution as a Public Good: The Paradox of Redistribution and the Paradox of Universal Externality' *Public Finance* XXVIII (1973) pp. 1–10.

D. NICHOLS, E. SMOLENSKY, and T. TIDEMAN 'Discrimination by Waiting Time in Merit Goods' *AER* (1971) pp. 312–23.

B. NIGHTINGALE *Charities*, Allen Lane (1973).

H. NIKAIDO 'The Core of a Large Economy with Public Expenditures' *Zeitschrift Für Nationalokonomie* 36 (1976) pp. 73–84.

R. NOZICK 'Distributive Justice' *Philosophy and Public Affairs* 3, (1973–4) pp. 45–126.

———————— *Anarchy, State and Utopia*, Oxford University Press (1974).

J. NYERERE *Freedom and Socialism: A Selection from Writings and Speeches*, Oxford University Press (1968).

W. E. OATES *Fiscal Federalism*, Harcourt Brace (1972).

D. J. OBORNE *Aspects of Blood Donor Motivation* ref. HR 2863, Social Science Research Council, (1975).

E. O. OLSEN 'A Normative Theory of Transfers' *Public Choice* (1969) pp. 39–58.

———————— 'Some Theorems in the Theory of Efficient Transfers' *JPE* LXXIX, (1971a) pp. 168–76.

———————— 'Subsidised Housing in a Competitive Market: Reply' *AER* 6, (1971b) pp. 220–4.

M. OLSON JR *The Logic of Collective Action*, Harvard University Press (1965).

L. L. ORR 'Income Transfers as a Public Good: An Application to AFDC' (Aid to Families with Dependant Children) *AER* (1976) pp. 359–71.
H. OSANA 'Externalities and the Basic Theorems of Welfare Economics' *JET* 4, (1972) pp. 401–44.
————— 'On the Boundedness of an Economy with Externalities' *R Ec Stud* XL (1973) pp. 321–31.
R. OWEN *The Book of the New Moral World*, Effingham Wilson (1836).

J. PASSMORE *The Perfectibility of Man*, Duckworth (1970).
P. K. PATTANAIK 'Risk, Impersonality and the Social Welfare Function' *JPE*, (1968); reprinted in Phelps (1973).
————— *Voting and Collective Choice: Some Aspects of the Theory of Group Decision Making*, Oxford University Press (1971).
M. V. PAULY 'Efficiency in the Provision of Consumption Subsidies' *Kyklos* XXIII (1970) pp. 33–57.
————— 'Income Redistribution as a Local Public Good' *JPE* 2 (1973) pp. 35–58.
E. A. PAZNER and D. SCHMEIDER 'Social Contract Theory and Ordinal Distributive Equity' *J Pub Ec* 5 (1976) pp. 261–8.
D. W. PEARCE and J. ROSE (eds.) *The Economics of Natural Resource Depletion*, Macmillan (1975).
I. F. PEARCE 'Resource Conservation and the Market Mechanism' in Pearce and Rose (eds.) (1975) pp. 191–203.
R. B. PERRY *General Theory of Value*, Longmans (1926).
M. PESTON *Public Goods and the Public Sector*, Macmillan (1972).
E. S. PHELPS (ed.) *Economic Justice*, Penguin (1973).
————— (ed.) *Altruism, Morality and Economic Theory*, Russell Sage Foundation (1975).
————— 'The Indeterminacy of Game Equilibrium Growth in the Absence of an Ethic' in Phelps (1975) pp. 87–102.
————— and R. A. POLLACK 'On Second Best National Saving and Game Equilibrium Growth' *R Ec Stud* XXXV (1968) pp. 185–99.
J. PLAMENATZ *Karl Marx's Philosophy of Man*, Clarendon Press (1975).
A. C. PIGOU *Economics of Welfare*, Macmillan (1920).
A. M. POLINSKY 'Shortsightedness and Non-marginal Pareto Optimal Redistribution' *AER* 61 (1971) pp. 972–9.
R. POLLACK 'Interdependent Preferences' *AER* (June 1976) pp. 309–20.
P. J. PROUDHON *What is Property?* (1840); Dover (1970).

E. L. QUARANTELLI and R. R. DYNES 'Community Conflict: Its Absence and Its Presence in Natural Disasters' *Mass Emergencies* 1 (1976) pp. 139–52.

F. P. RAMSEY 'A Mathematical Theory of Saving' *EJ* (1928) pp. 543–59.
D. D. RAPHAEL 'The Impartial Spectator' from Skinner and Wilson (1975) pp. 83–99.
A. RAPOPORT *Fights, Games and Debates* Michigan University Press (1960) pp. 173 *et seq.*
————— (ed.) *Game Theory as a Theory of Conflict Resolution*, Reidel (1974).
————— and A. M. CHAMMAH *Prisoner's Dilemma: A Study in Conflict and Cooperation*, University of Michigan Press (1965).
J. RAWLS *A Theory of Justice*, Clarendon Press (1972).
LORD ROBBINS *Political Economy Past and Present: A Review of Leading Theories of Economic Policy*, Macmillan (1976).

214   *References and Bibliography*

T. A. ROBERTS *The Concept of Benevolence: Aspects of Eighteenth Century Moral Philosophy*, Macmillan (1973).

D. H. ROBERTSON 'What Does the Economist Economize?' from *Economic Commentaries* (1956) pp. 147–54.

J. ROBINSON *Economic Philosophy*, Franklin Watts (1962).

B. RODGERS *Cloak of Charity*, Methuen (1949).

T. ROMER *Individual Welfare, Majority Voting and the Properties of a Linear Income Tax*, Research Report 7402, University of Western Ontario (February 1974). See also *J Pub Ec* 4 (1975) pp. 163–85.

K. W. ROSKAMP 'Pareto-optimal Redistribution, Utility Interdependence and Social Optimum' *Weltwirtschaftliches Archiv* 109 (1973) pp. 337–44.

J. ROTHENBERG *The Measurement of Social Welfare*, Prentice-Hall (1961).

W. G. RUNCIMAN and A. K. SEN 'Games, Justice and the General Will' *Mind* 74, (1965) pp. 554–62.

J. RUSKIN *Selections: 1860–1888* 3rd edn, George Allen (1898).

B. RUSSELL *Sceptical Essays*, Unwin (1935).

P. H. M. RUYS *Public Goods and Decentralisation*, Tilbury University Press (1974).

P. A. SAMUELSON *Economics* 9th edn, McGraw-Hill (1973) p. 505 (in appendix to Ch. 25).

———— 'The Pure Theory of Public Expenditure' *R Ec Stats* 36, (1954) pp. 387–9.

T. SANDLER and V. K. SMITH 'Intertemporal and Intergenerational Efficiency' *Journal of Environmental Economics and Management* 2 (1976) pp. 151–9.

A. A. SAMPSON 'A Model of Optimal Depletion of Renewable Resources' *JET* 12 (1976) pp. 315–24.

J. SAWYER, 'The Altruism Scale: A Measure of Cooperative, Individualistic and Competitive Interpersonal Orientation' *American Journal of Sociology* LXXI (1965–6) pp. 407–16.

L. D. SCHALL 'Interdependent Utilities and Pareto Optimality' *QJE* (1972) pp. 19–24.

———— 'Interdependent Utilities, Charity and Pareto-optimality: A Reply' *QJE* LXXXIV (1975) p. 482.

D. T. SCHEFFMAN 'The Aggregate Excess Demand Correspondence and the Structure of Economies with Externalities' *R Ec Stud* XLII (1975).

E. F. SCHUMACHER *Small is Beautiful*, Abacus (1974).

J. A. SCHUMPETER *Capitalism, Socialism and Democracy*, Allen & Unwin (1943; 1970).

B. SCHWARTZ 'The Social Psychology of the Gift' *American Journal of Sociology* 73 (1967) pp. 1–11.

R. A. SCHWARTZ 'Personal Philanthropic Contributions' *JPE* LXXVIII, (1970) pp. 1264–91.

H. K. SCHNEIDER *Economic Man; The Anthropology of Economics*, Free Press (1974).

R. H. SCOTT 'Avarice, Altruism and Second Party Preferences' *QJE* LXXXVI (1972) pp. 1–18.

L. A. SELBY-BIGGE *British Moralists* 2 vols., Oxford University Press (1897).

A. K. SEN 'Labour Allocation in a Cooperative Enterprise' *R Ec Stud* XXXIII (1966) pp. 361–71.

———— 'Isolation, Assurance and the Social Rate of Discount' *QJE* LXXXI (1967) pp. 112–25.

———— *Collective Choice and Social Welfare*, Oliver & Boyd (1970).

———— *On Economic Inequality* Radcliffe Lectures 1972, Clarendon Press (1973a).

——————— 'Behaviour and the Concept of Preference' *Economica* n.s. XL (1973b) pp. 241–59.

Shaftesbury, Third Earl of *An Inquiry Concerning Virtue* (1669); reprinted in Selby-Bigge (1897) vol. 1.

L. S. Shapley and M. Shubik 'On the Core of an Economic System with Externalities' *AER* 59 (1969) pp. 678–84.

J. Sherburne *John Ruskin, or the Ambiguities of Abundance: A Study in Economic and Social Criticism* Harvard University Press (1972) p. 366.

E. Sheshinski 'The Optimal Linear Income Tax' *R Ec Stud* (1972); Reprinted in Phelps (1973) pp. 409–16.

M. Shubik *Games for Society, Business and War: Towards a Theory of Gaming*, Elsevier, New York (1975).

H. Sidgwick *The Methods of Ethics*, Macmillan (1874).

——————— *Principles of Political Economy*, Macmillan (1963) p. 540.

P. Simmons *Choice and Demand*, Macmillan (1974).

——————— *Intertemporal Fairness as Equality of Opportunity* Working Paper 7518, Institut des Sciences Economiques (December 1975).

P. Singer 'Altruism and Commerce: A Defence of Titmuss against Arrow' *Philosophy and Public Affairs* 2 (1973) pp. 314–20.

A. Skinner and T. Wilson (eds.) *Essays on Adam Smith*, Oxford University Press (1975).

J. J. C. Smart and B. Williams *Utilitarianism, For and Against*, Cambridge University Press (1973).

A. Smith *The Theory of Moral Sentiments*, (1759); reprinted in Selby-Bigge (1897) vol. 1.

——————— *The Wealth of Nations*, (1776); R. H. Campbell and A. S. Skinner (eds.) Oxford University Press (1976).

J. Smyth 'The Prisoners' Dilemma II' *Mind* 81 (1972) pp. 427–31.

Social Audit Vol. 3 (1973–4).

R. M. Solow 'Blood and Thunder' *Yale Law Journal* 80 (1971) p. 170.

——————— 'The Economics of Resources or the Resources of Economics' Richard T. Ely Lecture, *AER* (Papers and Proceedings) (1974a).

——————— 'Intergenerational Equity and Exhaustible Resources' *R Ec Stud* Symposium (1974b) pp. 29–45.

H. Spencer *Principles of Ethics*, Williams and Norgate (1904).

D. Starrett 'A Note on Externalities and the Core' *Econometrica* 41 (1973) pp. 179–83.

G. Strotz 'Myopia and Inconsistency in Dynamic Utility Maximisation' *R Ec Stud* XXIII (1955–6) pp. 165–80.

P. Suppes 'Some Formal Models of Grading Principles' *Synthese* 16 (1966) pp. 284–306.

R. H. Tawney *Equality*, Allen & Unwin (1931); 1964 edn with introduction by R. M. Titmuss.

L. G. Telser *Competition, Collusion and Game Theory*, Macmillan (1971).

L. C. Thurow 'The Income Distribution as a Public Good' *QJE* LXXXV, (1971) pp. 327–33.

——————— 'Cash Versus In-kind Transfers' *AER* (Papers and Proceedings) (1974) pp. 190–5.

——————— 'Government Expenditures: Cash or In-kind Aid?' *Philosophy and Public Affairs* 5 (1976) pp. 361–81.

R. M. Titmuss *The Gift Relationship*, Allen & Unwin (1970).

G. Tintner 'A Note on Welfare Economics' *Econometrica* 14 (1946) pp. 69–78.

J. TOBIN 'On Limiting the Domain of Inequality' *JLE* 13 (1970); reprinted in Phelps (1973).

F. TONNIES *Community and Society* Gemeinschaft und Gesellschaft (1887); trans. C. P. Looms, Harper and Row (1957).

R. L. TRIVERS 'The Evolution of Reciprical Altruism' *Quarterly Review of Biology* 46 (1971) pp. 35–57.

G. TULLOCK 'The Social Rate of Discount and the Optimal Rate of Investment: Comment' *QJE* LXXVIII (1964) pp. 331–6.

———— *Private Wants, Public Means*, Basic Books (1970).

———— 'Subsidised Housing in a Competitive Housing Market' *AER* 61 (1971) pp. 218–9.

I. S. TURGENEV *On the Eve*; trans. G. Gardiner Penguin Classics (1972).

S. VALVANIS 'The Resolution of Conflict when Utilities Interact' *Journal of Conflict Resolution* II (1958) pp. 156–69.

H. R. VARIAN 'Equity, Envy and Efficiency *JET* 9 (1974) pp. 63–91.

———— 'Distributive Justice, Welfare Economics and the Theory of Fairness' *Philosophy and Public Affairs* 4 (1974–5) pp. 226–47.

———— 'Two Problems in the Theory of Fairness' *J. Pub Ec* 5 (1976) pp. 249–60.

W. S. VICKREY 'One Economist's View of Philanthropy' in Dickinson (1962).

———— 'An Exchange of Questions between Economics and Philosophy' in Phelps (1973).

D. WALL *The Charity of Nations: The Political Economy of Foriegn Aid*, Macmillan/ Basic Books (1973).

V. WALSH *Introduction to Contemporary Microeconomics*, McGraw-Hill (1970).

B. A. WEISBROD 'Toward a Theory of the Voluntary Non-Profit Sector in a 3 Sector Economy' in Phelps (1975) pp. 171–95.

J. K. WHITAKER 'Some Neglected Aspects of Alfred Marshall's Economic Thought' (mimeo).

———— *The Early Writings of Alfred Marshall* Vols. I and II Macmillan (1975).

J. M. WHITWORTH *God's Blueprints: A Sociological Study of Three Utopian Sects*, Routledge (1975).

P. H. WICKSTEED *The Commonsense of Political Economy* Bk. 1, Macmillan (1910) ch. V, pp. 174 *et seq.*

A. WILLIAMS 'Need as a Demand Concept (with special reference to health)' in A. J. Culyer (ed.) *Economic Policies and Social Goals*, Martin Robertson (1974).

E. WILSON *To the Finland Station* (1940); Fontana (1960).

———— *Sociobiology*, Harvard University Press (1975).

S. J. WINTER, JR 'A Simple Remark on the Second Optimality Theorem of Welfare Economics' *JET* 1 (1969) pp. 99–103.

K. WOLFF (ed.) *The Sociology of George Simnel*, Free Press (1950).

R. J. ZECKHAUSER 'Optimal Mechanisms for Income Transfer' *AER* (1971) pp. 324–34.

O. ZINSER, J. S. PERRY and R. EDGAR *Journal of Psychology* 89 (1975) p. 301; reported in *New Society* (16 October 1975).

Author Index

Subject Index